# Britain's Economic Renaissance

# Britain's Economic Renaissance

MARGARET THATCHER'S REFORMS
1979–1984

ALAN WALTERS

An *American Enterprise Institute
for Public Policy Research* Book

New York   Oxford
OXFORD UNIVERSITY PRESS
1986

Oxford University Press

Oxford   New York   Toronto
Delhi   Bombay   Calcutta   Madras   Karachi
Petaling Jaya   Singapore   Hong Kong   Tokyo
Nairobi   Dar es Salaam   Cape Town
Melbourne   Auckland

and associated companies in
Beirut   Berlin   Ibadan   Nicosia

Published by Oxford University Press, Inc.,
200 Madison Avenue, New York, New York 10016

Oxford is a registered trademark of Oxford University Press

Library of Congress Cataloging-in-Publication Data
Walters, A. A. (Alan Arthur), 1926
Britain's economic renaissance.
An *American Enterprise Institute for Public Policy Research* book
Includes index.
1. Great Britain—Economic policy—1945–
2. Fiscal policy—Great Britain.
3. Monetary policy—
Great Britain.   I. Title.
HC256.6.W334   1986   338.941   85–15563
ISBN 0–19–503739–1

Printing (last digit): 9 8 7 6 5 4 3 2 1

Printed in the United States of America
on acid-free paper

# *Preface*

The main pretext for this book is the reform program of Mrs. Thatcher's first government, 1979–83. The economic policies of that government were a negation of the conventional wisdom of some four decades. As a personal economic advisor to Mrs. Thatcher from January 1981 to October 1983 (and subsequently part-time), it is clear that I thought that the general thrust, if not all the details, of policy was correct.

Although this book is derived, in part, from dissatisfaction with received macroeconomic theory and policy, it discusses the reforms of both ideas and policy in a way readily accessible to the generally well-informed reader, such as the commuter who devours *The Economist* on the Clapham omnibus. The arguments do not require the technical complexities and the nice abstractions that many earnest students pay substantial sums to imbibe. In my view the errors of received doctrine are simple and basic rather than sophisticated and esoteric. Similarly the reform of ideas and policy owes much to the central propositions of the theory of demand and supply and little to explorations in mathematics and econometrics.

My debts are many and large. I owe most to Mrs. Thatcher, who really is responsible for this book. She looked at the manuscript and corrected some of my errors. Colleagues at No. 10, the Treasury and the Bank of England were also generous in reading the manuscript and pointing out where I had gone wrong or had articulated infelicities. Patrick Minford and Tim Congdon, who have been pursuing independently somewhat similar ideas, were early readers who steered me onto new paths. My colleagues at Johns Hopkins University and at the American Enterprise Institute—including Bela Balassa, Lou Maccini, Phillip Cagan, Gottfried Haberler, Herb Stein, and the late William Fellner—gave me most useful comments. My new colleague but old friend, Esra Bennathan, read the manuscript in its final form and eliminated a number of howlers. Veronique Bishop shepherded the manuscript through the final stages of revision and checking and liaison with the press.

I am particularly grateful to the American Enterprise Institute for the resident fellowship of 1983–84 and to Thomas Johnson, the director of economic studies, who encouraged me to embark on writing this account of the British reforms. I am solely responsible, however, for what follows.

*Washington, D.C.*                                        A.A.W.
*October 1985*

# Contents

Britain's Economic Renaissance

# *Prologue*

## Britain in the Postwar Years

The relentless decline of the United Kingdom from the pinnacle of a world power and economic giant to the secondary status of one of the less affluent states of the European Community has frequently been chronicled and lamented. Explanations have ranged far and wide—from fundamental faults in British character, education, and institutions to complaints about the smallness of the home market and the uniqueness of British tastes. Whatever the diagnosis, however, the main remedy was thought to be some change in government policy.

For some 50 years, from 1930 to 1979, the path to British prosperity and power was thought to be found in greater state intervention in decisions which had hitherto been the responsibility of the worker, the firm, or the family. When socialist governments were in power, as in 1945–51, the pace of socialization increased rapidly. The advent of Conservative governments in 1951–64 and 1970–74 slowed, but certainly did not reverse, the process of socialization. Indeed, conservative leaders generally recognized that their role was to moderate, rather than reverse, the tide of socialism; it was thought that, were they to pursue a radical policy of liberating Britain, the electorate would not tolerate such a reversal and power would be lost to the increasingly socialist Labour party.

Dissatisfaction with the Conservatives' role surfaced shortly after the demise of the Heath government in 1974. The rapid erosion of people's savings during the great inflation of the 1970s and the demonstrable

3

and overwhelming power of the trades unions were probably pivotal events in inducing a change of approach and policy in conservative circles.[1] With the election of Mrs. Thatcher to the leadership, the party showed that it believed that it was time for reversing the tide of socialism. In 1979 the electorate thought so too.

## The Policy of the Government, 1979–83

The policy of the Conservative government envisaged a long period, perhaps as long as eight or even ten years, in which major reforms would be completed. Mrs. Thatcher's government of 1979–83 was only the start of this long program of reform.

The most urgent business of the early years was to secure *financial stability,* particularly the reduction in the rate of inflation to low and stable levels. The Medium Term Financial Strategy, with its planned reductions in the growth rate of the money supply and public-sector borrowing, was the centerpiece of the policy. The government expected no quick results from this policy; it was thought, quite properly, that more than two or perhaps even three years would elapse before a substantial and sustainable reduction in inflation would appear in the statistics. This policy and its effects are the central focus of this book. Most members of the parliamentary Conservative party accepted that financial stability was a necessary but not sufficient condition for the achievement of the other major objectives of reform. Without financial stability, little could be achieved. With such stability, many other reforms were at least feasible.

The second area of urgent reform was the *deregulation or freeing of the economy* from the complex and confusing network of controls. The objective was to get a market economy functioning efficiently without suffocating government intervention. After the 1979 election the government moved swiftly to abolish exchange controls and general regulations on prices and incomes. With certain important exceptions (of which the main ones are rental accommodation, minimum wage arrangments, and some transport fares), the market rather than the bureaucracy determines the price and allocation of resources.

The third field of reform was the *privatization of state-owned indus-*

1. An interesting account of the change of opinion in the party and the process by which Mrs. Thatcher became leader is to be found in William Keegan, *Mrs. Thatcher's Economic Experiment,* Allen Lane, London, 1984.

*tries.* Both experience and scholarly study had shown that the state industries were over-mighty and tended to be used by powerful unions and other special interests for extortion and political purposes. The general policy of the government was to return these industries to the people. Some rather hesitant progress was made in 1979–83 as a prelude to the great disposals of 1984–85.

The fourth package of reforms applied to the *trades unions.* The basic thrust was to try to reduce the overweening powers of the unions, as exercised through their leaders and shop stewards, by abolishing or modifying the legal immunities conferred on them 80 years ago. In addition the policy envisaged that unions would evolve from their feudal form and would become increasingly democratic and responsive to the wishes of their members. This fundamental change was bound to take a long time and was planned as a series of "stepping stones," consolidating past reforms and then pushing on to the next step.

Underlying all these reforms was the belief that the uncertainties of inflation, regulations, the lethargy and waste of nationalized industries, and the restrictive practices of trades unions had retarded Britain's economic growth and made her perform well below her potential. The government sought to provide the conditions for an economy of opportunity and enterprise within a stable financial environment.

As for external economic relations, Mrs. Thatcher's government remained as committed to membership of the European Economic Community as it was to the need for reform of Community finances. Even under the exigencies of the recession the government maintained, with one or two significant exceptions, its general policy of keeping trade barriers low. Free trade remained the central aim of policy.

Even viewed in terms of its ten-year horizon, the reform program was ambitious. Many cognoscenti opined that the government's will would wilt or that the people would protest the pain of such a metamorphosis and throw the government out. Neither of these events had occurred at the time of writing this book, but someday they will. Then there is likely to be a recantation of many of these reforms. There is little to prevent a Labour government from inflating, regulating, renationalizing, and handing over power to their paymasters, the trades unions. Yet I suspect that some of the reforms will remain (e.g., the disposal of public housing, many aspects of trades union law, and more dubiously fiscal and monetary constraint). Ultimately, the test will be for the electorate to decide.

## A Briefing Note on the Government Financial System and Economic Advisers in the UK

*Government Ministers and Their Responsibilities*

In the UK the ultimate authority for economic policy lies in Parliament. The Treasury ministers—collectively through the cabinet—are responsible to Parliament. The First Lord of the Treasury is the Prime Minister. Usually, however, the Prime Minister delegates much of the responsibility to the Second Lord—the Chancellor of the Exchequer—who is the minister responsible for running the Treasury. (Under Mrs. Thatcher's government the First Lord has played a much more informed and active role than has been the norm.)

The Treasury—through the Chief Secretary—is responsible for reviewing the public-spending proposals of departments and producing an overall coherence and discipline in public expenditure in conformity with the broad outlines adopted by the Cabinet. Bilateral meetings between department and treasury (Chief Secretary) attempt to compromise between departmental ambition and Treasury parsimony—but the ultimate referee is the Cabinet (or some so-called "star chamber" committee of cabinet). Public-expenditure plans (intentions for the following fiscal year) extending over some three or four years are published in the (November) Autumn Statement by the Chancellor and are usually approved by Parliament.

Treasury responsibility for taxation is much greater than for expenditures. The annual budget (usually in March) is the occasion for tax reform proposals and the changing tax rate in order to finance the published spending plans. (The United States budget is virtually all about spending and says little or nothing about taxes—just the opposite of the British system.) There is virtually no discussion with the ministers, except the Prime Minister. Even the Cabinet is not informed of the budget proposals until the morning of budget day, when at 3 PM the Chancellor gradually reveals his intentions. These are enshrined in the Finance Bill which then threads its way gradually through the committee system of Parliament. Although there may be changes in detail, all the main proposals of the Chancellor will be approved in the Finance Bill.

*The Bank of England*

The Bank, nationalized after World War II, is a wholly government-owned public corporation. It advises the Chancellor, and if asked, the Prime Minister, on the views of banks and finance houses both foreign and domestic. It is, so to speak, the ears and eyes of the government in the City. It also interprets policy for the denizens of the City. Correspondingly, the Treasurer is discouraged from contacting the City; in principle, any Treasury official wanting to get the views of financial houses should consult the Bank as the "normal channel." The Bank has no independent policymaking role; it consults and receives instruction from the Treasury.

The main executive functions of the Bank are:

1. The supervision and control of the banking and financial system (the watchdog role)
2. The management of the public debt including issues, sales and redemptions, and "lender of last resort" in supplying liquidity to the financial system
3. Bank for the government and leader of government "rescue missions" for financially troubled firms
4. Currency issue and management

To a foreign observer perhaps the only surprising function is that of managing the public debt. In virtually all other countries this is carried out by the Treasury and not the Central Bank. This implies that the Bank is the executive agency for monetary policy through its open-market operations and discount-window lending.

Although the formal arrangements imply that the Bank has no power to evolve and lay down policy, it would be naive to imagine that the Bank as executive agency does not play a considerable role. The Chancellor may instruct the Bank in policy, but if the Bank takes the view that the policy is infeasible, inconsistent, or just plain wrong, it would take a very brave Chancellor to ignore the Governor's warnings.

*Economic Advisers and Their Role*

Since World War II the expansion of economic advisers has been enormous, probably near 100 fold. The official (or civil servant) economic advisers have organized in the Government Economic Service (GES) as a differentiated group of professionals. The cream of the GES is employed in the Treasury, and the Head of the GES is the chief economic adviser (in 1980, Sir Terence Burns) who in turn advises the Chancellor.

Apart from the considerable team in the Treasury, most of the GES personnel are scattered throughout the departments and are responsible to the normal career civil servant (ultimately to the Minister) in the department. The role of an economic adviser in a department should be to ensure that the policy makes economic sense; however, many advisers appear to be, in fact, arch-rationalizer for the policy proposed by officials or ministers.

Formally, the Prime Minister has no economic adviser. The convention is that she relies on the Chancellor for such advice. (On one occasion in 1981 when I met Sir Harold McMillan—now Lord Stockton—it was clear that McMillan, when Premier, regarded the Chancellor as his economic adviser.) Clearly if a member of the Government Economic Service (other than the Head) were appointed to No. 10 Downing Street, the advice that the Prime Minister received would be very similar to that which the Chancellor imbibed.

Yet some Prime Ministers have taken the view that they need their own economic adviser and not one that is a captive of the Treasury. In the Labour government of 1964, an entirely new department—the Department of Economic Affairs—was established to provide an alternative to the Treasury view with the Minister as a member of the Cabinet. Although the "alternative department" approach did not survive the test of time, the idea of an alternative view did persist. Harold Wilson (now Lord Wilson) did have Thomas Balogh (afterward Lord Balogh, dcd.) to assist him, although he was lodged in the cabinet office rather than No. 10 itself.

It was natural that a Prime Minister as involved in economic policy as Mrs. Thatcher should also look for some independent advice. This had to be in the form of a *political* appointee, like Balogh, whose term would certainly cease in the advent of a general election. It was on this basis that I agreed to serve from January 1981 for a two-year term or until a general election.

Unlike in the United States or every major European country, political appointees are very few in number. In 1981 there were only 16 in all of the United Kingdom, usually attached to particular ministers. The regular civil service were uneasy with such irregulars and were anxious to somehow contain their activities. Thus, when the prospect of my return to advise the government was aired, there was considerable pressure to put me in the Treasury or possibly the Cabinet Office rather than No. 10. However, I took the view (and still so hold) that independence of the Treasury establishment and the Cabinet secretariat was important and this could be achieved only by being in No. 10.

Unlike the Chairman of the Council of Economic Advisers in the United States, I had no formal legislated office. I had no staff (except a splendid secretary, Mrs. Rose Padwick). But I also had no formal responsibilities for reporting or testifying—nor did I have a public persona. My advice was confidential and for the Prime Minister alone. I did not give media interviews except on a background, unattributable basis.

The terms of reference were equally simple. The Prime Minister said, "You know what you can do best, and you know what it is best that you do." In practice I spent more than half of my time on Treasury and Bank matters, such as financial and budgeting policy. The remaining time was occupied primarily with labor market issues, trade, and industry problems. To some extent the distribution of advice was related to the political priorities of the Prime Minister. But this did not preclude my pursuit of issues which were important and which, I thought, needed her attention.

Any further details of my relationship with the Prime Minister might clearly betray a confidence and, thus, must await the 30-year rule. It is, however, not betraying any confidence to say that my relationships with the Treasury—with both ministers and officials—and with the Bank were friendly and cooperative. For my part, and I hope for theirs, I cannot complain that the policy of 1981–83 differed *fundamentally* from that which I thought desirable.

## The Purpose and Shape of This Study

In the decade of the 1970s, there was a pronounced shift in macroeconomic policy. The decade began with policymakers fairly sure about the effects of macroeconomic measures. Fiscal policy ruled the roost, and fine tuning was the fashion. The objective was clear—keep unemployment low by trading off against a little more inflation. Through fiscal policy, demand was injected or extracted from the economy to provide buyers for the forecast supply of goods at the forecast level of prices. Monetary policy had no crucial role in this drama—it merely echoed the fiscal themes and provided support and backing for the ever more frequent budgets.

But even before the decade of the 1960s was out, the winds of change were eddying, even into the stuffy offices of Whitehall. First, it was clear that the Bretton Woods system was gone, never to return.[2] Secondly,

2. In fact the Bretton Woods system proper lasted only from the end of 1950s, when most of the major currencies became convertible, to the sterling devaluation of 1967 and "two-tier" gold of 1968.

and partly as a consequence of the breakdown of Bretton Woods and partly by the IMF's insistence on some degree of monetary constraint, there had been a distinct revival of concern about the role of the money and monetary policy in the economy. Thirdly, in his famous address at the December 1968 meeting of the American Economic Association, Milton Friedman showed that, in the long run, if a government pursued real objectives (such as maximizing employment or real GNP) by using monetary means (such as expanding money demand or fiscal deficits), then the real reward will elude it, and it will reap merely the monetary consequences—inflation.

As the 1970s wore on, governments became painfully aware of the faults of fine fiscal tuning, on the one hand, and of the dictum that monetary and fiscal expansion begets inflation not growth. Policy changed perceptibly. In 1975–76, for example, Britain witnessed the development of monetary targets and the eschewing of finely tuned fiscality. The Medium Term Financial Strategy of the government of Mrs. Thatcher was a lineal descendent of these brave measures of Mr. Healey.

Policy changed but doctrine remained broadly the same. The textbook wrote and the professors spoke broadly the same message about the efficacy of fiscal expansion and the dangers of "dogmatic monetarism." The professional economist and the practicing politician not only parted company but found communications, if not cut, then most difficult.

This is one of the central themes explored in this book. I have tried to confront ambient doctrine with current policy, and with the experience of the British economy during the years 1979–83. As the flag-bearers for the neo-Keynesian or post-Keynesian view, I have chosen Professors Willem Buiter and Marcus Miller. In my judgment they have produced the most sophisticated and rigorous version of the current doctrine and its application to the United Kingdom. But there are legions of less articulate and less rigorous exponents of the ambient doctrine.

And what of the alternative theory of fiscal policy? Alas, one cannot call on any representatives of large schools of economics which have produced a well-articulated alternative theory to serve as the basis for economic policy in the 1980s.[3] I am certainly not equipped to develop

3. The fiscal policy aspects of Patrick Minford's writings are close to the themes which I attempt to articulate. But I would not wish to follow Professor Minford to the end of the road of rational expectations.

an alternative theory of fiscal policy with all its reliability and rigor. But it is impossible to write this sort of study without touching on the salient features which such a theory ought to encompass. Most of these suggestions appear in Part I, Chapters 1 to 4. As the assiduous journal reader will know, I have entertained these notions for more than twenty years, but I fear they are still largely half-baked, certainly in their empirical assessment. This is, in part, because when I started this study what has been called Mrs. Thatcher's Economic Experiment had been in operation only about four years. The final results will have to await the lapse of another five years or so. Thus, the assessments of fiscal policy in Part I and monetary policy in Part II must be considered provisional and subject to later revision. We do, however, have the history of these four years and it seems worthwhile to provide an interpretation at this point so that we can discard it or perhaps chew it over at a later stage.

In the last chapters, Part III, I attempt to deal with some of the consequences, and some of the puzzles, of the performance of the economy during these years. Some quite dramatic trends asserted themselves—the swing of the current account of the balance of payments to a surplus, the buoyancy of exports in the face of a massive appreciation, the persistent high rate of growth of productivity, and rising real wages and unemployment—and at least they deserve some comment. However, I cannot claim to have found any new solutions; but I hope to contribute a little to enlightenment—even when that involves no more than defining what we do not know and should not make claims about. The reader may be none the wiser, but I hope somewhat better informed.

This account is, of course, partial. It would be dishonest if it attempted a perfect balance of evenhanded assessment. I cannot insulate this manuscript from the role which I played in Downing Street. But the reader should be warned: there are no revelations in this book. It is neither a diary nor a denouement. It is just a plain old piece of applied economics.

# I
# FISCAL POLICY

Chapter 1 reviews the propositions of Keynesian economics, focusing mainly on the potency of fiscal policy. The basic point is that if there is substantial unemployment, then fiscal expansion will result in a short-run (up to two years or so) expansion of output and employment with little effect on the level of prices or the rate of inflation. If, on the other hand, the economy is fully employed, then fiscal expansion is likely to result only in a rise in prices.

A brief survey of experience and statistical evidence, from the simplest of models, suggests that the British economy (and probably other economies such as that of the United States) not only failed to conform to the Keynesian pattern but, on the whole, behaved perversely. The results from the standard econometric models reviewed in the second section of the chapter seem to confirm this perversity. During the years of low unemployment there appeared to be a powerful fiscal effect on real output. Yet in years of high unemployment the effect was much reduced and certainly not increased, as suggested by the theory.

In the third and fourth sections of Chapter 1 an attempt is made to develop an explanation of the phenomena in terms of the determinants of "confidence," its association with unemployment, and uncertainties and convictions about policies. The final sections of the chapter suggest that the size of the deficit, as well as the change in the deficit, may be a critical determinant of "confidence." In particular, confidence will depend on all elements, both political and financial, which render the government's policy *credible,* and among these elements, the expected path of future deficits must rank high on the list.

Chapter 2 examines the contentious issue of crowding out—the displacement of private-sector spending by an expansion of public-sector spending. [The reader who is not interested in the professional disputes on this issue may skip the chapter, although the first section (entitled, "Crowding Out, Real, Macro and Micro") is recommended for all readers. In this section there is a description of the various forms of crowding out and, in particular, the micro crowding out or the substitution of public provision (e.g., of hospitals) for private provision.] The second section discusses the traditional versions of crowding out through financial markets in which government borrowing replaces private borrowing. The statistical evidence—unfortunately worth very little—is examined in the third section. Although the evidence is equivocal, inevitably some financial crowding out will be characteristic of modern economies. Finally, in this chapter, we review the Pre-Ricardo proposition that it is the increase in public expenditure which crowds out private spending, and that the form of finance, whether through taxes or borrowing, is irrelevant. This proposition, which implies that the variation in the budget deficit, with public spending unchanged, has no effect on private spending, seems to be eroded when one takes into account aspects of reality, such as the finiteness of human life. Yet it does embody an important principle, which one should not ignore.

In Chapter 3, we return to examine the effects of fiscal policy on real output paths (the fiscal multipliers) in the context of econometric models of the United Kingdom. It is now suggested that instead of the value of 2, the fiscal multipliers in the United Kingdom may be as low as 0.24 to 0.62. But as we show in the second section, the interest of fiscalists tends to wane after about two years, yet the dynamic behavior of the economy after the fiscalists' short run is of immense importance for policy formulation. The difficulty is to reconcile the long-run neutrality of fiscal policy (that is to say, there is no way of increasing permanently the wealth and income of the economy through fiscal manipulation) with the dynamic path of the reaction process. We show that there is likely to be a substantial backlash effect after three or four years which will plausibly be procyclical and, thus, require yet a larger fiscal stimulus to offset the backlash effect.

Chapter 4 examines the context of fiscal policy in the United Kingdom and the measurement and meaning of the deficit. First, there is a discussion of the definition of deficit and the role of the deficit in macroeconomic policymaking. The widely recommended practice of using the full-employment budget deficit, or the capacity working deficit, in order to push the economy back onto its potential path presupposes that the private sector will react passively to such public commitments to promote full employment or growth. Yet logic and evidence clearly contradict such passive reaction. The private sector is neither stupid nor incapable of learning. In the remainder of the chapter, we describe and discuss the various other amendments to the deficit concept, beginning with the weighting of expenditures and receipts to reflect their relative punch; continuing with the consideration of future obligations and receipts; and, finally, considering the proposed adjustments for inflationary erosion of the debt. After all such amendments and adjustments, the reader will be able to judge the degree of precision and objectivity of the public sector borrowing requirement (PSBR) or deficit as a basis for policy.

Chapter 5 covers the recent fiscal policy of the United Kingdom, beginning with the policies of the Labour governments from 1974 to 1979. The main bequest of the Labour government was a deficit of 6.6 percent of GDP—and that at the top of a boom. We discuss the budgets of 1979 to 1983, and the Medium Term Financial Strategy (MTFS). The MTFS was the centerpiece of financial reform, but although produced in 1979 and announced in 1980, implementation did not really occur until the budget of 1981. Then the government firmly established that break with the past which had been envisioned in the MTFS. In spite of rapidly increasing unemployment and falling output, the government introduced the toughest peacetime budget in memory. The budget succeeded admirably in its main long- or medium-term objective to bring confidence back to the financial markets and to establish the credibility of government strategy. Contrary to the overwhelming condemnation of the 1981 budget by professional economists, the economy began to grow under conditions of quite sharply declining inflation. One may adduce some lessons about the power of monetary policy, compared to fiscal policy, from the experience of 1981. The budgets of 1982 and 1983 were mainly concerned with holding and improving the balance achieved in 1981, and gradually reforming microeconomic conditions, through raising tax thresholds, indexing capital gains tax, etc. In conclusion, we examine the tightness of fiscal policy over the critical years from 1981 to 1984 relative to other countries in the European Community. Using European Economic Community (EEC) statistics, we show that yet again, contrary to the conventional view, Britain pursued budgetary policies that were *less* restrictive than those of the other countries.

The revisions of fiscal theory and policy which emerge from Part I are considerable and pervasive. They are also tentative and uncertain. They lack rigor and have passed only the sketchiest empirical tests of validity. We are engaged, like the process of capitalism itself, in what Schumpeter called "creative destruction." The exposure of the flaws and exaggerated claims of fiscal policy is the easier of the tasks of this chapter. The development of an alternative policy, such as the MTFS, is a much more tentative and uncertain business. One might simply say, "So far, so good." However, the reader must make up his own mind on this issue.

# 1

# *The Propositions of Fiscalism*

The central question for economic theory and policy is the reaction of the economy to changes in fiscal conditions. The main proposition of macroeconomics is that looser (sometimes called expansionary) fiscal conditions will give rise to an expansion of nominal GNP. And, symmetrically, tighter fiscal conditions will lead to a contraction of GNP.

By tighter fiscal conditions we shall normally mean a decrease in the public-sector financial deficit; and, symmetrically, by looser, an increase in the deficit, after making such adjustments as are necessary for variations in the level of activity. (This will be discussed below.) In this proposition, it is supposed that monetary conditions are held constant and are not accommodating. Precisely what is meant by "constant" may vary according to the model, but for our purposes we can assume that the rate of growth of the monetary aggregates is not changed.

## Multipliers and Unemployment—The Proposition

The *real* justification for a fiscal expansion is when there are substantial *unemployed resources* in the economy, or when the level of actual output is below the level of capacity. Then the increase in the deficit will inject additional demand, and resources hitherto idle or underused will be put to work. Little of this additional demand will be reflected in higher prices. The idle machines and the dole queues will give a pause to price and wage increases. So, with unemployment there is a pre-

17

sumption of a powerful real multiplier—and only a small or insignificant price multiplier.

With *fully employed resources,* per contra, there is little scope for increased real output, and the additional demand impinges almost entirely on the level of *prices* or the *rate* of inflation. There are, however, two constraints. First, even in a closed economy, the fact that the money supply is not affected by the fiscal expansion means that any additional inflation must not merely be transitory but also result in later reversal. Ultimately, the price level must be the same whether or not there has been fiscal expansion or contraction.[1] Secondly, in an open economy some of the additional demand would leak away, not merely in savings, but also in the form of increased imports and reduced exports.[2] Depending on the exchange-rate regime, the external accounts will modify the multipliers. However, since the external leak, although quantitatively important, does not centrally affect any of the issues discussed in this chapter, it will be largely ignored.

The benign role of fiscalism is, therefore, to nudge the economy back onto its full-employment track. If this expansion is achieved by increasing public spending (on goods and services), then, considered as a public spending "project," the appraisal would show that there was a net present value greater than zero. The general rule is clear; if there is unemployment in the economy, which is not expected to disappear in the near future, then expand public spending.

What happens if one makes a "mistake" and expands public spending under conditions of either current or incipient full employment? Output does not increase, or at least not much, *but it does not decrease either.* True, there will be a temporary surge of prices and then a backlash as the long-run stability of the monetary aggregates asserts its effect. But in fiscalist models there are no *real* consequences of this instability in prices. Output does not fall because of an inflationary surge followed by a relapse—indeed, the presumption is that there will be an *increase,* albeit *transitory,* of output in a temporary situation of "over-full employment."

In this description I have brushed aside doubts about the definition

1. This is supposing the monetarist position that ultimately inflation is caused by the rate of growth of the money supply relative to the trend of real output and that the level of output is, in the long run, not affected by fiscal policy. Alternatively, fiscal policy cannot indefinitely change the velocity of circulation.
2. The leak will be greater, the smaller the gap between actual and capacity output.

and observation of the states of less-than-full-capacity output. As we shall see, the concept of full employment is the most slippery of fish. But in the context of these fiscalist ideas, such refinements of definition and measurement were not of momentous consequence. If in doubt, the best policy is to expand public spending; you may do some good and you can do little or no harm. A little transitory flutter in prices, and that is all.

Many fiscalists, however, would argue that, with full employment, inflation can take place without any change in the growth rate of the money stock. Velocity is a malleable magnitude.[3] So an expansionary fiscal policy under full employment conditions and with an unchanged money supply would increase demand and, in the absence of a *permanent* increase in output, would result in more inflation. Removing the monetarist constraint, however, does not change any of the general tone of fiscal policy. True, one would prefer less to more inflation, but at the same time none of the models formulated any deleterious effects on GDP of the greater inflation. Indeed, it was pointed out that all that was required was that prices be marked up higher than before.[4] Real output would hardly be affected, and full employment would be maintained.[5]

The state of employment was thought to be the only dominant "state variable" that discriminated between output and prices. And the state of employment (or more often, unemployment of resources—particularly labor) was susceptible to quantification. So it was readily incorporated not merely in economic and econometric models but also in the central thinking of economists on questions of policy.

To show that this proposition is central to policy discussion and proposals by the profession, we can examine the most recent accounts of the most modern versions of macroeconomic theory.[6] Hahn's theoreti-

3. In the Radcliffe Report it was said that there is no reason to suppose that "there is any limit to the velocity of circulation" (p. 391).
4. For an exceptionally clear statement of this position, see Frank Hahn, *Money and Inflation,* MIT Press, 1983, Chapter III.
5. Indeed, many antimonetarists are at pains to point out that countries which have very high inflations have also enjoyed very high growth rates (e.g., Brazil, Israel) and that there is little or no negative correlation between price stability and growth.
6. Frank Hahn (*op. cit.*). Prof. Hahn, who holds a chair of economics at Cambridge University, is perhaps Britain's most distinguished economic theorist. But he is no mere theorist. He was also one of the two marshals of the charge of the 365 in March 1981.

cal reflections lead him to propose a rule for macroeconomic policy: when unemployment rises above some predetermined threshold, then pursue an expansionary policy.

## Multipliers and Unemployment—The Evidence

The literature of macroeconomics treats the differentiation of the multiplier between real and price, especially under full and less-than-full-employment conditions, as self-evident. So strongly is this belief held that most economists would require an enormous volume of cast-iron evidence of results to the contrary in order to budge their basic beliefs. Yet I suspect that the cumulation of evidence and experience is now so large that the certainties of ten or twenty years ago have been seriously eroded.

The first batch of evidence is derived from simple multiplier models following the original work of Friedman and Meiselman.[7] The work on similar data for the United Kingdom exhibited a number of seeming anomalies or paradoxical results. It seemed that the multipliers for each period were the reverse of what one expected from the concurrent conditions of unemployment.

Clearly, the most interesting period is the interwar years 1922–39, when there was clear evidence of massive unemployment and considerable excess capacity. If there is a high Keynesian fiscal multiplier, it must have been manifest in these years. Unfortunately, the simple reduced-form models which have been used to explore the power of the multipliers have not been suitable for distinguishing between the fiscal multiplier and the effects of other variations in autonomous expenditure (net exports, for example). The separation of the fiscal effect can be achieved only through simulating the results from a structural model. Such simulation results as are available will be reviewed later in this chapter and in Chapter 3. If we examine the multiplier of autonomous expenditure (government spending plus exports, plus gross domestic fixed capital formation) in *current prices* on *nominal* income (or nominal consumption), we find that there is a very strong and well-defined multiplier.[8] One might then conclude, as I did, that the interwar years were predominantly Keynesian. But this interpretation is incorrect. The

7. Commission on Money and Credit, *Stabilization Policies,* Washington, D.C., 1953.
8. See Appendix on Multipliers, Section A, at the end of this chapter. For those who wish to follow the mathematics of multipliers, this Appendix is provided.

Keynesian proposition is about *real,* not nominal, multipliers. It is, of course, tempting to assume that prices were sticky during the interwar years and so the price multiplier is near zero, all the effect is real and the nominal multiplier translates readily into a similar real multiplier. That Keynesian assumption, however, is quite discredited by the evidence.

*The real multipliers for these interwar years were found to be virtually zero.* Taken in conjunction with the high positive multipliers for the nominal magnitudes, this implies that all the multiplier effect was on prices and not on quantities. If anything, there was a slight negative effect on quantities.[9] I had first come across this curious relationship between prices and quantities when I examined monetary multipliers in the early 1960s.[10] I was then inclined to treat it as an anomaly or, at most, a paradox which had yet to be explained away.[11] Now, however, new analyses of old data and the new information from the 1960s, 1970s, and 1980s suggest that the interwar years were no anomaly but part of the general pattern.

Perhaps the most important reassessment of the evidence of the interwar years has come from the study by Friedman and Schwartz (FS).[12] FS examined the reaction of the United Kingdom economy to variations in the "output ratio," which measures the ratio of actual output to capacity output. They showed that, for the years 1873 to 1975 as a whole, the relationship between this output ratio and the growth rate of output over cyclical phases was slightly negative. Even during the interwar years, when the output ratio dropped to very low levels, the relationship was not significantly positive.

In a reassessment of the Great Depression and recovery of 1929–37, it has been shown that the recovery of 1931–37 was associated with a

9. See Appendix on Multipliers, Section B.
10. Some of these results appeared in A. A. Walters, "Monetary Multipliers in the U.K.," *Oxford Economic Papers,* November 1966. Keynes was quite right in his assessment that *real* GNP and the volume of employment were insensitive to variations in the monetary magnitudes, but they were also immune to variations in autonomous expenditures.
11. See, however, A. A. Walters, "The Radcliffe Report—Ten Years After: A Survey of the Empirical Evidence," in David R. Croome and Harry G. Johnson (eds.), *Money in Britain 1959–1969,* Oxford, 1970. By 1969 I had found only evidence to support rather than discredit the perverse relationship.
12. Milton Friedman and Anna Schwartz, *Monetary Trends in the United States and the United Kingdom,* National Bureau of Economic Research, Chicago, 1983, particularly Chapter 9. This discussion merely skims the surface of the scholarly and sophisticated work of Friedman and Schwartz.

sharply contractionary fiscal policy[13] as well as an expansionary monetary policy demonstrated by the growth in all monetary aggregates from early 1932. Contrary to the widespread view, still current among economists, that a fiscal expansion is necessary for a recovery and that monetary expansion will be merely "pushing on a string," the British economy expanded at more than 4 percent a year until 1937.[14]

It is worthwhile contrasting these results for the interwar years with those for the years before World War I, 1881–1914. Although the data for these years are more sparse and suspect, it is widely believed that the degree of unemployment of resources, particularly labor, was on the average much lower than during the interwar years. Yet in contrast to the negative multipliers during the interwar years, Sheppard calculates a significantly positive multiplier.[15] Clearly, the dubious data give one pause before too much is adduced from such a result. It is worth adding, however, that in their detailed survey of these years, FS found that there was no significant effect on either prices or output due to variations in the cyclical phase average levels of the extent of unemployment (in their study this was measured as the "output ratio"). In other words, the Keynesian-Phillips proposition was negated by the evidence.

The years after World War II, at least up to the late 1960s or early 1970s, were characterized by very full employment. Expansionary policies, whether fiscal or monetary, should have had their dominant effect on prices and not quantities. Yet the remarkable result is that such expansionist policies, up to 1962, had a marked effect on real income; the

13. See P. N. Sedgwick, "Economic Recovery in the 1930s," *Bank of England Paper No. 23,* April 1984, p. 47. It is remarkable that the change from 1931 to 1932 in the general government deficit, as a percentage of GDP at factor cost, was a reduction by 2.7 percentage points. This corresponds to a change of 1.2 percentage points in the same magnitude (except as a percentage of GDP at market prices) in 1980–81. The inflation–adjusted figure for 1931–32 was even more remarkable—an increase of 9.1 percentage points!

14. There are still many aspects of the 1920s and 1930s that do not fit easily into any single simple theoretical explanation. For example, although the Sedgwick research clearly points to the primacy of monetary policy, and perhaps perversity of fiscal policy, in promoting the recovery in real output growth, this does not appear (albeit including the 1920s in the analysis) in the comparative multiplier study of Barrett and Walters. It would be strange, but interesting, if the relative dominance of the Keynesian multiplier appeared in the 1920s and was reversed in the 1930s! Such conjecturing, however, cannot be pursued here. C. R. Barrett and A. A. Walters, "The Stability of Keynesian and Monetary Multipliers in the United Kingdom," *The Review of Economics and Statistics,* Vol. 48, No. 4, November 1966, pp. 395–405.

15. See Appendix on Multipliers, Section C.

statistics suggested that, if anything, the short-run effects on prices were negative—that is to say, perverse.[16] One example of this perversity is the Butler downturn of 1955. A combined monetary and fiscal squeeze saw a fall in the production index, which remained in the doldrums; but prices went on increasing at the same rate of growth for some three years.[17]

Again this perversity is confirmed by FS. In their study of the nine cyclical phase averages, they found that unemployment increased and output dropped below capacity; the main effect of an expansionary policy was on prices and not, as expected by the Keynesians, on output. And the Butler downturn of 1955 is merely one illustration of this process.

Of course it may be objected—one can safely say that the objection is certain to be raised—that the simple models used in this discussion do not capture the complex reality of modern economies. Alternative specifications may reveal the subtleties of powerful real multipliers, under conditions of low utilization of resources—as suggested by the theory. Similarly, the new complexities may reveal that the high real multipliers under full-employment conditions are merely an optical illusion. We had, therefore, best look at the economic models. Unfortunately, there are few sophisticated models in the United Kingdom that have been running and have simulated results for any long period. And even in the United States, the models are numerous only for the postwar (World War Two) years. Fortunately for the analyst, the postwar years have produced very substantial variations in the extent of unemployment. Up to the early to mid 1970s, employment in both the United Kingdom and the United States was high and the unemployment rate in the U.K. rarely exceeded 3 percent, while that in the U.S. rarely exceeded 6 percent, with an average in the region of 4.5 percent. In the ten years from 1975 to 1984 the U.S. unemployment rate has rarely dipped below 6 percent and has averaged 8 or 8.5 percent.

With these ambient conditions, on Keynesian principles one would expect that the main effect of fiscal (or strictly autonomous expenditure) multipliers (with no monetary accommodation) would be on price for the years up to the early 1970s and then on quantity for the years of the last decade. Yet simulations of these models produce quite

16. See Appendix on Multipliers, Section D.
17. This period was reviewed in my *Money in Boom and Slump*, Institute for Economic Affairs, London, 1968. One of the most distinguished Keynesians, Sir Roy Harrod, attempted to rationalize these results by arguing that firms were operating under decreasing costs and, therefore, cutting back volume and increasing costs and prices. (*The Economist*, July 19, 1969.)

the opposite results. As we shall see subsequently, models of the post-war years up to the early 1970s all show very substantial *real* multi-pliers—ranging from two to three for many years—and in some cases more or less permanently.[18] In these full or near-full employment years one would have expected the main effect to appear on prices; although the models do show (ultimately, after two or three years) some positive effect on prices, it is very muted and quite small beer compared with the great effects on real output. For the years after the mid 1970s, however, when there was such widespread and substantial unemploy-ment, the simulations of U.S. models show very low real multipliers and much higher price multipliers.[19]

For the Federal Reserve Board Model—the MCM or Multi-Country Model—which was estimated over the period from the early 1960s to 1979/80, fiscal multipliers have been simulated for the period 1977–81. Average civilian unemployment over these years was 6.5 percent with the initial conditions in 1977 at 7.1 percent. The fiscal multiplier aver-age over a two-year period amounted to only 1.2.[20] This clearly illus-trates the proposition that as unemployment has increased the multi-pliers have fallen—from the "safe assumption" of Blinder and Solow or Ando and Modigliani of 2 down to 1.2.[21]

The obvious second question is: does the expansionary fiscal policy (no monetary accommodation) simply result in additional inflation?

18. Carl Christ, "Judging the Performance of Econometric Models of the U.S. Economy," *International Economic Review,* Vol. 16, No. 1, February 1975, pp. 54–74.
19. The reduction in the real fiscal multipliers is most readily seen in the econo-metric models. But the modelers, whatever their errors and omissions, do faithfully reflect current history. They make sure that the equations and simula-tions fit the current time series. Thus, the decline in the multipliers shown in the models mirror their decline in the real world.
20. Gilles Oudiz and Jeffrey Sachs, "Macroeconomic Policy Coordination Among the Industrial Economies" paper presented to the Brookings Panel on Eco-nomic Activity, April 1984, p. 25, Table 5. The authors actually calculated the increase in public spending as a percent of GNP (0.83) required to produce a one percentage point increase in GNP, so the multiplier is the reciprocal of 0.83. (The results also show that there is almost a 50 percent leakage of the original fiscal stimulus in the decay of the current account of the balance of payments.) Simulations for Germany and Japan show similarly low multi-pliers of 0.97 and 1.4, respectively.
21. Alan S. Blinder and Robert M. Solow, "Analytical Foundations of Fiscal Policy," ed. Alan Blinder, *et al., The Economics of Public Finance* (Wash-ington, DC: Brookings Institution, 1974); Franco Modigliani and A. Ando, "Impacts of Fiscal Actions on Aggregate Income and the Monetarist—Contro-versy, Theory and Evidence," *Monetarism,* ed. J. Stein (North-Holland, 1976), pp. 17–68.

The simulation clearly shows inflation increasing over the average of two years at about 0.15 percent for every additional 1 percent of government spending. But one knows that the time lag for the full effect on the inflation rate is far longer than two years; thus, the appearance of only a small price effect is misleading as an indicator of the *final* effect. The small value in no way discredits the proposition that the main effects of fiscal multipliers were on the rate of inflation.[22] However, to show this we need to examine the longer-term dynamics of the process, to which we turn in Chapter 3. From these sophisticated and complex models of the United States, it is clear that the consensus opinion is that the fiscal multipliers have fallen from 2.0 to 3.0 in the 1950s to the early 1970s, to 1.0 to 1.5 in the 1980s. So far as they go, therefore, the complex macroeconometric models give results which are not inconsistent with the simple models of the interwar and pre-World War I years.

In the United Kingdom, although models are not so ubiquitous as in the United States, the same sort of revision has taken place.[23] The high fiscal multipliers of the 1950s and the 1960s—somewhere in the range of two to three—have given way to the more modest claims which we shall later review.[24] As unemployment has increased, so the power of the real fiscal multipliers has declined, and inflation has been the main outcome. As Ball (op. cit.) puts it:

> . . . none of the models of which I am aware suggest that important permanent gains in real output and employment can be obtained by major fiscal expansion without an unacceptable cost either in terms of inflation or in terms of the effect on the current account of the balance of payments. (p. 27)

In the United Kingdom the modelers and the policymakers have learned the same lessons. Seemingly, under the full-employment conditions of the 1950s and 1960s, it was possible to use fiscal policy to

22. The deterioration in the current account of the balance of payments might be thought to be the first sign of an ultimate depreciation of the exchange rate and a rise in the domestic price of traded goods.
23. See the perceptive remarks of R. J. Ball, *Macro-econometric Model Builders in the United Kingdom,* Discussion Paper 121, London Business School, February 1984.
24. Michael Artis, "Fiscal and Monetary Policy—an Introduction to the Issues," *Essays in Fiscal and Monetary Policy,* ed. Michael Artis and Marcus Miller, Institute for Fiscal Policy Studies, Oxford, 1981, p. 6. As Artis concludes, "a feature of the fiscal policy simulations reported below is that the output multipliers are rather low."

steer the real economy because there was a real fiscal multiplier. These were the years of high fiscalism—the "touch on the tiller" operated the real fiscal multipliers. This disappeared, however, as the volume of unemployment rose in the 1970s—and, paradoxically, with mass unemployment, the response to fiscal expansion was inflation, not growth.

## Multipliers and Unemployment—The Conclusion

The simple conclusion is that the evidence seems to be inconsistent with the basic proposition that the real multipliers will be higher the larger the degree of spare capacity (or unemployment). Yet the review of the evidence does not support, alternatively, the null hypothesis—namely, that the potency of the real and price multipliers is *unconnected* with the degree of unemployment. The evidence of a hundred years suggests that there *is* a connection between unemployment and the multipliers, but that it is the *opposite* of that accepted by fiscalists.

I am sure that the first reaction of professional macroeconomists is that the statistics must be wrong. Perhaps so. But it is remarkable that not merely the simpler models but also the macroeconometric models seem to be in some degree of agreement—at least for the years after World War II. I doubt whether an effective challenge is possible on this basis. And I believe that most economists would concede that fiscal policy has been less potent in the 1970s than in the 1950s and the 1960s. The statistics are consistent with "experience."

A second objection would be that the concept of unemployment and spare or idle capacity has changed, so that simple measures of unemployment or unused machines, etc., are now inappropriate. In particular, the increase in unemployment benefits and the increased monopoly power of the unions in the 1950s and 1960s have given rise to a larger permanent hard core of unemployment. For this to be the explanation it would also have to be argued that there was greater *real* unemployment in the 1950s and 1960s than in the 1970s. It is, of course, a possible way out, but not one which would readily appeal to fiscalists (or others) as plausible.

Instead of trying to wriggle around the results, it might be more useful to accept them, albeit tentatively, and ask what might be implied. One possible implication is that fiscalists have wrongly identified the factors that give potency to real multipliers and price multipliers. The main factor is not the quantity measure of unused resources, but perhaps something which is perversely related to unemployment.

One candidate which deserves some discussion is the mysterious factor "confidence." It may well be that over the historical record confidence has been negatively related to the extent of unemployment—as the latter has been associated with dislocations of activity and financial crises. We shall consider briefly the effects of confidence, the determinants of confidence, and possible surrogates in the next section. It is worthwhile, however, to quote Keynes[25] on this subject:

> The state of long-term expectation, upon which our decisions are based, does not solely depend, therefore, on the most probable forecast we can make. It also depends on the *confidence* with which we make this forecast—on how highly we rate the likelihood of our best forecast turning out quite wrong. If we expect large changes but are very uncertain as to what precise form these changes will take, then our confidence will be weak.
>
> The *state of confidence,* as they term it, is a matter to which practical men always pay the closest and most anxious attention. But economists have not analyzed it carefully and have been content, as a rule, to discuss it in general terms. In particular it has not been made clear that its relevance to economic problems comes in through its important influence on the schedule of the marginal efficiency of capital. There are not two separate factors affecting the rate of investment, namely, the schedule of the marginal efficiency of capital and the state of confidence. The state of confidence is relevant because it is one of the major factors determining the former, which is the same thing as the investment demand schedule.
>
> There is, however, not much to be said about the state of confidence *a priori.* Our conclusions must mainly depend upon the actual observation of markets and business psychology.[26]

## Multipliers and Confidence

A possible, even plausible, generalization from the empirical results is that there was mainly a real multiplier when confidence was high and predominantly a price multiplier when confidence was low. Although there is no obvious formal measure of confidence and although it waxes and wanes with great rapidity, we can be fairly certain in ascribing periods of "low confidence" and "high confidence."

25. John Maynard Keynes, *The General Theory,* Chapter 12, pp. 148–149 (London 1936).
26. I believe that there is "much" to be said *a priori* about confidence. In particular, in the United Kingdom the uncertainties of strikes and "industrial action," the draconian changes in tax rates (usually but not always associated with changes of government) and the effects of regulation: all affect "confidence." But there is no easy way of quantifying it.

The interwar years in the United Kingdom comprised a period which no one would dispute was characterized by both great political and economic uncertainty. Such lack of confidence was reflected in the high interest rates which obtained for most of the period.[27] Although confidence picked up from the trough of 1931–32 through to 1937 (when there was the sharpest of downturns in the United States), there were still many doubts about the path of the economy and the stability of the financial system.

By contrast the postwar years to 1972–73 or so have been characterized by great, perhaps overweening, confidence not only in the economy but also in fiscality.[28] There was little doubt about the ability of government to maintain full employment and about the continued high growth of the economy. True, inflation was becoming more of a problem as the 1960s wore on, but was still thought to be just tolerable at about 5–6 percent average during the 1960s. The early 1970s saw a sharp reversal of confidence, as the economy sank into a deep depression (which many economists thought was a thing of the past) and which was perversely associated with the biggest inflationary surge in Britain's peacetime history. A depressed but inflationary economy has been characteristic of the decade from 1971–81. There is little doubt that the confidence of the 1950s and 1960s has rapidly eroded. In the wake of the long, slow recovery from the depths of the 1981 recession, confidence is being slowly restored, but seemingly far short of the heady heights of the 1960s.

It is not surprising that confidence should be low during periods of substantial unemployment. In the historical record, periods of high unemployment have seen vast oscillations in real interest rates, the collapse and recovery of equity and bond markets, and many bankruptcies. In response to an increase of aggregate demand under these kinds of conditions, entrepreneurs tend to mark up prices and wages rather than expand production, increase investment, and hire more labor.

A positive real response required a commitment to the future. This applies not merely to the conventional purchase of investment goods but also to the investment in labor through training and implicit contracts.

27. Nominal interest rates were particularly high, since they were maintained by the threat of an optional redemption of a large 5 percent government stock until the conversion of 1931–32.
28. For example: Sir Alec Cairncross said, ". . . I doubt whether bad theory has played a major part in forecasting errors in the country over the past decade or two." "Economic Forecasting," *Economic Journal 79*, December 1969, pp. 797–812.

In times of high uncertainty, the businessman will try to limit his future commitments and restore his profit margins on his existing labor, machines and production. Indeed, the reluctance of entrepreneurs to take on more labor, particularly in the manufacturing industries, because of the cost of reducing manning, should the occasion arise, is one of the factors that is commonly thought to have prevented an expansion of employment in the 1981–84 recovery.[29]

Correspondingly, under conditions when confidence is high entrepreneurs are willing to take on future commitments since the risks of catastrophic loss are trivial. And periods of high confidence have usually been associated with a fair degree of stability in prices—or at least a low and *stable* rate of inflation.[30] But the important feature to explain away is why, under these "full employment" conditions, entrepreneurs and workers did not mark up their prices and wages to absorb virtually all the increase in aggregate demand? The answer must be highly conjectural and tentative. I suspect that part of the answer lies in the plasticity of a fully employed economy. There are always incipient workers to be tempted into employment, even though they do not register as unemployed, particularly part-timers, married women, etc. Employment grew dramatically in the 1950s–60s. Similarly, the concept of machine capacity is extraordinarily flexible, as has been illustrated recently in many industries.[31] If the main response is in this quantity form, under conditions of malleable capacity, then there is little room for increase in prices. But there is also an incentive to "stay-in-line" with the confidently expected stable growth of the price level and the economy.[32]

In conclusion, therefore, one possible but highly tentative explanation for the perversity of the multiplier with respect to the level of unemployment can be put forward. When there is a high level of unemployment—or in circumstances when it is widely expected that unemployment will

29. In spite of rapidly increasing productivity (about 5 to 7 percent a year) in manufacturing and a modest increase in real wages, considerably less than the productivity increase, employment has fallen. See Chapter 10.
30. Such stability may be due to a Bretton Woods type peg or, before 1914, the gold parity, or simply trust in the authorities.
31. In discussing the weaknesses in modeling the supply response of econometric models of the United Kingdom, Ball observed that the problem "is not so much of determining capacity in any physical sense but in determining and measuring the degree of *economic* capacity." (op. cit. p. 25).
32. Although the United States is not specifically the subject of this monograph, it must be noted that in the interwar years the United States is an exception to this proposition. Friedman and Schwartz discuss this exception in detail and at length.

soon sharply increase—governments have been tempted to increase demand by drastic fiscal and monetary expansion. Perhaps the most striking case in recent years was the Heath-Barber expansion of 1971–73 in anticipation that, without such expansion, the level of unemployment might exceed 1 million. The expectation of the cynical market is that the reaction by the authorities will be too much and too late, and thus it will merely add to inflation, price-dispersion and uncertainty. The additional uncertainty (which can be enormous as in 1973) more than negates any direct positive expansionary effect of government spending, etc. In effect, the state of high unemployment, combined with experience of government behavior, itself *creates* the high level of uncertainty which emasculates the real multiplier.

## Confidence and Deficits

So far this discussion of confidence has been loose, woolly, and evocative, rather than tight, incisive, and analytical. In one sense all we have done is give a name to our ignorance, just as Keynes did in *The General Theory*. We can make a little more progress by trying to delineate the main ingredients of low confidence and show that it is not merely a consequence of unemployment and recession.

It is clear that political change can shatter or restore confidence; and the expectation of likely dramatic political change will be a potent factor in redirecting the economy's response to changes in aggregate demand.[33] In the 1950s and much of the 1960s the United Kingdom enjoyed the stability of Butskellism—that wide measure of agreement on the basic macroeconomic policies between the two contending parties. Since the mid 1960s, and more markedly since the early 1970s, there has been emerging an evidently larger division between the party economic policies. The swings in policy have been more dramatic and more frequent than in the previous two decades.[34] This increasing political uncertainty has eroded confidence.

It would be useful, however, if one could identify a *quantitative* indicator of confidence. One such tentative candidate is the public-sector budget deficit, taken in conjunction with expectations of government behavior. If the underlying deficit is "high" (both with reference to the

33. The reaction to and the anticipation of the Mitterrand election in France in 1981 is an interesting case which would repay study.
34. In addition, there has been the rise in the price of energy.

historical record and with respect to the expected growth and savings rate), then the markets will anticipate some very considerable increases in tax rates and, possibly, in the rate of inflation. The markets may also anticipate increased uncertainty about the *level* of interest rates. These are the elements that erode confidence and inhibit irrevocable future commitments. In other words, a "high" deficit *forces* a change in government policy which can only generate additional uncertainty, with respect to form, extent and timing of response. If, on the other hand, the underlying deficit is "small," then there is no such pressure to change policies through tax increases or financial squeezes or inflationary "melt-downs" of the mountain of debt. Fiscally, the government's present policy is *credible*.[35]

## The Effect of a Change in the Deficit
## Depends on the Level of the Deficit

Thus, it seems intuitively likely that the behavior of the private sector will depend not merely on the *change* in the deficit but also on the *existing size* of that deficit relative to GDP. There is a great deal of difference between, say, increasing the deficit (cyclically adjusted for the sake of the argument) from 8 percent of GDP to 12 percent, and expanding it from minus 2 to plus 2 percent of GDP. The market would judge the first as foolhardy and a premonition of financial crises and of increases in taxes, inflation, interest rates and regulations; whereas the latter would be regarded as quite consistent with a stable financial policy.

In the former case I would expect that the increase in the deficit would have a depressing effect on real activity. Expectations of imminent disaster are not the stuff of expanding economies. In the latter case,

35. It might be thought that confidence and credibility would depend on the public debt as a ratio of GNP, rather than the rate at which that debt is accumulating. Although the debt ratio does play a role, it is rather ambiguous and depends critically on current and immediate–past policies. For example, a very large debt/income ratio is sustainable under noninflationary conditions if government runs a surplus or a small deficit, such that real debt cumulates at a rate less than the growth rate. But a country that had inflated or expropriated debt-holders will find it difficult to achieve a credibly sustainable policy even with quite low debt ratios. This principle can be seen most readily with respect to international indebtedness where, as Deepak Lal has demonstrated, Argentina in the years before World War I enjoyed a very high debt ratio and the highest possible confidence of investors. In 1982–83 the debt ratio was lower, but confidence had also plummeted.

it is likely that there would be per contra an expansionary effect of the deficit increase. This is the traditional Keynesian result and one that emerged from the analysis of the 1950s and the 1960s.[36]

If there were a nice, smooth path of interpolation between the high deficit case and the low (Keynesian) case, discussed above, then it would follow that at some moderate deficit, between the high and low, a change in the deficit would have virtually no real effect. However, it seems a rather narrow fence on which to sit. It cannot be recommended as a comfortable, permanent perch.

It will also be noted that the proposition that, at high levels of the deficit, an increase in the deficit will be contractionary is made with no reference to the pervasive level of unemployed resources. There may well be considerable unemployment of labor and capital. An increased deficit from a high level will generate the expectation, or reinforce the expectation, that a financial crisis must soon ensue—followed by increased tax rates, perhaps by more regulations, and a collapse of financial markets. A high level of unemployment may actually reinforce these expectations, since at such times governments come under great political pressure to "do something" (i.e., expand public spending), thus making the deficit even larger.

It would be nice to have estimates of the level of the deficit at the switch-over point. At this stage I would conjecture that in the United Kingdom, provided the PSBR is less than 3 percent of GDP, the deficit increase is likely to be expansionary. But if the PSBR is more than 5 percent of GDP, there is a good chance that the blow to confidence and expectations will ensure that an increase in the deficit will be contractionary in real terms. These numbers are guesses, based on examination of budgets over the 1970s.[37] It would be unwise to suppose that, fragile as these guesses may be, the figures would remain immutable through time or with respect to such fundamental propensities as the savings rate. However, they will be useful guides in assessing the effects of the budgets of the Thatcher government and any attitude to the policies pursued.

36. This also emerged from Feldstein (1982), and is broadly consistent with the time period that he analyzed (i.e., 1930–49 and 1946–77). Except for 1975, the deficits were small as a fraction of GNP.

    Martin Feldstein, "Government Deficits and Aggregate Demand," *Journal of Monetary Economics* 10 (1982), pp. 1–20.
37. They must also be placed in the context of the cumulation of deficits in the past years.

## Appendix on Multipliers

### A.

For the period 1921–38, Barrett and Walters (1966) fitted the equation:

$$\Delta c(t) = .0049 + .118\ \Delta m_t - 0.92\ \Delta m_{t\text{-}1} + 0.128\ \Delta a_t + 0.256\ \Delta c_{t\text{-}1}$$
$$\qquad (.0014)\ (.087)\qquad (0.88)\qquad (0.026)\qquad (0.106)$$

(standard errors in parentheses) $\qquad \bar{R}^2 = 0.788 \qquad DW = 1.55$

where

   $c$ is the logarithm of consumer spending in current pounds

  $m$ is the logarithm of the money supply

   $a$ is autonomous expenditure (the trade surplus plus government spending
     plus gross capital formation) in current pounds

Note: In this nominal-nominal result, the autonomous expenditure variable is
by far the main determinant of nominal consumption; money hardly puts in
an appearance. And considering that the regression is for differences, the
correlation coefficient is very high.

### B.

David Sheppard reports the following results:

1921–39

$$(c\text{-}p)_t = 1.456 + 0.262(ea\text{-}p)_{t\text{-}1} - 0.000(a\text{-}p)_t\ \bar{R}^2 = 0.98\ DW = 1.15$$
$$\qquad\quad (7.8)\quad (2.9)\qquad\qquad (0.0)$$

1922–39

$$\Delta(c\text{-}p)_t = 0.007 - 0.003\ \Delta(a\text{-}p)_t\ \bar{R}^2 = -0.06\ DW = 1.27$$
$$\qquad\qquad (3.6)\quad (0.0)$$

              and a similar result for lagged $\Delta(a\text{-}p)$

where

   $c$ is the log of UK consumption expenditure.

   $a$ is the log of UK autonomous expenditure,
     = exports + government expenditure + gross fixed capital formation.

   $p$ is the log of retail price index: 1958 = 100.

  $ea$ is the log of encashable assets—money stock + Post Office and other
     savings bank deposits + outstanding National Savings instruments +
     life assurance funds.

  $\bar{R}^2$ is the square of the correlation coefficient corrected for number of
     degrees of freedom.

 $DW$ is the Durbin-Watson statistic.

Table 5.3, p. 78. *The Growth and Role of U.K. Financial Institutions 1880–
1962*, Methuen 1971. The "e" variable is a measure of very broad money—or
"encashable assets." The values in parentheses are the "$t$" values.

## C.

Thus, from table 5.3, of Sheppard (1970):

1882–1914

$$\Delta(c\text{-}p)_t = 0.006 + 0.195\ \Delta(a\text{-}p)_t\ \bar{R}^2 = 0.24\ DW = 1.98$$
$$\quad\quad\quad (12.2)\quad (3.3)$$

where the $t$ statistic is reported below the estimate.

However, the monetary multiplier dominated the fiscal multiplier during this period, and was especially important in determining movements in prices. For example, Barrett and Walters show for 1881–1914:

$$\Delta c_t = .0031 + 0.576\Delta m_{t\text{-}1} + 0.087\Delta a_t \quad\quad \bar{R}^2 = 0.579 \quad\quad DW = 1.87$$
$$\quad (.002)\quad (0.088)\quad\quad\quad (0.031)$$

where standard errors are in parenthesis.

## D.

See Walters (1966) and Walters (1970). The reduced form multipliers from simple regressive equations of autonomous expenditure (gross capital formation plus exports of goods and services plus government expenditure) are:

| | | | |
|---|---|---|---|
| 1948–72 | *Nominal* | $\Delta c_t = 0.055 + 0.176\Delta a_t$ | $\bar{R}^2 = 0.407$ |
| | | (3.973) (1.993) | $DW = 1.84$ |
| | *Real* | $\Delta(c\text{-}p)_t = 0.025 + 0.254\Delta(a\text{-}p)_t$ | $\bar{R}^2 = 0.360$ |
| | | (2.289) (2.160) | $DW = 1.59$ |
| 1973–82 | *Nominal* | $\Delta c_t = 0.083 + 0.377\Delta a_t$ | $\bar{R}^2 = 0.289$ |
| | | (3.281) (2.445) | $DW = 1.816$ |
| | *Real* | $\Delta(c\text{-}p)_t = 0.026 + 0.206\Delta(a\text{-}p)_t$ | $\bar{R}^2 = 0.405$ |
| | | (3.277) (1.760) | $DW = 1.670$ |

For the low unemploymnt years, the real multiplier is higher than the nominal. For the high unemployment years, the real multiplier is lower than the nominal. The statistics do no more than confirm the common observation that real demand management became ineffective and even perverse by the 1970s.

# 2
## Crowding Out

### Crowding Out, Real, Macro and Micro

The proposition that an increase in government spending on goods and services will have some effect in reducing (or perhaps increasing) private spending has long been accepted. Equally, the extent and effects will depend on the method of financing the deficit; thus, *financial crowding out* (or portfolio crowding out) will appear when private borrowing and capital formation is displaced by public borrowing. The best definition of "crowding out or in," however, is not in terms of the displacement of investment but the change in sustainable output (formally, the net present value of output). The central concern is with real crowding out (or direct crowding out), whether it is induced through the financial mechanism, and the way in which the spending is financed.

At the real level, it is obvious, although rarely invoked, that government spending can both crowd out and crowd in—and it can be done by more than 100 percent. This arises clearly from the supply side of the economy, and the fact that government is often a *de facto* and usually *de jure* monopolist in the provision of certain goods and services. For example, a government may expand water, sewer, and other services (as well as planning permission) and so open up land for housing and industrial development.

In principle, the government should simulate (or actually improve upon) the conditions of competitive supply of such services and goods.[1]

---

1. The "improvement" due to government provision arises because, again in theory, the government not only can but will take into account all the manifest externalities which arise from the alleged "market failures."

If the pattern of investment and production were exactly the same as (or better than) that which would occur under competitive conditions, then any crowding out or crowding in is a "good thing." These are the ordinary rules of resource allocation, under conditions of "full employment."

Under less than full employment conditions, the true cost (or shadow price) of resources is less than that conveyed by the market price. Expansion of spending, either private or public, may well employ some resources otherwise idle, and so, if there is crowding out it would be less than 100 percent, and a possibility exists that the total level of sustainable output would be increased. Increased efficient spending by government or subsidies to private spending—both financed either by lump-sum taxes today or by borrowing today, duly requited by lump-sum taxes in the future—may therefore increase output, so that there may be less than 100 percent crowding out.[2] Alternatively, there may not. It may well be that such public expenditures or subsidies merely increase costs, either labor or capital, thus being dissipated in inefficiency or increased rents to unionized labor or capital owners.

Summarizing the evidence in 1974, Blinder and Solow were led to remark: "a fiscal policy planner will not often be led astray if he uses a [real] multiplier of 2 in his back of the envelope calculations."[3] This result, which did not seem remarkable a decade ago, now invokes much skepticism. (True, it was fitted to the economies of the 1950s and 1960s—but then one would have expected yet *more,* not less, crowding out than in the underemployed 1970s.) But the really striking aspect of the result is that it appears to provide a painless system of levitation for real output, and a superb rationalization for increased public expenditure. After all, this shows that there is not merely no crowding out but

2. As with all such statements, they are very dependent on the particular expenditures and subsidies as well as the presumed reaction of saving and spending patterns to them. Later we attempt some generalizations about such conditions—usually called "model specific." (This is a euphemism for "don't know.") Readers acquainted with microeconomics may see that this is a standard recipe which goes back at least to Pigou's *Wealth and Welfare* (1921) for the treatment of monopolies that restrict output—encourage them to expand with a per-unit subsidy and raise the revenue for such subsidies from some (mysterious) lump-sum tax. In the underemployed environment all firms and government agencies (on the above assumptions) are similarly producing too little because marginal costs are less than price. It is the same remedy.

3. Blinder and Solow (op. cit., p. 88), reflect the modelers in the sense that they did not think that the way in which the expenditure was financed was crucial to such figuring.

actually 100 percent crowding *in*. You can really eat your cake and have it![4] And if real marginal tax rates are more than 50 percent (as they have frequently been alleged to be during inflations), then government spending will be self-financing. With no conceivable financial crowding out the deficit will be unchanged; but since one gets "a bigger bang per buck" with government spending than one loses on tax receipts, the only way is up. Increased government spending, matched by increased taxes, is the road to nirvana.[5]

Credulity is stretched beyond the breaking point. Such macroeconometric modeling produces results which are inconsistent with common sense and casual observation. And they give rise to implied policy measures that are unlikely to improve the performance of the economy.

Oddly enough, there has been little effort devoted to the *micro*economic study of crowding out, possibly because of the contempt many macroeconomists display for what they regard as mere anecdotal evidence. Yet studies of particular elements of government spending in their institution and market environments can tell us a lot about the effects of changes in the level of spending. Again, this is no place to give a definitive survey of the evidence. All that can be done here is to touch on the kinds of evidence that seem to be relevant and to adduce some general but highly tentative results.

Perhaps the clearest evidence on government spending is that which pertains to the nationalized industries and other state enterprises. A most comprehensive study, at the micro-level, has been carried out by Richard Pryke.[6] This study demonstrated that the efficiency of resource use, including capital and labor, in the nationalized industries was significantly lower than that in private industry. Indeed, much of the capital investment had a negative rate of return, and it was also clear that there were significant areas where the marginal productivity of labor was negative. This, however, does not establish unequivocally that ad-

4. Since this is a *real* result, it can in principle be associated with any inflationary effects or conditions.
5. This real multiplier effect of a balanced budget increase in public spending is set out in T. Haavelmo, "Multiplier Effects of a Balanced Budget," *Econometrica 13*, pp. 311–18, 1945. For a subtle reversal of this Haavelmo principle, see Knoester, Anthonie, "Stagnation and the Inverted Haavelmo Effect," *De Economist 131*, 4, pp. 548–84, 1983.
6. Richard Pryke, *The Nationalised Industries*, Oxford, Martin Robertson, 1983. The strictures which Pryke brings to bear on nationalized industries in the UK does not *necessarily* apply to other countries. But with the possible exception of France pre-1973, there is good reason to believe that Pryke has enunciated a principle of wide application.

ditional public spending on the nationalized industries would not generate a net increase in output. Investment which takes the form of digging useless holes in the ground, analogous to much of the investment in, for example, the steel industry in the 1960s and 1970s, *may* be claimed to increase wealth because of the secondary effects of the spending out of the increased incomes, and the employment of additional idle resources in producing something of value. We must dig a little deeper to establish that much of the expenditure involves 100 percent or more of crowding out.

One illustration, by no means trivial, from the critical year of 1981 may illuminate the issue. The problem arose because the British Gas Corporation (BGC), in association with others, proposed the construction of a gas-gathering pipeline (GGP) in the North Sea. The cost of public provision by the BGC was put at about £2.5 billion, but with the various ancillary investments it would have totaled some £4 billion or more. This public-investment option necessarily involved continuation of the monopsony purchases of gas by the BGC, the no-export restriction, and various other conditions including the proscription of pipeline construction by the private sector. Approval of such a public-investment program did not involve merely the construction of an asset; it involved also the monopoly restrictions and the preclusion of the exploitation of many potential and some existing gas fields.[7] The evidence was clear: the GGP would have been a net wealth *reducing* investment. The alternative to public provision, *inter alia,* was simply to open the gas fields up for private exploitation by the oil companies. Opening up the North Sea gas regime, so that it was similar to the oil regime, would give rise to private investment in pipelines, etc., and somewhere near the "best" exploitation of the natural assets. There is a good case for suggesting that the GGP is an example of more than 100 percent crowding out of the private sector.

The usual versions of the crowding out process appear to either ignore the efficiency with which resources are used or implicitly assume that the same productivity is achieved whatever the public/private sector distribution of activity. This seems to be a crucial distinction and not one to be tucked away in an implicit assumption of macrotheory. Hence, I stress the net wealth implications rather than the employment

7. There was also considerable evidence that the GGP would have been constructed to a high capacity long before there was gas to fill it. Thus, it fulfilled the normal indictment of public investments—it was too early and too large (and one would also add, in the wrong place!).

of resources. This is particularly important when public expenditure substitutes largely for some private provision, and above all for *competitive* private provision.

Although there are many methodological and statistical difficulties in comparing the efficiency of public and competitive private provision of goods and services, the evidence is hardly equivocal. For example, Feibel and I carried out a study of urban bus services in various cities of the world where, at the same time, there was a publicly owned and operated bus authority and fairly competitive private bus owners operating in similar environments.[8] In no case did private costs exceed those of the municipal buses, and on the average the private costs were about half of the public costs—and the latter are appropriately subsidized. Similarly, comparisons of the publicly owned British Airways, as well as other state airlines in Europe, with private airlines and with competitive airlines in the United States, show that adjusted costs tend to be about doubled by state ownership.[9] All these data are consistent with "Friedman's Law," namely, that public provision doubles the cost.[10]

The treatment of public-sector provision in the national accounts and in calculating GDP and GNP ensures that it takes the resources absorbed as a measure of the output of many public-sector services. The output is priced at the average *cost* of producing the public services. Consequently, when there is a switch from private to public provision, and the same resources are used with a fall in productivity, the real GDP, as measured by the national accounts and used by macroeconomists, will remain the same. This imparts a potentially serious bias to the estimate of fiscal multipliers and perhaps goes part of the way toward explaining why they have been more disappointing in practice than their estimated statistical magnitude would predict.[11]

The real crowding-*in* hypothesis has been deployed rather vigorously by critics of the first Thatcher government to justify a substantial increase in the program of public investment. It has been argued that

8. C. Feibel and A. A. Walters, "Ownership and Efficiency in Urban Buses," World Bank Staff Paper, No. 371, February 1980.
9. Although airlines operate with very similar equipment, costs have to be adjusted for variations in landing fees and fuel prices. For comparable trips, United States airlines (which are normally in the long run profitable) charge fares of about 40 to 60 percent of the European state airlines (subsidized) fares.
10. David Friedman, *The Machinery of Freedom*, New Rochelle, Arlington House, 1978, p. 116.
11. If we combine Friedman's Law with Blinder and Solow's fiscal (expenditure) multiplier of about 2, we can see that in *output* terms as distinct from resource-use terms, the multiplier falls to 1.5, if expenditure is wholly on services.

there is an enormous program of "potentially high yielding (public) investment projects" which it would be worthwhile to undertake.[12] Few analysts would deny that there are a number of *"potentially* high yielding projects"—indeed, there always have been. The difficulty has been to realize that potential. It can hardly be claimed that such a potential has been realized in the past. To imagine it can be achieved in the future is "a triumph of hope over experience."[13]

Finally, it is necessary to correct a common error in interpreting the Thatcher government's policy on public investment. It is widely held by the most eminent authorities that the "obsession with that most myopic of indicators, the PSBR, means that even worthwile projects which are self-financing over a number of years are discriminated against [, and that] [a]ny new scheme which yields a return that does not take the form of a cash inflow into the public sector stands no chance at all."[14] Such statements are the product of a vivid imagination rather than a cool survey of the facts. In my experience, which encompassed such great projects as Rail Electrification and the GGP, the PSBR effect, calculated over a number of years, played very little part in the decision-making process. Of course, it would be stupid to ignore cash flow effects, but they constituted no constraint to the project evaluation. The real deciding factor was that the projected investments were not superior to alternative low public-investment strategies. The returns projected by the sponsors, when subjected to critical appraisal, were greatly exaggerated and the investment was very likely to be a waste. The government was anxious to undertake any project in the public sector, almost irrespective of the effects on the PSBR, provided that it could be shown that the benefits clearly exceeded costs, using the test rate of discount of 5 percent real. There were many extravagant claims but few convincing cases.

## Financial Crowding Out

Instead of crowding out being achieved through the direct substitution of, for example, publicly owned for private transport, financial crowd-

12. See Willem Buiter, "False Dilemma on Public Investment," *The Times,* Nov. 23, 1983.
13. More sophisticated commentators recognize that there need to be many changes in the control of public investment before any such program can be confidently launched. See Christopher Foster, "A Cautious Dose of Investment Could Cure the Ailing Economy," *The Times,* November 15, 1983.
14. Buiter, op. cit., 1983.

ing out appears because of substitution of financial assets and liabilities which, in turn, affect real expenditures. In its simplest and most convincing form, financial crowding out occurs when the government issues a bond to finance expenditure, and that gilt-edged security is substituted for an industrial debenture in the portfolio of the private sector. Government borrows money hitherto borrowed by private industry (or persons), and so the private sector will have that much less to spend. As distinct from the real crowding out discussed above, there is no reason why the contraction of spending in the private sector should be associated with substitutes in the public sector. The link is entirely through the provision of finance.

In this financial crowding out, it must be recalled that the portfolio decision is thought to be free from money illusion.[15] It is the *real* stocks of financial assets that affect decisions. Similarly, the additional demand for credit by the government will put upward pressure on *real* interest rates. But if private spending is highly elastic with respect to real interest rates, and if portfolio holders are more or less indifferent between government and private debt at the margin, then it is possible to conceive of 100 percent crowding out with little or no change in real interest rates. It is then the analogue of a perfect substitution of public spending and debt for private spending and debt. The size of the public sector, at least for the range of spending and debt for which this approximation is valid, is of no consequence—but, of course, only if public- and private-sector expansion are equally efficient and productive. If the public-sector spending generates returns either in cash or noncash terms which are sufficient to offset the financing of future interest payments, then the equivalence is virtually complete. However, this would be a rare event indeed.

## Substitution of Gilts, Equities and Money

The central result for complete crowding out depends critically on the high substitution of gilts for private assets, particularly equities and corporate debt.[16] Whether gilt-edged securities and equities (or the myriad

15. Thus, if there is a constant inflation *and* if the interest rate reflects this plus a positive real rate, then the inflationary erosion of the real value of debt will mean that asset-holders will readily absorb additional debt to replace that erosion. One might imagine, however, that if the real rate of interest had been substantially negative for some time such enthusiasm would wane.

16. It has been recently argued that the data are more consistent with a high substitutability between financial assets and money. Financial assets earn a margin,

of bank CDs, and other financial deposits which are the liability counterpart to bank loans to industry) are significantly high substitutes is an
empirical matter of immense complexity and difficulty.

Statistical analyses of the degree of substitution have tended readily
to founder on the problem of calculating convincing measures of the
anticipated real rates of return, after tax.[17] Except for quite short maturity instruments, the expected rates of return have large arbitrary elements. Inflationary expectations will differ over different maturities and,
in the absence of indexed debt, there is no agreed method of divining
market expectations. Thus, although we wish it well, it is unlikely that
statistical analysis will shed revealing and trustworthy light on this
issue.

But whatever the statistical analysis reveals or denies, there is no
doubt that the opinion of men in the market is that there *is* crowding
out of private investment by bond financing, and there is certainly no
crowding in. Although at one time government bonds were fairly close
substitutes for money (such as during 1945–51 when there was virtually no chance of any substantial unexpected real capital loss), the volatility in recent years has shown that there is a good chance of a sub-

---

approximately constant, over the implicit yield–liquidity preference–on money
balances. But since the nominal return on money (assumed to be noninterest
bearing) is zero, the real (explicit) return is minus the rate of inflation. Thus,
the real rate of return on financial assets will be the more or less constant
liquidity premium minus the expected rate of inflation. The results of this
analysis suggest that there is much more of a dichotomy between financial and
real rates of return on capital assets than has been supposed. See, J. Carmichael
and P. W. Stebbing, "Fisher's Paradox and the Theory of Interest," *American
Economic Review,* Vol. 83, No. 4, September 1983, pp. 619–30.

17. For a very sophisticated test of crowding out, see Jeffrey A. Frankel, "A Test
of Porfolio Crowding Out and Related Issues in Finance," NBER Working
Paper No. 1205, September 1983. Using United States data for 1954–80, he
shows that the hypothesis that there is no crowding out is not discredited by
the data. Indeed, he shows that, statistically insignificant though it may be, the
evidence is more consistent with crowding *in.* That is to say, federal debt
substitutes for money, and not for equities and real capital; thus, additional
federal debt will drive *down,* not up, the relative rate of return required for
real capital, thus stimulating investment and "crowding in." See Benjamin
Friedman, "Crowding Out or Crowding In? Economic Consequences of Financing Government Deficits," Brookings Papers on Economic Activity (March
1978), pp. 593–641. This is consistent with the Carmichael and Stebbing
(1983) results. Phil Cagan has pointed out, however, that this result arises
from an inefficient increase in "money" since the debt substitutes for money.
Yet, the *sine qua non* of such exercises is to hold the quantity of money constant. So the Frankel and Friedman exercises confound fiscal with monetary
policy.

stantial loss. And the long inflation and high nominal rates have resulted in a reduction of money balances—and I mean here money in the non-interest-bearing transactions sense—to a minimum level.[18]

Although government bonds may substitute for term deposits, it is unlikely that they will substitute for notes and coin and non-interest-bearing sight accounts. Since term accounts and CDs are the basis for bank lending to the private sector, there is a high likelihood of financial crowding out. In principle, with other things being equal, this would give rise to an increase in the required real rate of return on bank credit, and so on real capital.

## Pre-Ricardo Neutrality of Debt and Tax Financing

However, it is unlikely that other things would remain equal. In particular, the increase in the public debt would mean that people would expect to have to pay larger taxes in the future in order to offset the higher interest payments and the amortization of the principal. Thus, people would be induced to save more this year, so that they can maintain consumption in subsequent years when the increased taxes are paid. In its extreme or pure version of this theory, people will save *just sufficiently* more of their income to take up the additional government debt. Then it is irrelevant whether taxes are raised in the current year to finance the spending, or whether debt is raised in the current year and taxes in future years to pay interest and principal. Whichever form of finance is used, the private sector will save in order to achieve the same path for consumption and net wealth (i.e., net of tax liabilities). Then there is no crowding out or in.

This superficially surprising result seems relatively commonplace and all of a piece with much post-1970 experience when one reflects that it simply asserts that the private sector will plan its own wealth and spending-saving plans, taking into account not only what government does today but also what is implied for future government exactions.[19] It will

18. This is shown in the increase over the last decade in the velocity of currency (notes and coin) by a 4 percent per annum trend.
19. The original idea was certainly around in Ricardo's day, although Ricardo rejected the conclusion that the form of finance, either through bonds or current taxes, did not affect the economy. The seminal article that developed the pre-Ricardian concept is by Robert Barro, "Are Government Bonds Net Wealth?," *Journal of Political Economy*, Vol. 82, No. 6, November–December 1974, pp. 1095–117. The Barro process does not deny the crowding out of increases in public spending; the issue is the form of financing.

be readily seen that the principle could also be applied to monetary expansion, where expenditure is financed through short-term borrowing from the banking system. People will then save more in order to pay the inflation tax—or they will try to restore their eroded financial wealth, which has been expropriated by borrowers. This, as we shall see, is thought to be an explanation for the high personal savings rates in the United Kingdom in the inflationary 1970s (see note 36, Ch. 1; Feldstein, 1982, p. 15). There is an important kernel of truth in this proposition of neutrality of finance. One need not embrace, however, the extreme proposition that financing does not matter.

Clearly, a reduction of taxes today with the promise that they will be higher next year, etc., is bound to have an effect on the level of activity today compared with that in the future.[20] Similarly, the principle supposes that people think as much of the welfare of their heirs as they do of their own—but perhaps heirless people may be quite happy to consume today's seed corn at the expense of someone else's children.

All these sorts of reflections suggest that deficit finance should still have some effect, but probably not so much as those models of the 1960s imply. The empirical evidence on the "neutrality" proposition is not as clear cut as one would wish. But it is difficult to conclude that debt and tax finance are equivalent in their effects on the economy.[21]

20. It would be possible to preserve the extreme version of neutrality if one were able to impose taxes that had no effect on activity—so called "lump-sum taxes" which are always and everywhere bolts from the blue. In reality, however, there is no such animal. Lump-sum taxes are impossible.
21. The most recent and most convincing discrediting of the neutrality proposition is contained in Martin Feldstein's "Government Deficits and Aggregate Demand," *Journal of Monetary Economics,* Vol. 9, 1982, pp. 1–20. In terms of the discussion of the importance of confidence above, it seems clear that debt-finance is likely to generate expectations of future exactions, the form of which may be highly conjectural, whereas the pay-as-you-go form of tax finance creates no future obligation to cloud the outlook.

# 3

# *Fiscal Multipliers in Econometric Models*

## Multipliers in the United Kingdom

Since the heady days of the 1960s and early 1970s, there has been a considerable change in the evaluation of the statistical fiscal multipliers; they are now thought to be much lower than the two to three of those pre-oil-shock years. A recent survey suggests that the long-run multiplier with respect to government spending might be as low as 0.24 to 0.62.[1] One's first impression is that such low values of the multiplier (excluding the Cambridge estimate) are much more "reasonable" and consistent with the Treasury's recent views and current opinion on the relative impotence of fiscal policy as a countercyclical stabilizer. Nevertheless, with *any* positive long-run multiplier, one is always tempted to increase government spending in order to maximize GDP. There is still

---

1. See Michael Artis and Marcus Miller (ed), *Essays in Fiscal and Monetary Policy,* Institute for Fiscal Studies, Oxford, 1981. The value of 0.24 was found by a simulation of the NIESR model, with earnings and exchange rate endogenously determined, whereas the value of 0.62 comes from a more explicitly monetarist model of the London Business School, see Ball, R. J.; Burns, T.; and Warburton, P. J., *The London Business School Model of the U.K.: An Exercise in International Monetarism,* mimeo., London Business School, Discussion Paper No. 49, 1978. The Cambridge fiscalists, however, still believe that the multiplier is 3.27—as demonstrated in the paper by M. Fetherston and W. Godley in Artis and Miller, op. cit.

The European Economic Commission reported that a multiplier of GDP with respect to public investment could be increased from 0.9 to 1.6 percent after two years if the policies of the Community were "coordinated." See "European Economy," *Annual Economic Review 1983–1984,* No. 18, November 1983, Commission of the European Communities, Brussels.

a free lunch, if not a sumptuous one. If the simulations are valid, then sizable gains to GDP can be made by expansion of the public sector.

Of course, the critical presumption in all these expansive policies is that there are unemployed resources which will be brought into production by the new government spending.[2] Since these multipliers were calculated, the levels of unemployment have increased two- to threefold; so simulations of an expanding public sector borrowing requirement in 1984, 1985, etc., should now show more substantial increases in output. The National Institute for Economic and Social Research seems to have made such claims in proposing an expansionary fiscal policy in their Review No. 106 of November 1983. Since the change in the financial deficit and PSBR were not revealed, it is difficult to calculate any sort of implied multiplier. The results on GDP, however, are set forth; the cumulative gain over five years is almost 12 percent, and in the fifth year, GDP, under the larger deficit, is about $2\frac{1}{3}$ percent higher than it would otherwise have been, with the clear implication that it will persist above 2 percent and not drop to negative values in subsequent years.[3] By not adopting their policy it is alleged that Britain will lose some £35 billion (12 percent) of GDP at end 1983 market prices over these five years—a very large claim indeed. Furthermore, strong effects overlap the length (4 to 5 years) of the average cycle. This is then no countercyclical strategy. It is a bootstrap policy for secular expansion and growth.

2. For example, in the Fetherston and Godley case, it is *assumed* that the growth rate of full employment or capacity output is 4 percent per annum, whereas the "growth rate of the baseline economy" is 3 percent. If this went on for "ever," then ultimately unemployment will settle at about 25 percent. In the case of Ball, *et al.*, and the NIESR, the result is a consequence of the analysis of the data from 1964 to 1967. The LBS simulations take 1976 as the base year when unemployment was 5.7 percent. But the initial conditions for the NIESR simulation for 1972 were a year in which the unemployment rate was 3.8 percent.

3. The alternative fiscal policy was developed using "optimum control analysis" designed to minimize the squares of the deviations of the outcome from some "desired" values for growth and inflation, with a trade-off of 1 percent growth for 3 percent inflation, and with some "penalties" for too large a debt or current foreign balance. Although the PSBR profile "may be large relative to the government's declared intention, . . . we do not believe it is inconsistent with prudent finance" (p. 18). The NIESR claimed that there would be no effect on real interest rates and market confidence would be maintained. There is neither argument nor evidence (nor even the PSBR's) produced to support such extraordinary and extravagant claims. It was reported that monetary policy was "neutralized" by maintaining the same real interest rates. Artis and Miller, *op. cit.*

The general result, however, is clear: whatever the length of the dole queue, there is always a permanently sustainable free lunch at the fiscalists' counter. They vary, of course, from the heady gourmet delights of the Cambridge high table to the meager fare of the monetarists' manqué.[4] The policy implications are also clear; public spending promotes a higher standard of living and should be increased. Over the twenty years before Thatcher from 1960–79, public spending as a percentage of GDP increased from 33.2 percent in 1960, to 37.6 in 1970, rising to a peak of 46 percent in 1975.[5] Similarly, over the period 1960–74, the financial deficit as a percentage of GDP also roughly trebled. Governments certainly acted *as though* they believed the promises of the fiscalists. In the marked slowing of growth in the 1970s from 1972–73, which was experienced by all Western industrialized countries, there is no obvious evidence that the extravagant claims of the fiscalists were justified. Lower growth was also associated with higher inflation.[6]

## Dynamics from Econometric Models— The United States and the United Kingdom

So far we have treated the dynamics of the adjustment of real output (and the price level) in a rather cavalier way. Now we must try to make amends.

In the long run with a stable state economy the fiscal multiplier is simply the inverse of the marginal rate of taxation.[7] This simply says that in the long run all expenditures must be financed by tax revenues;

4. As in the "optimum control" system of the NIESR, it is argued that there is, or should be, a trade-off between more inflation and more output. I cannot see why, except insofar as GDP is a bad measure of output or welfare and that inflation has unfortunate distributional effects which are masked in the aggregate. Policies should be judged by their *real* effects, and the real effects of inflation, due to uncertainty, loss of confidence, etc., should appear in the measure of GDP appearing in subsequent years.

5. For some comparative figures, see Frank Gould, "The Development of Public Expenditures in Western Industrialized Countries," *Public Finance*, Vol. 38, No. 1, 1983, pp. 38–69. In Table II, p. 42, Gould shows that relative to GDP, the UK increase was little more than average in its behavior from 1960–62 to 1977–79 (which, it must be recalled, was *after* the Healey cuts of 1977).

6. As we have seen, however, the *ex post* adjustment of the deficits for inflation in the 1970s has been used to claim that the 1970s saw fiscal *tightness*, rather than ease, which retarded the economy. Thus, the fiscalists would have preferred yet larger financial deficits of more than the 8 percent of 1975–76!

7. See Appendix on Multipliers at the end of this chapter for references and mathematical discussion.

when government spending is increased, in the long run *it must be financed by additional taxes*. And if the marginal tax rate is fixed, the only way to increase taxes to match the increased spending is to increase the level of nominal income. If prices are "fixed," as in Blinder and Solow (see note 21, Ch. 1), then the only way to increase tax revenue is a sizeable increase in *real* income. If prices are not "fixed" and there are no unemployed resources in the long run, then the rate of inflation will increase and impose an "inflation tax" to balance the long-run budget. Alternatively, prices may be considered fixed if the *rates* of taxation eventually are increased to finance the debt created by the increase in spending.

In the long run—far longer than a business cycle—the appropriate model must be one which recognizes that there is no "permanent" or transcyclical core of involuntarily unemployed resources. There *is* an economic problem in the allocation of *scarce* resources. This would imply that in the long run either inflation or increased tax rates or some combination of the two would be the appropriate outcome—with no effect on real income.[8]

The path of adjustment to the new equilibrium is one which must be studied by reference to the fitted macroeconometric models. Since the models of the United States economy are more numerous and detailed than those of the United Kingdom, I shall first review the time pattern of the multipliers in the simulations of the United States before examining those for the United Kingdom.

There is a considerable measure of agreement between non-monetarists and monetarists that by the time a new long-run equilibrium is reached, the macro fiscal actions will have no significant effect, at least on real income.[9] However, in the non-monetarists' view, this long-run equilibrium will require a very long time (if not forever); it is, therefore, hardly more than a *curiosum* which tells us nothing about the response relevant to the design of policy—say the first two or three years.[10]

8. There is a logical possibility that in response to a bond-financed increase in government spending, the tax revenues can be raised by increasing the capital stock of the economy and, with unchanged employment, increasing real incomes. But to bring about a higher capital stock requires a lower nominal interest rate and a fall in the price level—not the normal ambience of increased bond-financed spending.

9. Modigliani and Ando (*op. cit.*) argue that the "[increase in real GNP] would dwindle to zero or first turn negative (something one would hardly expect much before two or three years)" (p. 25).

10. Modigliani and Ando (*op. cit.*) pp. 18–19. It is most important to note that this statement does not specify initial conditions of "spare capacity" or unemployment. The boost is always there.

The simulation reported by Modigliani and Ando was based on the initial conditions of 1958 when unemployment averaged 6.6 percent.[11] In the operation of the multiplier, it is supposed that the additional government spending nudges the economy onto a higher level of employment, thus filling in the trough of the recessionary shortfall of employment and output. If one could be sure that, after this process of filling in the trough, the net effect would fall to zero, there would be little more to be said. Relatively small amounts of countercyclical public spending would have a net present value (benefits minus costs) greater than zero. One should expand public spending until the marginal project produces a net present value just equal to zero. Then public spending is optimized.[12] One would imagine that the troughs are almost wholly filled.

The attention of fiscalists is concentrated on the two years of the expansionary effects of additional spending—indeed, Modigliani and Ando dismiss the succeeding effects as a mere *curiosum*. But clearly what happens in subsequent years is more than a *curiosum* if we are examining the effects of an active fiscal policy on the long-term health of the economy. A fast fix may also be a slow poison. The argument that fiscal policy will have no long-run real effects also must be applied not merely to the rate of growth of the economy but also the *level* of GNP. One possible scenario is illustrated in Figure 3.1 where the reaction of real GNP, in terms of changes over the quarter, is in response to an initial increase, duly sustained in perpetuity, in government spending on goods and services.

The usual positive stimulus is shown for the first three or four years. This is consistent with the claims of the fiscalists. But after that period we have supposed that the negative effects are strung out, as Modigliani and Ando say, "forever." This means that the increment in output due to government spending, after the first four years, is forever slightly negative. In fact, the increase in government spending would displace private capital investment, so reducing the stock of capital that would be otherwise available to contribute to output "forever."[13] The cost of the

11. This was the highest value for unemployment for the 32 years from 1942 to 1974. Although the authors do not say so, it is difficult to think of any other initial conditions which, using their presuppositions, would produce larger multipliers.
12. The process is, however, very complicated. The analyst must predict the path of the economy with and without various doses of public spending for future periods. I do not intend to extend this study to the consideration of optimum control systems.
13. See footnote 3, pp. 22–23, of Modigliani and Ando (*op. cit.*). Figure 3.1 is, I believe, consistent with their propositions.

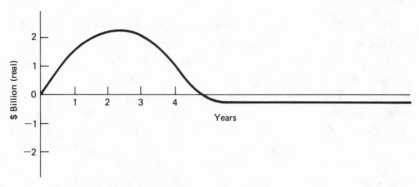

Figure 3.1 Cumulated effect on real GDP of a $1 billion expansion of public spending.

stimulation in the short and medium term is a slightly but permanently depressed output for all future years.[14]

In a sense the time distribution of the effects in Figure 3.1 is the best outcome for those who believe in discretionary fiscal policy. Provided that in the long run increases in government spending are about as frequent and of the same magnitude as decreases, the effects of discretionary fiscal policy should cancel out. There would be no permanent depression of the level of equilibrium long-run output. We should merely be filling the trough.

But it is also an unlikely response path. It is more likely that the oscillations persist from year 4 onward. One possible path is shown in Figure 3.2. The first three years have been taken from Modigliani and Ando (1976); then I have assumed that the effects become negative, finally giving the zero effects in year 10.[15]

This sort of reaction in years 4, 5, and 6 is no *curiosum*. The negative effects then, although somewhat less than the high positive multipliers (about 2) during the first 18 months, are considerably depressing factors on the economy. The really worrying aspect of this pattern is that in years 4, 5 and 6 one may well be encountering yet another recession which will be exacerbated by these negative hangover effects of the previous stimulus.

14. In principle one should add the increment in investment, which is generated by the higher savings from the four-year increase in income, to the capital stock and so to the long-run level of output. However, this line of reasoning rests on dubious stabilities in savings functions and investment incentives. It would be unwise, if not fatal, to rely on such doubtful evidence as a basis for policy.
15. The results which one would get from the MPS model were not reported by Modigliani and Ando.

It is easy to see that, if the average length of the cycle is about 4.5 or 5 years, and if the original countercyclical expansion of spending was undertaken at the onset of the recessionary stage of the cycle, then the negative effects, or "backlash," of the original stimulus will occur just as the economy is entering another recession. What was initially a countercyclical stimulus becomes a procyclical depressant. Then, to offset this backlash and to provide the stimulant necessary to counter the normal forces of cyclical recession, the government must inject almost twice the stimulus that it put in four or five years ago. And so as this process continues, the required injection becomes larger and larger. It will appear as though the patient is becoming immune to the drug. Seemingly, the larger the dose, the smaller the effect.

This explanation is at least consistent with the widespread view that in spite of *increasing* slack in the economy, the efficacy of fiscal policy is not what it once was in the balmy days of the "touch on the tiller" and the "new economics." But, of course, one does not *know* whether this is the explanation. It would be useful if we could trace the effects through the MPS type of model over, say a 10- to 12-year horizon. But such models do acknowledge that the predictions become more and more unreliable the further one gets away from the base. This is not unreasonable. These models were primarily constructed to answer short- or medium-run problems. They were not intended to trace the longer-

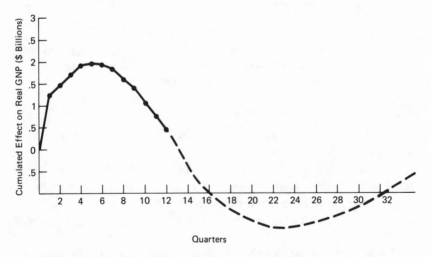

Figure 3.2 Real GNP multiplier with respect to an increase in government purchases of goods of $1 billion. Quarters 1-12 from Modigliani and Ando (1976), p. 25. Quarters 13-32 extrapolations using hypotheses of text.

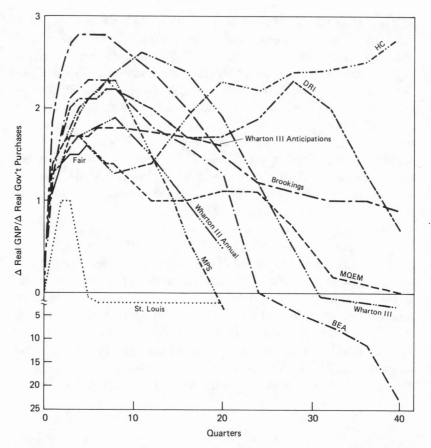

Figure 3.3 Dynamic multiplier effects of a maintained $1 billion increase in real government purchases upon real GNP without accommodating monetary policy as a function of time elapsed. From Christ (1975).

term effects—whether benign or mordant—that follow from short- or medium-term policy proposals.[16]

It might be thought that the Modigliani and Ando description of the fiscal multiplier is somehow atypical. Figure 3.3 shows the multipliers from a variety of econometric models for varying periods within the time span 1951 to 1973, but concentrating generally in the mid 1960s

16. If one *did* fit a model which was intended to answer such questions concerning the long-run effects, then it would be wise to constrain it so that the long-run effect nets out at zero; one could then merely examine the oscillations on the way.

to early 1970s. All are consistent with the Modigliani and Ando pattern, for the first two or three years with peak effects at one to two years. Clearly, there were enormous benefits to be derived from expanding government purchases, notwithstanding the historically low unemployment and high utilization of those days.[17]

The simulators seem reluctant to thrust, or perhaps trust, their multipliers into the negative ranges. Slight negative effects appear in the MPS model only after five years and in two Wharton III and BEA models after eight and ten years. The BEA is probably closest to an explicitly "full-employment" simulation since they maintained the unemployment rate at 4 percent throughout. Yet the effect is positive for *six years*. As Christ remarks, however, the uncertainties certainly increase—and I think more than proportionately—as one projects further and further forward. There is no measure of the confidence in simulations, but the spread of the models tells something of modeling procedures. Negative values, as Modigliani and Ando suggest, are quite likely after 20 quarters or so.

The results for dynamic multipliers in Britain suggest a similar time profile to those of Modigliani and Ando, but the efficacy is about half that in the United States. (See Table 3.1.)

After four (or five) years no negative values appear for the change of GDP. In fact it is remarkable that two of the three models show the multiplier actually increasing in the final year. I suspect that, in the Budd and Burns and in the Ball *et al.* models, this is merely a statistical aberration due to the fact that one is a long way from base. As in the case of the United States studies, the negative values did not appear over the first four years.

The fact that the measured multipliers in the United Kingdom (excepting Fetherston and Godley) are about (or less than) half as large as those found for the United States is consistent with the history of countercyclical fiscal policy. Fine fiscal tuning has been a central concern of U.K. policymakers since the end of World War II, whereas in the United States such policies date from the mid 1960s. If the decay rate of the multipliers, after repeated doses, is the same in the two countries, then we would expect this result.

17. Carl F. Christ, "Judging the Performance of the Econometric Models of the U.S. Economy," *International Economic Review*, Vol. 16, No. 1, February 1975, pp. 54–74. See Table 3 for the description of the models and periods of simulation. As a rough guide, most unemployment percentages before 1974 were in the 3 to 6 range, but after 1974 the range moved to 6 to 11.

Table 3.1. Simulations of fiscal policy

Dynamic multipliers for fiscal policy: ratio of GDP increase ($\Delta Y$) to government spending stimulus ($\Delta G$) or real tax cut ($-\Delta T$)[a]

|  | | NIESR ($\Delta G$) | Budd & Burns ($-\Delta T$) | Ball, Burns & Warburton (1978) ($\Delta G$) | Featherston & Godley ($\Delta G$) |
|---|---|---|---|---|---|
| Quarter | 1 | 0.68 | 0.07 | 1.01 | |
| | 4 | 0.81 | 0.17 | 0.85 | Year 1: 1.15 |
| | 8 | 0.68 | 0.14 | 0.74 | |
| | 12 | 0.43 | 0.02 | 0.54 | |
| | 16 | 0.24 | 0.03 | 0.62 | Year 5: 3.27 |

Source: Michael J. Artis, "Fiscal and Monetary Policy—An Introduction to the Issues," in Artis and Miller (eds.), 1981, p. 9.

a The simulation results quoted assume—except in the case of Fetherston–Godley (F–G)—endogenous earnings, interest rate, and exchange rate. In F–G, the exchange rate is chosen to clear the current account.

The model for the United Kingdom that is most closely associated with the ideas advanced in this monograph is that of Minford and his colleagues at the University of Liverpool.[18] In his model Minford tries to capture some of the effects of confidence through an application of the principle of rational expectations. I suspect that this is as far as formal modeling will take us. But the interesting result is that Minford finds a multiplier equal to about one half, which lasts about four years—then output drops back to its base level.[19] The initial conditions for this simulation were from the high-unemployment year 1981 compared with 1976 (I) for Ball and Budd and the boom year of 1972 (I) for the NIESR. Considering the initial conditions, the Liverpool multiplier was indeed a damp squib.

However, as we shall see, I believe that even the Liverpool model got the 1981 multiplier wrong (and I suspect Professor Minford would acknowledge this). An increase in public spending and the PSBR of another £2 billion would have generated a deterioration of confidence which would have ensured a *negative,* not positive, multiplier. But this needs to be examined in the context of the Thatcher budgets—to which we now turn.

18. Patrick Minford, Satwant Marwaha, Kent Matthews and Alison Sprague, "The Liverpool Macroeconomic Model of the United Kingdom," *Economic Modelling,* January 1984, pp. 24–62.
19. See simulation 2 on p. 45, where an increase of government spending of 1 percent of GDP, financed by bonds, gives rise to a 0.5 percent increase in output.

# Appendix on Multipliers

See Alan S. Blinder and Robert M. Solow (*op cit.*), James Tobin and Willem Buiter, "Long-Run Effects of Fiscal and Monetary Policy on Aggregate Demand," *Monetarism*, North Holland, J. Stein (ed.), 1976. F. Modigliani and A. Ando (*op. cit.*) pp. 17–68.

This proposition can be easily generalized to a growing economy where the government has, in the long run, two sources of revenue to finance the deficit. These are from the issue of high-powered (or base) money and from the issue of gilts, where both issues must be consistent with the growth rate of the economy. In formal terms:

$$D = (p + g) M_0 + gB$$

where

$D$ = deficit including net interest payments on public debt
$p$ = "steady state" rate of inflation
$g$ = growth rate of GDP
$M_0$ = monetary base
$B$ = stock of government debt outstanding

The monetary base and the gilts, etc., must be willingly held by the public, and so the real interest rate and the rate of inflation must be such that they induce people to hold these supplies of government liabilities.

Taking each side of the equation as a percentage of GDP, we can find the deficit that is consistent with constant prices ($p = 0$) and a growth rate of, say, 2 percent. We obtain:

$$\frac{D}{\text{GDP}} = 0.02 \, \frac{M_0}{\text{GDP}} + 0.02 \, \frac{B}{\text{GDP}}$$

The value of $M_0/\text{GDP}$ is small (0.05) and falling whereas $B/\text{GNP}$ is about 0.45, and in recent years has been fairly stable. This then gives a rough estimate of the long-term deficit as 1 percent of GDP. This implies that if real interest rates are sufficient to induce the public to hold a bond portfolio of half the GDP, then 1 percent of the deficit can be financed without inflation.

Of course, a large noninflationary deficit could be feasible if the public were willing to hold a greater quantity of bonds (as they did in the 1950s and early 1960s). But higher real interest rates would be required to induce such behavior. And, ultimately, there is a limit (total national, including human, wealth) to the quantity of bonds that the public will willingly hold.

# 4

# *Measuring the "Fiscal Stance"*

## The Deficit and Adjustments

The modeling of fiscal policy in Britain has come around a complete circle. Before and during World War II, attention was more or less entirely concentrated on the additions to aggregate demand contributed by the budget deficit. Then during the development of more sophisticated Keynesian models in the postwar years, attention was shifted to the various individual components of the budget, both spending and revenue sides, with the tax package as the ultimate instrument on budget day. In particular this enabled the Chancellor to adjust personal disposable income so that, with the forecast savings rate, people would spend just enough to take up the expected supply of goods at the next year's expected price level. The targets were unemployment and the price level. The deficit was merely the residual in this sophisticated calculus. However, even a residual is a reality, and it clearly had to be financed.

It was largely the difficulties of financing such deficits, usually called the public sector borrowing requirements (PSBR), that ensured that once more the PSBRs have a central role—as target and as instrument—in the formulation of macroeconomic policy.[1] It linked fiscal policy to

---

1. The first important emphasis on the PSBR as a target was during the visitation by the IMF in the late 1960s. The elevation of the PSBR to a central target of policy came with the IMF visit in 1976. So it has remained.

56

what was thought to be "financeable." In the MTFS the proposed path of the PSBR was just as important a target as the rate of growth of the money supply (sterling $M_3$).

The usefulness of a *single* measure to encapsulate the government's fiscal policy—and in particular the use of such a single measure as a target—has been much questioned. After all, different expenditure and revenue flows have markedly different effects on aggregate demand, supply, and the rate of inflation. Nevertheless, there is a good case for a step-by-step approach by ignoring these differentials at first, then later taking what account one can of these differences. The experience of the last twenty years with large-scale econometric models suggests that it is difficult (and may mislead) if we try to account in one grand design for all the manifold complexities of reality. Better, as Alfred Marshall observed, that reason's chain be forged with a number of short simple links. The economic significance of the deficit is in many ways different, at least in emphasis, from the financial consequences—so we shall leave the latter aside for the time being and concentrate on its traditional Keynesian (or post-Keynesian) role.

The traditional view of the deficit is that it is expansionary. With unchanged monetary conditions, an increase in the deficit will expand nominal aggregate demand. But nominal aggregate demand will affect the budget deficit—partly because of the effects of money GNP on tax receipts and because of the effects on other spending categories, such as unemployment and supplementary benefits. Thus, the budget deficit can be decomposed into:

*Autonomous* spending plus spending induced by *cyclical* variations in GNP
minus
*Autonomous* receipts plus receipts induced by *cyclical* variations in GNP.

In the autonomous components we have included the *trend* over time in the paths of spending and receipts as well as the discretionary spending and taxing of the authorities. Thus, the cyclical elements of both spending and taxing should, in the absence of random variations, average out at zero over the cycle. All the "structural deficit," as well as the authorities' countercyclical fiscal policy, will appear in the autonomous components only.

It is widely believed that the cyclical elements of the deficit will be countercyclical—the deficit expanding on the downswing and turning to a surplus on the upswing—hence, the concept of the automatic stabilizers.[2] It may be agreed, however, that the cyclically adjusted deficit is the appropriate measure for describing the fiscal stance of the authorities.

The main difficulty with this decomposition is that there is no reliable empirical basis for discriminating among trend and cycle, and, indeed, random shock. Trends change, sometimes quite dramatically, as the world discovered in the 1970s. At the time of the downturn from 1973, it was widely thought by industrialized countries that this change was another, albeit severe, cyclical downturn. However, now the evidence a decade later is that the slowdown also heralded a significant change of trend.[3]

Nevertheless, undaunted by such doubt, practitioners of macroeconomics who use these concepts have apparently had few qualms in defining a "target" or "potential" GNP or GDP which is sometimes designated as a "full employment" GDP. Connecting cyclical peaks of *real* GNP appears to be the most preferred way of constructing "full-employment" or "capacity" GNP—and extrapolation of this peak-to-peak line or curve is thought to indicate the potential real GNP in the cycle. Thus, the reference peak for the "Thatcher" cycle is naturally the year 1979.

The normal practice is then to calculate the *changes* in the cyclically adjusted budget from the peak year.[4] Buiter and Miller have followed

2. But in the United Kingdom during 1955–65 this was not so. The UK central government automatic stabilizers calculated by the OECD were not stabilizers at all. They were automatic destabilizers! See Bent Hansen, *Fiscal Policy in Seven Countries 1955–1965,* Table 2.6, p. 69 (Paris, OECD, 1969). This remarkable result of OECD seems to have been largely ignored by the fiscalists. This result implies that compared with the late 1960s, 1970s, and 1980s, when OECD discovered that the fiscal automatic stabilizers were positive and large, more discretionary fiscal expansion was needed to offset a given automatic contraction. It is indeed very odd that during the years when the Keynesian mechanism and policy seemed to work best the mechanism was seemingly *perverse.* Such results are inconsistent not only with the widespread view that the efficacy of deficit spending has diminished, not increased, but with much empirical evidence as discussed above. Although I am sure that it is possible to induce a statistical rationalization of these results consistent with the fiscalist views, it must give one some qualms in using any particular estimates.
3. Of course, one man's trend is another man's Kondratief, but this is the same point.
4. This is the practice followed by the pioneer of this concept, E. Carey Brown, "Fiscal Policy in the Thirties: A Reappraisal," *American Economic Review* Vol. 46, Dec. 56. See also Alan S. Blinder and Robert M. Solow "Analytical Foundations of Fiscal Policy," where they say "one should note that it is usually *changes* in a measure of fiscal impact that convey useful information" (p. 16, italics in original).

Table 4.1. Public sector financial balance
(percent of GDP at market prices)[a]

| Financial year | Actual balance | Change from previous year | Cyclically adjusted budget change |
|---|---|---|---|
| 1978/79 | −4.7 | | |
| 1979/80 | −4.0 | 0.7 | 0.6 |
| 1980/81 | −5.2 | −1.1 | 2.0 |
| 1981/82 | −2.5 | 2.6 | 4.1 |
| 1982/83 | −3.1 | −0.6 | −0.4 |
| 1983/84 | −3.8[b] | −0.7 | −0.8 |
| Sum of changes | | 0.9 | 5.5 |

Sources: This table corresponds to the first section of Table 6 of Buiter and Miller (1983). The figures, however, have been revised to reflect adjustments in 1983–85, as follows: *Actual balance* (column 1) is derived from CSO *Financial Statistics* no. 249, Jan. 1983, and no. 273, Jan. 1985, and *Economic Trends* Annual Supplement, 1985 edition. *Change from previous year* (column 2) is derived from column 1. *Cyclically adjusted budget change* is column 2 plus a built-in stabilizer from NIESR data in Table 4.2, which is the difference between the "unadjusted" and "cyclically adjusted" changes in surplus.

a Variations are due to rounding.
b HM Treasury *Financial Statement and Budget Report 1985–86* shows a 3.3% deficit.

this practice in assessing the fiscal policy of the Thatcher government— the results of which are repeated in Table 4.1.[5] The conclusions are dramatic. "The cyclically adjusted deficit was reduced by almost 8 percentage points." And even taking the *Central* Government financial surplus, as cyclically adjusted by the IMF, Buiter and Miller show that there has been a "seven percent shift to surplus" over the calendar years 1980 to 1983 (i.e., with respect to the reference year of calendar 1979).

Buiter and Miller do not explicitly state what their preferred fiscal policy would have looked like. However, it is possible to infer that *at least* they would have preferred that the cyclical stabilizers be allowed to work. This would have meant an increase of the budget deficit over the years 1980–83 of 5.5 percent. This additional deficit, added to the percentage of financial deficit of 1979 (or indeed 1980), would have produced a deficit for 1983 of about 9 or 10 percent GDP. Presumably, the authors would not wish to rely merely on the built-in stabilizers, but would, in principle, wish to pursue additional countercyclical spending and tax remission programs which would drive the deficit

5. Willem H. Buiter and Marcus H. Miller, "Changing the Rules: Economic Consequences of the Thatcher Regime," *Brookings Papers on Economic Activity* 2:1983. Note, however, that in these calculations Buiter and Miller used the NIESR assumption that the trend rate of growth of potential GDP was 2.5 percent experienced over the 1973–79 period. The different trend assumptions make a great deal of difference to the figures, but the conclusions remain.

even higher, producing a positive fiscal stimulus to combat the slump. So we may safely take it that 10 percent is the lower limit of their ambitions.[6] I believe these calculations should be regarded as *ex ante* targets rather than *ex post* outcomes. If such a policy were pursued, there would be no need for such large deficits since the slump in GDP would be quickly reversed and the *ex post* cyclical deficits would be much less than those which were actually registered in the three- or four-year periods. Perhaps so. But this hypothetical outcome does not change the general proposition that the *ex post* financial deficits would be very large. Consider, for example, the change from 1979/80 to 1980/81. Then the built-in stabilizers were a deficit of 3.1 percent of GDP. If this is added to the 1979/80 deficit, we have a deficit in the first full year of the downturn of almost 7 percent of GDP.

It is still true that, in any event, such an outcome is highly hypothetical. As we have seen repeatedly in 1967/68 and 1974/75, public-sector financial deficits of such magnitude have always proved to be unsustainable and have invariably been associated with financial crises—a collapse of confidence, a funding strike, a sterling slump, and recourse to the IMF. The Fund, however, insisted on a reduction in the financial deficit as a condition for financial assistance. So had we followed the Buiter-Miller prescription for 1980/81, it is likely that we should have been in the hands of the IMF, and this would have effectively ensured that there would be no more of that sort of thing.[7]

The basic difficulty with the Buiter-Miller proposal is that it treats the 1979 peak as though the conditions that then existed were a sustainable and normal objective. In 1978 and 1979 the unadjusted financial deficit was already about 4 to 5 percent of GDP. True, it had fallen from the 1975–76 period when it had been up to nearly 8 percent; but it is readily seen that the *average* deficit over the whole cycle from peak 1973 to peak 1979 was running at about 6 percent of GDP.[8]

6. Of course, GDP, the denominator in these percentages, would increase if the countercyclical policy were successful. But even assuming massive success (say, an increase by 1983 of GDP of 5 percent compared with the actual outcome), it would have only a slight effect on such percentages. No material change in the conclusions is called for.
7. If the 1976 experience of the Healey-IMF squeeze is anything to go by, the reductions in expenditure required by the IMF would have exceeded anything the Thatcher government succeeded in bringing about. So I do not think that there is any warrant for believing that Buiter or Miller envisaged any such contingency.
8. Although we only have two observations, it is worth noting that the percentage was larger in 1979 than in 1973—4.8 percent compared with 3.7 percent. And

By 1979, and indeed arguably by 1973, the public sector had accumulated a large structural deficit equal to at least 6 percent and perhaps as much as 10 percent of GDP, and it seemed that the core or structural deficit was continuing to increase. Clearly, this situation was unsustainable in an economy like the United Kingdom, with its slow growth rate (1 to 1.5 percent) and low savings rate. Such a high growth rate of the debt would be consistent with periodic expropriation of creditors, through controlled interest rates, exchange controls, and inflation. In theory it would be possible to continue with high deficits, but eventually the deficits would be dominated by the interest payments on the accumulated public debt. In that event the real limits to structural deficits of such magnitude arise from the fact that the private sector will not continue to absorb the financial liabilities of the public sector. There is a limit and a price. Financial markets anticipate such events and extract a present payment for such future contingencies. I suspect that the Buiter-Miller program would be feasible (and this does not imply that it is desirable) only under conditions where the economy is substantially regulated.[9]

Under the conditions of freedom—particularly of exchange controls and credit markets—which the Thatcher government rapidly introduced in 1979–80, the continuation of such a structural deficit was simply a recipe for disaster. The government recognized this danger and took upon itself the task of greatly reducing the structural deficit of the 1970s. The high deficits of the unhappy 1970s were not to be taken as a base from which to build even higher deficits for the 1980s.

The year 1979, or indeed 1978, cannot be claimed as a year in which output was at the "potential" level. Certainly it cannot be construed as "noninflationary" as in the definition of the noninflationary level of unemployment. Inflation was not only running at about 12 percent but was clearly artificially constrained by low public-sector price increases and was about to blossom in 1980 to its peak of 22 percent. Furthermore, 1979 was a year when the patchy system of regulation and control was coming under increasing strain—manifest in the "winter of discontent" of strikes. It seems that the "potential" output of 1979 was itself a function of the regulatory system which was necessary to prevent the 5 percent deficit from exerting its full influence; and it would be

---

1973 was in turn higher than 1969–70 (when there was actually a small *surplus!*). The trend is up.

9. Clearly, the authors are favorably disposed to some sort of wage restraint—but their views on exchange controls, etc., are not reported.

a brave presumption to suppose that the alleged boost due to inflationary pressures was just offset by the depressing effects of regulations.

The general analytical criticism flows from the fact that the concepts
of "potential" or "capacity" or "full-employment output," and indeed
the concept of "full employment" itself, are very slippery fish indeed.
However, it is not only that such states, as observed in the real world—
in 1973 and 1979, for example—are inherently unstable and must rapidly decompose; *the fundamental problem is that policies designed to
bring the economy back to the "potential" path may well so damage
the productive system that the calculated potential becomes not merely
an ambitious goal but an impossible dream.* Once it is known that the
authorities are committed to such expansionary programs, the expectations and behavior of the private sector will frustrate any hope of
achievement. One could hardly expect that the private sector would
continue with its old behavior patterns under such a dramatic change
of regime.[10]

The belief that the private sector (and the autonomous public sector)
will react passively to changes in government policy is at the basis of
all policies of direct incomes and price controls and is even the linchpin
of the so-called tax-based incomes policies (TIP). But if the private
sector knows that the government is committed to "full employment"
policies, then the income-policy constraints will be subverted or the
TIP taxes absorbed and incorporated in the price, and all that will remain is a bureaucratic nightmare or a much-derided tax. Neither will
affect employment, except perhaps in the short run, and both will reduce welfare and the material standards of life in the longer run.

## Weighting the Expenditures and Receipts

In seeking to improve the deficit concept it has been argued that the
different receipts and expenditures should be weighted according to
their presumed effect on aggregate demand. Thus, on the intuitive level
a reduction in the deficit which is brought about by a £1 million fall
in the government's spending on goods and services will be much more
effective in reducing demand than if the authorities collected an additional £1 million from North Sea oil revenues. The objective is to stan-

10. Without delving into the analytical point, the implications are mentioned by
    Blinder and Solow (*op. cit.*) in terms of numbers which are both nostalgic
    and instructive: "The weighted full employment surplus is a true measure of
    the impact of budgetary changes on a full employment economy; but such
    information may be of limited interest if the unemployment rate is (*as high
    as*) 6 percent," (*op. cit.*), p. 17 (My italics.)

dardize the money flows so that the weighted pounds have the same impact. This objective is, however, ambiguous since, for example, we know that different elements of the deficit have time profiles that differ very considerably. There is no attempt to weight differentially according to the long- or short-period effect. The weights are crude amalgams.

Weighted deficits have been calculated by the NIESR (see Table 4.2). For the years 1979–83 weighted deficits show that the Thatcher fiscal policies were only about half as restrictive as appears in the unweighted versions (3.7 percent compared with 7.8 percent). This was because the deficits were diminished or constrained primarily by increases in taxes (and, in particular, revenue from the North Sea), whereas government spending on goods and services was largely maintained or even increased during these years.[11]

If the weights are to be trusted, and I shall shortly argue that there is no warrant for such faith, then the severe fiscal squeeze—allegedly, the cause of the great recession—turns out to have been only the application of the most delicate of pressure. Indeed since the analysis is in terms of *outcomes* of the fiscal deficit rather than in terms of programs, one might reasonably attribute much of the statistical tightening to the ordinary chance outcomes of the budgetary process. The *average* difference, whether negative or positive, between the budget forecast PSBR and the actual outcome is about £3.5 to 4 billion or 1.5 to 2 percent of GDP. A cumulative total for four years of 3.7 percent is well within expected error.[12]

Although the weights calculated by the NIESR, or other research workers, such as the CEPG, are meant to reflect the relative punch of the items, they must nevertheless implicitly assume an enormous amount about the values and stability of the relationships of the economic system. For example, they must suppose that there is a given degree of

11. Government expenditure on final goods and services, at 1980 prices, was:

| 1973 | £ 42.8 billion | 1978 | £ 46.7 billion |
|------|------|------|------|
| 1974 | 43.5 | 1979 | 47.6 |
| 1975 | 45.8 | 1980 | 48.4 |
| 1976 | 46.2 | 1981 | 48.3 |
| 1977 | 45.7 | 1982 | 49.0 |

*Source:* CSO *Economic Trends,* No. 360, October 1983, p. 8.

12. This is a very rough conclusion amply justified by very rough data. I am assuming that the weighting of the deficits would not lead to any difference in the average error—and I conjecture that this should be a reasonable presumption. More important, I am supposing that the recorded errors in hitting the target PSBR are not systematically related in any serial correlation—in other words, the error is not related to the built-in stabilizers. Although I suspect this is correct, it would take a great deal of work to test the proposition.

Table 4.2. Change in financial surplus as a percent of GDP at Market Prices[a]

| Financial year | 1974/75 | 1975/76 | 1976/77 | 1977/78 | 1978/79 | 1979/80 | 1980/81 | 1981/82 | 1982/83 | 1983/84 | 1984/85[b] |
|---|---|---|---|---|---|---|---|---|---|---|---|
| Unadjusted | −2.57 | −0.26 | 1.79 | 1.84 | −0.81 | 1.12 | −0.96 | 2.6 | −1.3 | −0.3 | 1.5 |
| Cyclically adjusted | −1.15 | 1.97 | 1.94 | 2.23 | −1.06 | 1.04 | 2.13 | 4.1 | −1.1 | −0.4 | 1.1 |
| Weighted | −2.37 | −0.19 | 1.27 | −1.97 | −0.44 | 0.53 | −1.38 | 1.1 | −1.2 | −0.2 | 0.6 |
| Weighted and cyclically adjusted | −1.57 | 1.16 | 1.32 | 2.20 | −0.58 | 0.48 | 0.47 | 2.1 | −1.0 | −0.2 | 0.3 |

*Sources:* David Savage, "Fiscal Policy, 1974/5–1980/81: Description and Measurement," National Institute *Economic Review* 99, February 1982, p. 95; subsequent information from National Institute *Economic Review* 103, p. 8; 107, p. 8; and 111, p. 15.

a Percent change from previous fiscal year. Positive sign shows that the surplus was increased or the deficit decreased.
b Outturns partly estimated.

crowding out for each form of spending. Similiarly, they must suppose that there are precise, stable, and differential effects on leakages, through increases in savings. Indeed, the very basis of the post-Keynesian theory of the efficacy of deficits in promoting demand rests on the proposition that, for outputs less than potential, there is little or no crowding out (with a suitable fiscal monetary mix) and that savings coefficients are highly stable. In the United Kingdom, however, the savings rates over the last decade have been remarkably unstable. Economic forecasters were almost entirely wrong in their predictions of savings.[13] And we are probably on even more shaky ground in trying to predict "crowding out"; but most would agree that it is variable in the long and the short run. In another sense the weight will necessarily represent a view of how the details of the economy have actually worked in the past. And even if they did work well historically, they clearly would not be appropriate when there is a "change in regime" or any large change in ambient expectations and confidence.

## Adjustments for the Effects over Time

One of the obvious objections against using the deficit or PSBR as an index of fiscal stance is that it is the difference between only financial receipts (or receivables) and payments (or payables) *in that year*. But government obligations and exactions in this year reflect not merely history but also are affected and themselves affect future years. It is therefore natural to incorporate in an assessment of fiscal policy all the expectations of future receivables and payables by the government. Just as one supposes that the individual takes into account his expected future debits and credits in deciding how much to spend and save, so the government should also incorporate future commitments both from and to the private sector in its current policy.

To illustrate, suppose that the government reduced personal income standard rates of personal income tax to 20 percent from the previous 30 percent—thus approximately doubling the deficit from £10 billion to £20 billion. This is unequivocally an "expansionary budget" (or "inflationary budget" depending on the division between real and nominal effects). But if people widely expected that such a large deficit would give rise to a collapse of confidence and that the authorities would have to increase taxes dramatically the following year (say, to 42 percent), then it is at least not at all clear whether the budget deficit

13. See A. S. Deaton, "Involuntary Saving through Unanticipated Inflation," *A.E.R.* Vol. 67, No. 5 (1977), pp. 899–910.

increase could be counted as "expansionary."[14] True, there would be some shifting forward of activity to take advantage of the low income-tax rates this year; but there would also be an increase in savings this year from the higher post-tax income in order to maintain consumer spending next year at the high tax rates. Indeed, in the strict version of this process, people would increase their savings from this year's income by just sufficient to pay the increased tax bill that they expect next year.[15] Thus, the private sector does neatly offset the machinations of the public authorities.

In order to have a general concept of the deficit which reflects these future expected events, it is natural to consider the normal practice of finding the *present values* of these expected benefits and obligations. The difference should constitute the "value" or the "net worth" of the public sector. In principle, the "net worth" should be positive, for otherwise the government is bankrupt and no one would wish to hold its obligations. In practice, however, it is usually possible for governments to raise taxes and validate their claims of positive net worth.[16]

One difficulty with such a theoretically satisfying concept is, of course, that no one has the foggiest idea of any acceptably valid way of calculating it. The obligations of goverment are shrouded in the hot vapid air of vague contingent promises. For example, it is widely supposed that no government would ever let the ten largest firms declare bankruptcy; they would always be bailed out by government "loans" (as in the case of British Leyland). But how to value the present cost of that liability? Beyond a vague feeling that it is very large, perhaps far too large, little can be said.

## Inflationary Adjustment of the Public Debt

Some components are however thought to be susceptible to valuation—or at least to some form of measurement. The most obvious is the marketable public debt—excluding the indexed gilts. A correction for inflation is recommended by not only neo-Keynesians but also monetarists

14. In this hypothetical example, there is, of course, no reason why a government, fearing or even knowing these effects, should not entertain this sort of "go-for-growth" policy—especially just before an election. In the early 1970s the cuts in tax rates by the Heath government were followed by such increases that by 1976 Britain had higher tax rates on income than any country, save only Egypt and Algeria. *Hansard,* June 14, 1976, Written Answer 358.
15. This is the "pre-Ricardian debt neutrality" referred to above.
16. Whether a government will find it in its political *interest* to do so is another matter.

such as Milton Friedman. With such universal approval it behooves us to review it with a fine critical sense. An increase in the price level reduces the real value of outstanding obligations of both interest, if that be fixed, and of the real value of the principal. Just as it constitutes a capital loss to the holders of the debt in the private sector (or foreigners) so it should be counted as a capital gain in the public sector. In the view of many commentators, making an adjustment to the deficit for this particular capital gain is necessary for an appropriate measure of fiscal policy.[17]

The normal practice is to measure the capital gain by taking the market value of outstanding public-sector debt at the beginning (or the end or at the middle) of the year and applying to this valuation the realized rate of inflation in the retail price index during the year.[18] Table 4.2, which has been calculated by Marcus Miller is instructive in showing the considerable *size* of this adjustment—at least on what were regarded as reasonable assumptions.[19] The large financial deficits and PSBRs of the inflationary years from 1973 onward were more than offset by erosion of the real market value of the public-sector debt. The cumulative PSBR and financial deficits were £70.0 billion and £63.0 billion, respectively, compared with the cumulative inflation correction of £77.8 billion. (Strictly one should calculate these in constant pounds or as a percentage of GDP, but the conclusions would be broadly the same.) Thus, ignoring any cyclical element, *the deficits over these years were on the average really surpluses.* In terms of the Keynesian interpretation, the budgets of the 70s were contractionary or restrictive and the depressed conditions of employment and GDP from 1973 may be attributed to such tight budgetary conditions. And the

17. In acceding to this argument we are implicitly committing the error of elevating the importance of the measurable above the nonmeasurable. At this stage all we can do is acknowledge the error. See W. H. Buiter, "Measurement of the Public Sector Deficit and Its Implications for Policy Evaluation and Design," *IMF Staff Papers,* Vol. 30, No. 2, June 1983.

18. Another alternative, used in Table 4.2, is to employ the *ex ante* real interest rate. For various measures applied to the UK see Marcus Miller, "Inflation-adjusting the Public Sector Financial Deficit," in *The 1982 Budget,* J. Kay (ed.), London, 1982. The underlying objection to most of the suggested methods of adjustment is that they employ *ex post* rather than *ex ante* concepts. (This is in contrast with the adjustment for cyclical changes which are made with respect to an *ex ante* "full employment" standard—although practitioners tend to adjust that standard, after the event, so that the results are not patently absurd.) Thus, a large deficit which generates a sharp inflation will result in the elimination of the inflation–adjusted deficit.

19. Buiter, *op. cit.*

Table 4.3. United Kingdom: correcting the public sector deficit for inflation, 1967–81

| Year | Public sector debt (market value) (percent of GDP)[a] | Public sector borrowing requirement | | Public sector financial deficit | | Inflation correction | | |
|---|---|---|---|---|---|---|---|---|
| | | (billions of pounds sterling) | (percent of GDP) | (billions of pounds sterling) | (percent of GDP) | (1)[b] | (2)[c] | (3)[a] |
| | | | | | | (billions of pounds sterling) | | |
| 1967 | 81 | 1.9 | 4.6 | 1.5 | 3.8 | 0.5 | 0.6 | 1.0 |
| 1968 | 77 | 1.3 | 3.0 | 0.9 | 2.0 | 1.4 | 2.0 | 1.2 |
| 1969 | 70 | -0.4 | -1.0 | -0.5 | -1.1 | 1.2 | 2.0 | 1.3 |
| 1970 | 67 | 0.0 | 0.0 | -0.7 | -1.3 | 2.1 | 2.7 | 1.4 |
| 1971 | 59 | 1.4 | 2.4 | 0.3 | 0.53 | 3.0 | 3.2 | 1.5 |
| 1972 | 58 | 2.1 | 3.2 | 1.5 | 2.4 | 3.3 | 3.2 | 1.7 |
| 1973 | 49 | 4.2 | 5.8 | 2.8 | 3.8 | 3.0 | 4.0 | 2.3 |
| 1974 | 43 | 6.4 | 7.7 | 4.7 | 5.7 | 7.0 | 9.3 | 3.3 |
| 1975 | 41 | 10.5 | 9.9 | 7.7 | 7.3 | 10.3 | 11.9 | 3.9 |
| 1976 | 43 | 9.1 | 7.3 | 8.3 | 6.6 | 7.5 | 7.4 | 5.0 |
| 1977 | 47 | 6.0 | 4.2 | 5.9 | 4.1 | 10.1 | 9.3 | 5.8 |
| 1978 | 44 | 8.4 | 5.1 | 8.1 | 4.9 | 6.2 | 6.4 | 6.5 |
| 1979 | 42 | 12.6 | 6.6 | 8.1 | 4.2 | 12.3 | 13.8 | 8.2 |
| 1980 | 36 | 12.2 | 5.4 | 9.7 | 4.3 | 9.6 | 12.1 | 10.5 |
| 1981 | 38 | 10.6 | 4.1 | 7.5 | 2.9 | 10.8 | 11.7 | 11.8 |

Source: Marcus Miller, "Inflation-Adjusting the Public Sector Financial Deficit, in The 1982 Budget, J. Kay ed. (London, 1982).

a GDP = gross domestic product.
b Inflation correction (1) = annual rate of inflation times market value of public sector debt (midyear).
c Inflation correction (2) = annual rate of inflation times nominal value of public sector debt.
d Inflation correction (3) is based on the assumption of a long-run real interest rate of 2 percent.

prime reason for these tight fiscal conditions was the high level of inflation of about 20 percent a year from 1973 onward.[20]

It is at this stage, if not at some earlier stage in the argument, that such methods of economic analysis and common sense conflict. Most economists would hold that it was the persistence of deficits (and monetarists would argue the persistent pressure to monetize the deficits) which produced the inflation of the 1970s. Persistent deficits are thought to herald an increase in the rate of inflation.

It is possible, although perhaps not easy nowadays, to rationalize a post-Keynesian interpretation if one is prepared to suppose that the level of inflation is largely independent of the deficits, either current or expected, and is determined by institutional forces such as pressure of trades unions, rises in the prices of imports, etc. Then with inflation so disposed of, the cumulative fiscal squeeze (adjusted for inflation) is consistent with the increasingly depressed conditions of the 1970s (whether measured in terms of unemployment, employment, or GDP). The theory and evidence hang together, albeit by the loose knots of a fragile thread. However, even the most distinguished Keynesians, after the experience of the 70s, would agree that inflation was substantially brought about by fiscal (and monetary) policies.[21]

Once this point is admitted—even if not as an irrefutable fact, then as a very likely occurrence—it is clear that there are possibilities of explosive inflation associated with ballooning (conventionally measured) deficits. For example, if in 1974 we had used the corrected financial deficit, it would have been calculated as a 2.3 billion *surplus* (or about 3 percent of GDP). This was compared with a nearly balanced (corrected) budget in 1973. And in 1975 during the depths of the slump, the surplus was maintained at roughly the same 3 percent. Clearly, the weight of Keynesian budget advice would be, at least, to turn these corrected surpluses into balance—and perhaps into corrected deficits. But in the circumstances of 1974 and 1975 this policy would have produced

20. Note that this effect is in addition to the normal "fiscal drag," whereby inflation pushes people into higher tax brackets and so tends to increase revenue at a faster percentage rate than the rate of growth of GNP.

21. In the words of James Meade: "By New Keynesianism I mean a policy of using the whole panoply of Keynesian financial policies to maintain a steady but moderate growth of total money expenditures on domestically produced goods and services and so of the national *money* income, and . . . to reform wage fixing institutions so as to promote *real* output and employment . . ." "A New Keynesian Approach to Full Employment," *Lloyds Bank Review* 150, October 1983, p. 8.

a massive funding crisis (i.e., more catastrophic than those that *did* occur), and much of the increase in the deficit would have been monetized and, some months later, added to the inflation rate. This would have produced then a larger (corrected) surplus, which would require, on these principles of policy, to be offset by more tax cuts and public expenditure. It is possible to formulate a familiar set of conditions where explosions are possible. But it would be unprofitable to explore any further what is patently an absurd policy. The lesson we draw is that the corrected deficits must be used with great circumspection and discretion.

These caveats can also be illustrated from the time-path effects of such inflation adjustments. Take an extreme case. Suppose that in a particular year, due to some natural catastrophe, the price level doubled, so that the value of the debt, which we may suppose was about 40 percent of GDP, is halved to 20 percent. Then if before the financial deficit was zero, the inflation-corrected surplus will now increase to 20 percent of GDP; and the Keynesian demand analysis would suggest that the surplus be reduced. But clearly this economy suffers from *supply deficiency* and *excess* demand. If the supply deficiency is known to be a transient one and will be offset in future years, then increasing the deficit this year, by borrowing either directly or indirectly from foreigners, is a sensible policy. Net imports would fill the transitory gap in supplies and moderate the price increase. Now, however, suppose that the inflation had been brought about not by a restriction of supplies but by a post-Keynesian trades-union push. The union barons decided to double their nominal wages; prices follow, thus halving the national debt in real terms, as before.[22] The appropriate policy, however, would not be to eliminate the 20 precent corrected fiscal surplus by expansionary spending and tax policies. There is no deficiency of supply. There may be a demand shortfall if the reduction in the wealth of bondholders induces them to reduce their spending on goods and services, and save more in order to restore their wealth to its desired level. But bondholders would do no such thing if they expected this year's inflation to be followed by a year in which precisely the same deflation occurs, thus restoring their wealth to its previous level. Such oscillations would in no way affect the real value at redemption of stock. The market value of

22. In accordance with the normal assumptions of Keynesians, the monetary policy is accommodating in the sense that either the velocity or the quantity of money adjusts smoothly to the new price level. See Nicholas Kaldor, "The New Monetarism," *Lloyd's Bank Review* 97, July 1970, pp. 1–18.

the stock would rise almost twofold during the year to reflect this expectation of reversal of the inflation. Such oscillations of the value of bonds would be regarded as a transitory phenomenon and would have little influence on the serious business of spending.

In any case, it is likely to be the *permanent wealth in real terms* that affects spending. Clearly, the variations in wealth, day by day, month to month, or even over a year, will not affect behavior much. It is the belief that one is permanently impoverished or enriched that will cause a change in basic spending plans.[23]

The measures that have been proposed or used for adjusting the PSBR and financial deficit for inflation have not been directed toward tracking permanent wealth. The valuations have been take on a particular day (COB)—either mid-year (Miller) or end of fiscal year [as in the case of the Economic Report of the President (of the United States) 1982]. This may well reflect all the peculiarities, financial and political, of that particular day—and is not a good estimate of permanent wealth. Similarly, the realized rate of inflation is a far cry from the *expected* real loss due to price level changes that is required to assess the effects on the savings and spending patterns in the private sector.

Of all the measures that have been used, perhaps the most likely candidate for "least-bad" is one suggested by Miller. He applies a notional 2 percent long-run real interest rate—as though, over the period 1967 to 1981, all debt were indexed at this real rate, and none matured during the period. However, to suppose that debt-holders behaved as if they had a real rate of return of 2 percent is quite inconsistent with the evidence.[24] The real rate of return on gilts, even before tax, was on the average substantially negative over these years—virtually irrespective of

23. This discussion is reminiscent of Joan Robinson's "widows and orphans" motives for holding bonds—they are concerned only with the coupon and are uninfluenced by the oscillations in market value. Equally, many observers would argue that today the gross funds which hold perhaps almost 50 percent of medium to long marketable gilts have their obligations specified in nominal terms. Thus, since they tend to match their maturity and coupon structure of their assets to their expected liabilities, and this is usually over a very long run indeed, changes in the price level and especially short-run changes will have only a modest effect on their behavior, or the behavior of their policyholders, etc.

24. See J. Carmichael and P. W. Stebbing, "Fisher's Paradox and the Theory of Interest," *AER 83,* (4) Sept. 83, p. 629, where we read "Contrary to some widely held beliefs . . . the impact of inflation has fallen dominantly on real rates of return with little influence on nominal interest rates either in the short run or the long run." See also The Bank of England *Quarterly Bulletin,* December 1983, for evidence on real rates.

the choice of the large numbers of ways in which one chooses to calculate it. Indeed, when Granny Bonds were introduced by the Labour government in 1975, it was anticipated that the demand would be so large that they were severely rationed by an age limit and by quantity per person. Yet those bonds paid a *zero* real interest rate.[25] Anyone who expected a long-term positive real rate of interest over these years clearly reflected a triumph of hope over experience.[26] If the real rate were changed to *minus* 2 to 2.5 percent, which is roughly the historical outcome of these years, then credibility in the implied massive adjusted surpluses would evaporate.

The general conclusion from this discussion of the inflation adjustment to the public sector borrowing requirement and the financial deficit is that it creates as many or more problems, confusions and uncertainties as it dispels. Furthermore, it is not clear that the inflation adjustment is either larger or better measured than those other changes in obligations between government and the private sector, such as pension commitments or industrial subsidies, which are rarely—if ever—suggested as possible adjustments to the deficit.

Yet there *does* seem to be some value in trying to allow for the obvious fact that in times of inflation it is likely that much of the interest payments received by private debt-holders represent repayment of capital rather than rate of return. This is especially the case when there is a free and fairly large market in index gilts—as there has been since the Spring of 1982. Clearly, the alternative of funding through indexed bonds instead of conventional gilts means that the deficit as conventionally calculated does depend on the way in which past deficits have been funded. The yield in indexed gilts has varied over a small range from 2.5 to 4 percent—averaging about 3.5 percent. Applying this to non-indexed nominal values would suggest that about £6 billion of the estimated borrowing requirement of 10 billion in 1983–84 was attribut-

25. Miller and Buiter (*op. cit.*, 1983) assume that the real interest rate in 1978–81 was 2.5 percent. There is no argument for this assumption. The OECD which they use extensively, and with general approval, clearly shows on the average *negative* real interest rates throughout these years—averaging some minus 2 percent. OECD *Economic Outlook 34*, December 1983.

26. Nevertheless, one must have some sympathy with Miller's 2-percent assumption—somehow, it seems consistent with the long run of history as Hicks showed in *Essays in Monetary Theory*, Chapter 7, Oxford 1967. Before the 1970s I would have argued that a long run of negative real interest rates was infeasible. However, with capital trapped by exchange controls, etc., these years showed it was entirely possible and, indeed, likely. The savers knew they were being robbed but could not escape.

# 5

# *Fiscal Policy:*
# *The Budgets of 1979-83*

## Before Thatcher

The fiscal environment in 1979 was very much a product of the trials and tribulations, albeit few, of the previous Labour Government. After being elected (and reelected) in 1974, the Labour Government, true to its electoral promises, implemented an expansionary public-spending program financed by borrowing. The financial deficit soared from about 2.5 to 3 percent of GDP in 1972/73 to 7.2 percent in 1975/76. (Although, of course, if adjusted for cyclical and inflationary effects it was, as in almost all postwar years, in surplus.) The government ran into increasing difficulties in trying to borrow such large sums; interest rates rose, sterling fell, and the Chancellor succumbed to the pressures to approach the IMF for finance with "conditionality," finally signing the letter of intent in December 1976. The requirements of the IMF in December 1976 had already been anticipated by the Treasury some months earlier. The paring of public expenditure plans had already begun, and the government had already taken the view that the financial deficit and PSBR (at record 9 and 10 percent) must be progressively reduced. Targets for $M_3$ were published which were to provide an overriding constraint on policy, and the authorities undertook to contain the quantity of domestic credit expansion.[1]

1. John Fforde in "Setting Monetary Objectives," *Bank of England Quarterly Bulletin 23* (2), June 1983, p. 203, argues that "other aspects of policy continued along broadly Keynesian lines." There was little enough left, however, at the Keynesian counter. In 1973 to 1974 unemployment increased from

able to implicit repayment of debt principal and not to real in rates.[27]

Finally, however, suppose that one rejects all these caveats an cepts the full inflation-adjusted deficit at its face value, then wha the consequential judgments which one must make about the infla impact on fiscal policy over the years of the Thatcher government us first accept the adjustments as percentages of GDP calculate Buiter and Miller (1983) in their Table 7.[28] These are:

| 1979 | 1980 | 1981 | 1982 | Average |
|------|------|------|------|---------|
| 3.0  | 3.2  | 3.3  | 3.1  | 3.2     |

Although the level of this adjustment accounts for about all the fina deficit for the latter years, that argument is of little relevance. By a other obligations, etc., we can make the *level* of the deficit more o what we wish. It is quite arbitrary. What matters, as Blinder and S pointed out, is not the level but the *changes* from year to year indeed *cumulative changes* over a period, as Miller and Buiter po out and calculated with respect to the cyclical adjustment. Unacc ably, however, they did not examine changes with respect to the tion adjustment.

The figures show that the inflation adjustment, considered as a *ch* from year to year, was quite trivial—and a maximum of plus or n 0.2 percentage points of GDP. The *cumulative* effect over the four period was even more trivial—only 0.1 percent of GDP from 197 1982 and, undoubtedly, entirely consistent with zero if one takes account rounding and measurement errors. In short, the inflatior justment is worthless.[29]

27. This is half the adjustment made by Miller for 1981—but this is be inter alia, (a) the real interest rate is 3.5 percent, not 2 percent, (b) th more indexed debt in 1984, (c) interest rates are lower, and (d) the of inflation is lower.

28. Miller and Buiter (op. cit.), p. 328. Figures for implied adjustment i public sector financial deficit to reflect the "true" cost of debt service, 1 1982.

29. It is also to be recalled that if the inflation adjustment in the public sec carried out, this requires corresponding reductions in the savings of the p sector. These should cancel out.

The *financial* success of Healey-Barnett's reform package was impressive. The financial deficit fell from a peak of £8.3 billion (6.6 percent of GDP) in 1976 to £5.9 billion (4.1 percent of GDP) in 1977. Inflation fell from 26 percent (end of 1975) to only a little more than 10 percent (end of 1977). In the course of 1977, the yield on Treasury Bills halved, and what had been a funding strike had turned into a funding flood.[2]

The *real,* as distinct from the financial, outcome of the 1976 policy, however, was deemed to be not quite so satisfactory by the Labour Right and an unredeemed disaster by the Left. True, output (GDP) did continue to recover from its cyclical low in 1975, but employment slid to a lower level. After its sharp rise in 1976 unemployment did not fall in 1977; on the contrary, in spite of being in the second year of the recovery, the number unemployed had increased over 1977 by more than 100,000.

The 1978 budget was the last occasion for a major change of course before the election. This followed the tradition of pre-election budgets with a clear intent to create a suitably prosperous environment for the occasion. But the markets judged it to be foolhardy, and by the summer the Chancellor had been forced to tighten fiscal conditions and to reimpose direct credit controls. Nevertheless, the net effect of this give and take was a small fiscal expansionary boost; the financial deficit increased from 1977 to 1978 by about £2.2 billion (or about 0.9 percent of GDP), and the PSBR as a percent of GDP expanded first by one percentage point, then another 1.5 percentage points to be in 1979 about 6.6 percent of GDP at market prices.

At last, unemployment did stop rising and in the month of the election (May) the numbers fell 100,000 below the level in May 1978. Whether this slight improvement was due to the fiscal measures of 1978

591,000 to 936,000 and the following year (1976) it went up to 1,305,000. On post-Keynesian principles, an increase in the deficit was called for but a reduction was planned. Fforde is, I believe, referring to the *use of budgetary instruments* to control the *money* supply—not to the use of budgetary instruments to promote GDP and employment—which is the *sine qua non* of post-Keynesian management.

2. A "funding strike" occurs when the government broker cannot get any offers for a tap issue of government bonds (gilts) at the specified price. More loosely, the term is used to describe market conditions when it is thought that even a cut in the tap price would not induce any substantial purchases since the market would expect more price reductions. Understandably, the authorities find a funding strike rather trying, and desperately seek to set conditions by changing prices or expectations so that dealing can again commence.

or whether it was the result of the early and "successful" stages of incomes policy that had been so prominent a part of the 1976 policy must be left to conjecture.[3]

## The 1979 Budget

The outgoing Labour Government bequeathed to the incoming Conservative Government a substantial financial problem in the form of a public sector borrowing requirement totaling £12.7 billion in 1979 calendar year (i.e., 6.6 percent of GDP). In the balmy summer months of 1979, the situation did not seem quite so bad—the £9.25 billion or 5.5 percent of GDP seemed a reasonable outcome for 1978–79. So the June 1979 budget, introduced soon after the May election, essentially marked time. It envisioned a reduction of £1 billion to £8.25 billion—to 4.5 percent of GDP for 1979–80.

Although VAT was raised from 10 or 12 percent to a uniform 15 percent, the additional revenue so obtained (£4.5 billion) was just offset (in a full year) entirely by the reduction in the standard rate of income tax from 33 to 30 percent, and the reduction in the maximum marginal rate on earned income from 86 to 60 percent.

The criticisms of the budget were severe. First, there was a substantial majority condemning the increase in VAT. And within this large number of commentators were many who believed that, with unemployment still at 1.3 million, a substantial cut in taxes, not an increase or a no-change package, was needed to get the economy moving (upward, presumably).[4] Supply-siders, of the extreme sort, who had some hearings in Tory councils, joined the call for expansion—but from the side of incentives rather than aggregate demand.[5]

3. The slowdown in nominal wages was striking: for example, the average hourly earnings of full-time adult males increased about 20 percent from April 1975 to April 1976, but the following year, 1977, the increase was only a little more than 10 percent. Yet in 1977 the output price index had increased almost 20 percent, thus giving producers a near 10-percent reduction in real wages. (CSO *Annual Abstract of Statistics,* Tables 6.20 and 18.1, 1983.) Even allowing for the subsequent increases in real wage costs, particularly during the winter of discontent 1978–79, and the alarming expectations so generated, it is difficult to conceive of such a reduction in real wages not having a substantial effect over the period.

4. This case has been most ably argued by Miller and Buiter (*op. cit.*), but similar arguments were put at the time by the NIESR, and other prestigious commentators.

5. Mrs. Thatcher's policies were roundly condemned by such commentators as Paul Craig Roberts and George Gilder because essentially the tax levels were increased rather than diminished.

But the main complaint against the VAT was that it was thought to add to inflationary pressures. The various arithmetical exercises showed that as a consequence of VAT and other outlay tax changes, prices would increase by as much as 3 percent during the year. It was suggested that this would be incorporated in expectations of the going rate of inflation for subsequent years, and would hinder the progress toward disinflation as well as giving a further fillip to nominal wage rates. Thus, the switch from direct to indirect taxes was thought to exacerbate inflation in spite of the fact that it left the PSBR and deficit virtually unaffected, and monetary conditions, if anything, slightly tighter.[6] In the absence of any perverse or magnifying expectational effects the switch should have produced a step or once-and-for-all increase in the prices subject to VAT (i.e., excluding food and some other services which enjoyed an increase in implicit subsidy).

It is difficult to see why such an obvious *step*-increase in certain prices, combined with *downward* pressure on the prices of excluded commodities, should lead to expectations of *higher* inflation (if, by inflation, we mean the *persistent* increase of prices year after year). Rationality would suggest expectations of lower price increases in future years.[7]

Price increases *remove* inflationary pressure; they do not add to it. Some light may be shed on the issue by pursuing the symmetrical argument for lower indirect taxes. If it were possible to excite inflationary expectations by a switch to indirect taxes, would it not follow that one could subdue such expectations by switches from indirect taxes to income tax? Or perhaps to more borrowing to finance some subsidies? I am sure that there is no doubt about the answer. Reducing indirect taxes—often associated with outright subsidies—had been a method of fighting inflation practiced by both the Heath and Wilson-Callaghan governments. Mr. Heath's famous "at a stroke" promise and increased subsidies, particularly to the nationalized industries and public housing, had been a prominent feature of the "social contract" of the Labour

6. If we suppose that the growth of the nominal money supply is not affected, then the increase of prices will mean that the growth rate of the *real* money supply is rather lowered by the tax switch, by 3 percentage points. If, however, we suppose that day-to-day operational control of the money supply is by controlling interest rates with respect to judgments about current market conditions, then the issue is much more muddy; a "no-change" assumption is perhaps about right.

7. Except insofar as people believe that monetary policy will be "accommodating." Then there can be no stability. The inflation will form a chain reaction and possibly explode.

Government. True, they kept many prices down for a while—as in 1974 when Mr. Healey claimed that "inflation was down to 8.4 percent." But everyone knew that the mixture of subsidies and regulation could not hold and that very rapid increases, particularly in public-sector prices, were bound to ensue. Such deceptions were facile rather than cruel; they misled only those who craved deception.

Although the increase in VAT did not contribute *per se* to inflation, it did help in promoting a more neutral tax system, and was one small step on the long and tortuous road to tax reform. VAT is the most natural tax in the Chancellor's present armory. It is a pity that the bad press accorded to the VAT increase of 1979 had tended to inhibit any further shift from income and capital taxes toward VAT. Until there is a more radical program of reform the 15 percent appears to be a political limit.[8]

To a large extent, the increase in the year-on-year changes in prices, which continued from 10.3 percent in May 1979 to a peak of 21.9 percent exactly one year later, were already in the pipeline. It was not merely the release of prices from the artificial constraints of social contracts and government dictates, but also the undertaking by the Conservatives, during the 1979 campaign, to honor the awards of the Clegg Commission on public-sector pay increases.[9]

These awards at levels of 16 to 25 percent combined with higher interest rates and deficits of nationalized industries soon rendered the budget plan of reducing the Labour Government's planned spending by £2.5 billion (about 3.5 percent) difficult if not entirely out of court. By the Autumn, additional measures were clearly needed. Tax increases were thought to be quite the wrong way to deal with the problem, although the government did warn that additional tax reductions were not to be expected! The focus was to be on cuts in expenditure to be implemented in 1980–81. Although the November 1979 White Paper argued for a substantial (5 percent) cut in the Labour Government's plans, it amounted really to holding expenditure at the level planned

8. There has been, however, some widening of the base of VAT.
9. The Commission on Pay Comparability, under the chairmanship of Professor Hugh Clegg. Precisely how the Conservative Party came to make such an open-ended commitment remains something of a mystery. A plausible explanation is that the party economic advisers were under the impression that acceptance of the Clegg recommendations did not necessarily involve implementing them—at least not in that year. It was thought that acceptance did not imply mandating the awards. Such mistakes in the euphoria of a campaign are as understandable as they are regrettable.

for 1979–80. The soaring borrowing requirement induced yet another search for additional cuts and gave rise to yet one more scrape of the barrel for another 1 percent, three weeks after the White Paper.

All such scrambling took place in a funding environment that had reached a crisis which was countered by the only weapon the government had left—the Minimum Lending Rate was raised on November 16th from 14 to a record 17 percent. The PSBR in the last nine months was in excess of £11 billion, and although some part was due to delays in tax payments, to be recouped in the first quarter of 1980, it seemed that the same sort of dreary round of frequent financial crises was to be a feature of the Thatcher Government as it had been of so many other governments past. *Plus ça change* . . .

But in March 1980 the government did firmly post its intentions for change in the form of the Medium Term Financial Strategy (MTFS).

## The Medium Term Financial Strategy (MTFS)[10]

Launched in March 1980, the MTFS was meant to be a medium-term (four-year) strategy in which the government would eliminate gradually the financial instabilities that existed when they took office in 1979, and which had been evident for the previous eight years. In 1979 the public sector borrowing requirement (PSBR) was about 6.6 percent of GDP, the monetary expansion was about 13 percent, and the rate of inflation was also 13 percent; however, partly because of the removal of some artificial constraints on prices, it was widely expected to rise.

The most remarkable feature of this situation was that it occurred in a year which was demonstrably the top of a boom—or more prosaically, the upper cyclical turning point. Inflation of some magnitude is the stuff of most booms, but a very large public sector borrowing requirement is not. The substantial public sector deficit showed that the financial system was out of joint. Normally, one would expect the top of a boom to have produced a surplus (a feat last achieved a decade before). Instead, there was a very large *structural* deficit the size of which one can only conjecture—but a figure of 6 to 10 percent of GDP would be broadly correct.

The centerpiece of the MTFS was the medium-term reduction of this

10. So much has been written about the MTFS that I will be very brief. The misinterpretations are legion, but it would be fruitless to consider them in this study.

Table 5.1. MTFS projected and realized PSBRs as percentage of GDP

| | 1980/81 | 1981/82 | Financial year 1982/83 | 1983/84 | 1984/85 | 1985/86 |
|---|---|---|---|---|---|---|
| (a) *Projected* | | | | | | |
| Date of projection | | | | | | |
| March 1980 | 3.75 | 3.0 | 2.25 | 1.5 | — | — |
| 1981 | — | 4.25 | 3.25 | 2.0 | — | — |
| 1982 | — | — | 3.50 | 2.75 | 2.0 | — |
| 1983 | — | — | — | 2.75 | 2.5 | 2.0 |
| November 1983 | — | — | — | 3.25 | 2.5 | — |
| 1984 | — | — | — | — | 2.5 | 2 |
| 1985 | — | — | — | — | — | 2.25 |
| (b) *Realized* | 5.7 | 3.5 | 3.25 | 3.25 | 3 | |

*Sources:* HM Treasury, *Financial Statement and Budget Report* 1980–81, 1981–82, 1982–83, 1983–84, and 1985–86; *Autumn Statement* 1983 and 1984, HMSO, London.

structural deficit to a manageable 1 percent or so. The MTFS, however, did not set out its program in terms of structural and cyclical elements. Although it was clear that the recession phase of the cycle had begun by the end of 1979, it was by no means clear how deep it would be and how long it would last. It was a strategic decision then for the MTFS to eschew cyclical effects and concentrate on the structural aspects. This implied that it would be quite sensible also to allow the deficit to go higher than had been envisioned in the MTFS if there was a clear cyclical shortfall of output and employment.[11] Thus, as we can see in Table 5.1, the original MTFS targets were revised upward by as much as 1.5 percentage points in order to allow for the depressed conditions in 1980 and 1982.

In order to promote the credibility of the MTFS, and in order to put all sides of the financial equation into context, the PSBRs were associated with projected public-spending plans and implied tax revenues as well as the growth rate of sterling $M_3$. This made it necessary to argue that, if for some reason the public-spending plans were exceeded (as happened in 1981), then corresponding increases in tax revenue would need to be secured in order to keep to the general strategy.

In reviewing the progress of the MTFS it is necessary to bear in mind that the PSBR is the difference between two very large numbers. Thus, there is a large expected error in the actual or realized PSBR and the PSBR that is envisioned at the time of the budget. Indeed, the *average error* over the 1970s was about £3 billion—some 1.5 percent of GDP. The reasons for the difference between forecasts and outcome are well

11. This was made clear by the Chancellor in the budget speech of 1981.

known: nominal and real incomes different from expectation, unexpected boosts or falls in spending (such as in the shortfall of defense spending or a Falklands conflict), or increases in revenue, such as oil duties (PRT), etc. There is some tentative evidence that the error has been reduced in the budgets since 1979, perhaps largely because of better control of spending; but it is too soon to claim any permanent improvement.

Considering these expected large errors, one must be wary of interpreting the *outturns* of fiscal policy as though they are evidence of the intentions of fiscal policy. For example, the budgeted PSBR in 1980/81 was 3.7 percent of GDP—whereas the actual outcome was about 5.6 percent. Yet the difference is well within the average error of such exercises. In essence it is best to judge fiscal policy by the *changes* from one year to another in *expected* PSBR at the time of the budget.[12] What is missed in terms of systematic adjustments by July measures or the November statement is usually small compared with the large "random" elements which tend to dominate the actual outturn.

In view of these wide margins of error, it has been argued by some distinguished economists as well as by politicians and media personalities that it is rather silly planning a precise figure for the PSBR. Many long nostalgically for the old days in the 1950s and early 1960s when the PSBR was a mere fuzzy residual in the economic planning process, and was the concern only of financial markets. Accuracy unachievable makes precision infeasible. In my view, however, it would be a great mistake to retreat from the sharp focus of setting one's sights on a particular number. The fact that one expects a wide margin of error is no argument for dispensing with a precise target. Just as in rifle practice, although experience shows that only a very small fraction of bullets hits the bullseye, the marksman will get a better score, on the average, if he *aims* carefully to hit the bull, rather than if he waves the rifle carelessly in the vague direction of the target! So it is with the budgetary process.

The statistical history of the MTFS *projected* deficits shows that the government has managed to maintain the strategy remarkably well. True, the projected deficits were pitched higher, by some 1.25 to 1.75 percent, than had been envisaged in March 1980. This upward revision was in response to the deep recession, and was entirely consistent with the medium-term framework.

The complaint by most professional academic economists was that

12. This does not imply that systematic laxity, either on spending or on revenue, should not be taken into account in the assessment. Obviously, we should judge by what governments do rather than what they say they will do.

the upward adjustment was far *too little*. But this is largely because they did not accept the underlying strategy of steadily reducing the structural deficit over the four- or five-year period. If one does accept this underlying strategy as outlined in the March 1980 MTFS, then the policy of increasing the 1980 projected deficits by some 1.25 to 1.75 percent does not seem outrageously perverse. On the contrary, it appears to be in the appropriate ballpark. This can be checked by examining the fall in real output from 1979 to 1981 and then calculating the countercyclical increase in the deficit required to offset the recession. The decline in the compromise estimate of real GDP from the top of the "boom" in 1979 to the bottom of the recession in 1981 was 4.2 percent. The objective of a countercyclical policy would be to fill in half this decline (2.1 percent), having first taken account of a modest underlying trend of (say) 1 percent per annum (giving another 2 percent for the two years). Most of the supporters of countercyclical policy believe that the real multiplier of the budget deficit is clearly greater than unity and some, the Cambridge Economic Policy Group, put it as high as 3 to 4.[13] If the multiplier were over 3, then the government could be plausibly accused of *overdoing* it! If one accepts the early 1970s' consensus estimates of about 2 to 3, then it must be admitted that the government got its cyclical adjustment about right.[14]

Of course, none of the fiscalists would agree with this judgment. But that is not necessarily because of the usual disputes about precise numbers for deficits and multipliers, but *because they do not accept the policy of reducing the structural deficit* over the five years from 1980 on. The reasons for eschewing a policy of reducing the structural deficit are many. As we shall see, perhaps the most cogent argument is that in 1979, if one takes into account the inflationary expropriation of debtholders, there was no structural deficit; on the contrary, there was probably a small surplus. At this stage of the discussion we may merely note that from 1974 onward, when the structural deficits became visible and large, there have been frequent and severe financial crises and funding strikes even under a floating-rate regime. Notwithstanding the sophistication of various "adjustments" of the figures, it is difficult to avoid the conclusion that the imbalance of the public finances was the basic cause

13. See Michael Artis and Marcus Miller, eds. (*op. cit.*), Chapter 3, footnote 1, in this book.
14. This rough calculation does ride roughshod over many obvious subtleties. For example, to the extent that countercyclical policy was successful, real GDP would record a smaller fall than otherwise. Thus, the required cyclical adjustment in the deficit is *under*estimated by taking *ex post* GDP outcomes as a basis for calculation.

of these difficulties.[15] Alternatively, one might accept the structural deficit in 1979 as a phenomenon that must be dealt with, but argue that a policy of medium-term (5-year) deficit reduction is not one to adopt in a recession. "The time is not yet ripe." But of course in *any* medium-term strategy it is virtually impossible to avoid a period of recession. This is tantamount to saying that reform of structural deficits should never be undertaken.

It would certainly have been more palatable to carry out a structural reform in a period of sustained inflation-free, full-employment prosperity. But it would have been naive to hope that one more push on the levers to increase aggregate demand would have moved the economy, except for a brief interval, in that direction. If increases in demand had been the cure, then the economy would have been fit and well since 1971–72. Alas, the reform had to start in 1979 with the dismal conditions at the top of the boom: with inflation at 13 percent (three times the average of the 1955–65 period), unemployment at 6 percent (again three times the average of 1955–65), and growth about 1 percent or so (half or one-third of 1955–66). There was no feasible or plausible way to reverse the sad history of the 1970s. Either the reform had to be implemented then or Britain would be allowed to endure yet another cycle of financial deterioration, yet another series of crises, and undoubtedly more "winters of discontent." The MTFS recognized that reforms must start from where we are—not where we would like to be.

In addition to its economic realism, the MTFS was also politically realistic. The objective was primarily the reduction in the rate of inflation, and it was believed that this could be achieved over a four-year period. Thus, the policy could be judged in the polling booths on its merits. So it was.

In its short history, it is difficult to exaggerate the importance of the commitment to the MTFS. It provided a frame of reference for all financial and economic policy. Never in the postwar history of Britain had the spending programs and the revenue and taxation consequences been so closely associated at the highest levels of government decision-making. On some occasions, as in the budget of 1981, the MTFS provided a powerful and effective discipline on policy, and gave rise to a financial rectitude which it would have been difficult if not impossible to achieve by other means. On other occasions, as in the budget of 1982, it has been less difficult or even easy to stay within the constraints of the strategy. Overall, it gave a coherence to all the financial aspects of policy. And it concentrated on those elements of the financial system

15. This was also the conclusion of the IMF and Mr. Healey in 1976.

over which the government had considerable control—as distinct from many previous "national plans" which dealt with concepts far beyond the reach of any government fiat.

Finally, the fact that the PSBR and other financial magnitudes were set out over a period of four or five years mutes one of the main criticisms of the use of *current* annual flow magnitudes. The MTFS peers forward and takes into some account the interactions between this next year's deficit and those which will be likely to succeed it. It envisions expenditures, taxes and other receipts and outgoings for a four- or five-year period. Of course, this is a far cry from the theoreticians' requirement that we evaluate the "comprehensive public balance sheet" taking into account *inter alia* the present discounted value of all future expected tax receipts, the real capital value of the states' note-issuing monopoly, the expected value of public-sector capital and its expected real rental value, in perpetuity, and so on. No such calculations are attempted. And if some empirical correlate could be found for such concepts as expected future tax receipts over a horizon that stretches infinitely forward or the present value of implicit real returns on the public stock of capital, looming long ahead, then the credibility attached to such estimates would indeed be zero. The choice of numbers would be arbitrary and would enable any investigator to have the "public sector wealth" of his choice. This is not the basis for a rational discussion of reality.

The MTFS, however, does represent a first achievable and credible step in setting out taxes, spending and borrowing over a time span—and that period of four or five years is approximately the horizon of a government. It is then credible because it passes one crucial political test—broadly, it is within the government's power to make it a reality. This can be checked readily by a cynical market. As distinct from guessing at public-sector wealth, the numbers are well-defined and well-known.[16] The hands of any masseur of the data will be soon identified and soundly rapped. Integrity of government policy requires transparency and consistency.

## The Budget of 1980

The forecasts of economic conditions during 1980 were quite grim. The world slump was clearly looming. The budget forecast was for a decline

16. The shifting forward of obligations, a common practice in private accounting, will clearly be exposed in the MTFS.

of about 2.5 percent in British GDP, which, during the calendar year, was just about realized. Yet, since it was the first year of the MTFS, the budget was formed in terms of a reduction of the PSBR from the £9.1 billion (4.75 percent of GDP) realized in 1979/80 to £8.5 billion (3.75 percent of GDP). Thus, there was some modest increase of taxes.[17] This increase, disappointing though it was to a government pledged to reduce the real burden of taxation, was needed to meet the increased spending on social security and the deteriorating deficits of nationalized industries.

Nevertheless, it became clear by the late summer that it was not sufficient to hold the PSBR at its planned £8.4 billion. This was largely because of the very rapid erosion of the finances of nationalized industries, the increase in subsidies to housing, various benefits and export credits. Hazardous though the exercise may be, it was quite clear by October that the PSBR would run at more than £10 billion—about £2 billion over the target. Nor could this overrun be excused as a chance event with no one to blame. Public spending was the main culprit. But it was far too late to do anything about it in 1980 or for the financial year 1980/81. Proposals were made to cut spending to hold the aggregate at least to the planning totals which had appeared in the MTFS.

The size of the cuts required was of the order of £3 billion—and this excluded the nationalized industries and any new measures being proposed to counter rising unemployment. The government, however, did not grasp this nettle in the Autumn statement. The expenditure cuts were modest (about £700 million), and the tax increases (National Insurance contributions and a new North Sea oil tax) were the main instruments for restoring the financial plans.

The deterioration of financial conditions was, however, even outside the forecasts of the Treasury and most outside observers. At the end of the financial year the borrowing requirement was £13.25 billion compared with the 1980 budget day forecast of £8.5 billion—almost £5 billion in overshoot. The extent of this deterioration, as is usual, was not known for sure until the summer months of 1981. But estimates of the outturn tended to creep upward, as budget day 1981 approached.

---

17. In particular, the abolition of the 25-percent range of income tax. This was the budget in which unemployment benefits and short-term social security benefits were made taxable from April 1982 but, unfortunately, that could not be implemented until 1983 because of "industrial action" by the civil service. However, in terms of the microeconomic consequences, this was a very important and long overdue reform.

## The Budget of 1981

In retrospect it seems that the budget decisions of 1981 represented a clear and resolute decision to restore financial integrity and to return the economy to the basic path of the MTFS. The objective was to reduce the PSBR from £13.5 billion in 1980/81 to £10.5 billion in 1981/82, but on "unchanged" tax rates (after indexing tax thresholds and specific duties to the inflation rate) the PSBR for 1981/82 would have come out of the forecasting machinery at about £14.5 billion. Thus the increase in the PSBR proposed—that is to say the amount to be taken out of the economy—was of the order of £4 billion.[18] Extra tax revenue of £3.6 billion was the target for 1981/82. The main adjustments of tax were:

1. the nonindexation of tax thresholds and most allowances (i.e., a 15 percent real reduction);
2. increases in excise duties at a rate exceeding the rate of inflation;
3. a once-and-for-all tax on banks' current accounts at 2.5 percent; and
4. a supplementary oil tax at 20 percent of the value of North Sea oil and gas.

Whatever one may think of the individual revenue measures in the budget, there is no doubt that on virtually any criterion the fiscal stance had been considerably tightened. Comparisons were made to show that it was one of the most severe fiscal squeezes in recent history. But the most vitriolic criticism concentrated on the undeniable fact that Britain was in the deepest depression since the 1930s. In the first quarter of 1981 there were only fleeting signs that the fall in output and the increase in unemployment were moderating, although the Treasury had suggested that there was a chance that the bottoming out of GDP would appear in 1981.[19]

The recommendations of many outside bodies varied, not merely be-

18. The £14.5 billion assumed complete indexing of all income-tax thresholds and specific duties.
19. The forecasts were (1975 = 100)

|                      | 1980 | | 1981 | | 1982 |
|                      | I | II | I | II | I |
|----------------------|-----|-------|-------|-----|-----|
| GDP                  | 109 | 105.5 | 104.5 | 105 | 105 |
| Manufacturing output | 98.5 | 90.5 | 87.5 | 88.5 | 88.5 |

*Source:* Treasury Committee (House of Commons) HMSO, London, 1981.

On similar assumptions the London Business School, however, forecast that output would expand by 2.5 percent, and the Liverpool University forecast was −0.2 percent for 1981 rising to 2.9 percent for 1982.

cause of the methodological disposition, but also because few, at the time of the budget discussions, realized the extent of the deterioration that had actually occurred. Most commentators expected that there would be *some* modest tightening to get the government within striking distance of the MTFS program. When the PSBR forecast for 1981/82 looked to be heading for £11 to £13 billion, opinion was that probably the Chancellor should reduce the PSBR by some £1 to £1.5 billion.[20] And this seemed sensible in the light of the original PSBR forecast of January of about £11 billion for 1981/82 (almost 4 percent of GDP). Then the PSBR would be some £2 billion above the MTFS figure of £1.5 billion (3 percent of GDP)—not at all out of line with what might be expected in a cyclical recession of this magnitude.

However, it was clear that the PSBR would be rapidly revised upward, just as the outcome had been so much larger than anticipated in 1980/81. The revisions soon arrived in February and added some £3 billion to the £11 billion to bring a forecast of about £14 billion.

In spite of the political difficulties and the delay to campaign commitments, the Prime Minister agreed to the final figure of a £10.5 billion PSBR as the centerpiece of the 1981 budget.[21] This was judged to be about the lowest figure that was politically acceptable. At the same time it could be claimed to be broadly consistent with the MTFS, and with a relaxation of interest rates (MLR) by two more percentage points.[22] Both judgments were proved correct. Politically, there was a

20. For example, Phillips and Drew, the stockbrokers, forecast a PSBR/GDP of £12.75 billion on unchanged policies and assumed that the budget would reduce it by £1.25 billion.

21. I would have preferred to have a figure below £10 billion but at that late stage of the budget process there were few alternatives left—and some did not seem at all attractive!

22. As the year progressed it became clear that the financial deficit was going to be even less than proposed in the 1981 budget. For example, the editor of the *National Institute Economic Review*, David Savage, published in 1982 the following indicators for 1981:

Changes in Public-Sector Financial Deficit as a Percentage of GDP

|  | 1979/80 | 1980/81 | 1981/82(Est.) |
|---|---|---|---|
| Unadjusted | −0.97 | 0.87 | −1.91 |
| Cyclically-adjusted | −1.32 | −2.12 | −3.89 |
| Weighted and cyclically-adjusted | −0.56 | −0.51 | −2.17 |

David Savage, "The Fiscal Stance," in John Kay (ed.), *The 1982 Budget*, Blackwell, Oxford 1982, p. 42. These figures, verbatim from Savage's article, differ from those reported in Table 4.2, since the latter have been constructed from later revisions of the data.

minor revolt of backbenchers against the sharp increases in petrol and derv (diesel) tax, and although a concession was made with respect to derv, the Chancellor made up the revenue by increases in other indirect taxes. In retrospect it is clear that if the Chancellor had proposed substantially larger indirect taxes to bring the PSBR well below £10 billion, the revolt would have been a serious one. It was a nice judgment.

There was no doubt, however, that the tightness of the budget was a surprise, and to some members a most unpleasant shock. More moderation, if not outright recantation of the MTFS, had been expected.

Although the budget was generally accepted in the City as courageous and correct, some academic economists, together with past chief economic advisers to previous governments, lost no time in condemning it in terms extreme and unequivocal. After the budget, in an unprecedented show of unanimity, 364 economists wrote a letter to *The Times* (March 31, 1981) condemning the policy of the government:

> Present policies will deepen the depression, erode the industrial base of our economy and threaten its social and political stability.[23]

This statement probably had an effect which was the opposite of what the signatories expected. If anything, it reaffirmed the government's resolve and frightened only the fearful. Academic economists had sunk so low in both ministerial and, I believe, popular esteem that the conjunction of so much academic opposition was taken as some faint confirmation that the policy must be right—or at least not obviously wrong.

The confounding of the forecasts of the 364 came quickly. At almost the precise time that the 364 were signing the letter, the decline was not only arrested but there was a decisive upturn in output. Of course, the Treasury had forecast this turning point when they had presented evidence to the Treasury Committee.[24] The aftermath of the 1981 budget provides an interesting and possibly instructive example of the relative power of monetary and fiscal policy.

I am convinced that the total thrust of the 1981 budget was substantially right, although the *individual* tax measures excited considerable criticism. The lowering of the *real* thresholds of income taxes by the entire 15 percent inflation of prices combined with the 1 percent in-

23. See Peter Ridell, *The Thatcher Government,* pp. 80–83, for a complete statement. (Note, however, that the date reported by Riddell is wrong.) The letter was organized by two professors of economics at Cambridge—Frank Hahn and Robert Neild on March 13th. The list of signatories included four former chief economic advisers to the government.

24. The increase in 1981 was even more pronounced than the Treasury forecast on *unchanged* assumptions.

crease in Employees National Insurance Contribution decreased the incentives to work and encouraged a resort to the benefits system.[25]

One other main revenue raiser, which slipped through unobtrusively but to which a few people raised constitutional objections was the "once-and-for-all" levy on bank deposits. This was thought to be a retroactive tax. From that body of lawgivers in the House of Commons, I anticipated the most profound and weighty objections. But only crocodile tears trickled down political cheeks.

To many supporters of the government's general policy, such as Patrick Minford, the 1981 budget was *macro good and micro bad*. But the bad aspects were rapidly reversed in the budgets of 1982 and 1983. In its general effects the budget did establish a decisive break with the past. The medium-term plans for financial stability were not to be jettisoned in another inflationary splurge. The MTFS still encompassed all.

The 1981 budget also ushered in a vast extension of the cash form of public-expenditure control. Hitherto, expenditures had been planned in survey (fixed) prices, and to find actual expenditure in cash one had to apply whatever increase in price had been experienced in that period. This was dubbed spending with "funny money." It gave rise to a laxity in control in the public sector and to considerable temptations in departments. Furthermore, the government never knew until after the event the resource implications of a "funny money" total.

The change was an extension of planning in cash terms. This does *not* mean that there are no plans in terms of quantities—such as the number of personnel, quantities of equipment, etc. In fact, much of the planning must proceed in terms of volumes. But to these overall volumes is applied a *general* expected inflation factor for prices, and then the constraint to the department is fixed in terms of that cash outlay. Thus, the department has a considerable incentive to keep the prices paid—and, particularly, wage and salary payments—under considerable pressure. No longer could they be effortlessly passed on to the Treasury, which would be expected to validate them.

This system of expenditure control seemingly gave a much vaguer idea about the real outcomes of public spending.[26] In the actual event, however, I doubt if that is the case. The use of cash limits is more likely

25. See Hermione Parker, *The Moral Hazard of Social Benefits,* IEA, London 1983; Patrick Minford, *Unemployment Cause and Cure,* Martin Robertson, London 1983; and C. N. Morris and A. W. Dilnot, "The Tax System and Distribution 1979–82," John Kay (ed.), *op. cit.*

26. This was powerfully argued by John Kay in *The 1982 Budget.* "Cash limits . . . are a very primitive form of control. . . . Large areas of public expenditure planning have simply been abandoned," pp. 104–105.

to lead to the expenditure plans remaining in place, than if the funny-money system is used. Without the discipline of cash planning, experience has shown that there have followed frequent and substantial revisions to public spending. The likelihood of a drastic revision in the realization of a real outcome in a funny-money system was much higher; as public expenditure got out of control, there was a great pressure to slash real programs. I believe that cash planning enables the government to adhere better to its initial plans. The reduction in uncertainty in this respect will more than counterbalance the additional uncertainty of having no pseudo-commitment in quantitative terms. Some tests of this proposition, although by no means conclusive, already suggest that cash planning is superior. Public expenditure was held at its target in 1982/83 and 1983/84.[27]

The main problem is that such cash control applies to rather less than 40 percent of government spending. Most of the programs are "demand-driven"—including most of the large benefits and social security system. Cash control has been effective but only over the non-demand-driven categories. There is still a great deal which needs to be done to bring these items of expenditure under control. The role of the contingency reserve is particularly important in meeting unforeseen expansions of demand-driven programs (such as unemployment and social security benefits).

It is noteworthy that although the switch to cash control has been condemned as a retrograde step by many economists, there is a classic argument for such an automatic control arrangement. Suppose that the rate of expansion of public spending as a whole is fixed at the expected rate of inflation for the next four years, which we can take illustratively at 5 percent. In a particular year the inflation rate may exceed 5 percent—suppose it rises to, say, 8 percent. Then automatically there is a 3-percent real squeeze on cash-controlled public spending in the year. This is just the kind of policy which, after undue lags, governments implement to fight inflation. Symmetrically, a fall of the inflation rate to 2 percent would give rise to a 3-percent larger real public spending—the sort of medicine long advocated for a recession.

Perhaps even more important, it gives the public officials and spending ministers a considerable incentive to support policies that reduce the rate of inflation. Of course, spending ministers would still compete with one another for their share of the nominal cake—that form of horse-

27. *The Financial Times* (February 17, 1984) agreed that the cash-control system had, after the initial chaos, proved to be a considerable success.

trading would not change. But there would be an incentive for public-sector labor unions to support disinflationary policies—at least as far as their members in work are concerned. (This does not, however, deal with the indexed pension problem and the associated temptations.)

These are considerable advantages of the fixed-nominal-trend spending rule over the alternative rule that has been much canvassed; namely, a maximum percentage of the GDP to be spent by the government. Although the government has made no commitment to the fixed-nominal-growth rule for public spending, the cash planning totals from 1982/83 through 1985/86 are not very far from such a rule.[28]

## The Budget of 1982

The background of the 1982 budget was the clearly emerging success of the measures of 1981. In spite of the high interest rates and sharp downturn in the United States—shortly to be followed by (surprisingly) Europe and Japan—Britain continued slowly to grow, and the underlying inflation continued to fall. The financial outturn during the year was clearly going to be favorable—something like a £2 billion undershoot in the PSBR was the common prediction.

Although there were the normal calls for reflation, they tended to be much more muted, and for much more modest stimuli. Even Sir Ian Gilmour called for an expansion of "only £5 billion" or 2 percent of GDP in a speech at the Conservative Party Conference at Blackpool, October 1982. This might be thought to be rather strange, granted that the judgment on the 1981 budget had been that it had been massively contractionary—and indeed that the outcome had been £2 billion more contractionary than the budget arithmetic had anticipated. Furthermore, unemployment had gone on increasing, although at a progressively slower rate, as forecast by almost all modelers. For if they were still convinced they were correct in requiring at least a neutral budget in 1981 (say a PSBR of some £15 billion), then the growth of unemployment and the increase in prices would require one of at least £19 billion in 1982, even if one did not make up completely for the 1981 contraction. So a net spending increase of some £10 billion should

28. There has been some considerable debate about the path of the ratio of public spending to GDP. A convincing and scholarly account of the public control and intervention in the economy is quite beyond my competence and means. Some notes on a cycle-free method of approach are contained in the Appendix to this chapter. These represent suggestions for an agenda for research rather than conclusions of close study.

have been on the cards of the critics. I suspect that this reluctance to propose a massive stimulus was partly associated with the fact that the dire consequences so confidently predicted did not follow the 1981 budget.[29]

The critics could only acknowledge—albeit tacitly and with reluctance—that the Prime Minister and the Chancellor had been substantially right; the policy was showing distinct and unmistakable signs of success, manifest in the opinion polls and suffusing the back benches.

As far as the general budgetary stance was concerned, the view was that little or no change was called for. The borrowing requirement was set to be reduced from the planned £10.5 billion in 1981/82 to £9.5 billion in 1982/83. However, there was precious little to "give away" in the form of tax reductions. This was largely because of the fact that proposed public expenditure in 1982/83 exceeded the amount which had been planned in March 1981, by nearly £5 billion. The culprits were the usual ones—augmented benefit payments associated with the higher levels of unemployment and some additional spending on employment measures, further money to cover the higher deficits of the nationalized industries, and more defense spending. This just about absorbed the additional revenue which was expected as a normal part of the fiscal adjustment.

All in all, the MTFS called for little to be done in the 1982 budget— but the Chancellor did that little very well. The main elements of the budget were:

1. a 1 percent reduction in the National Insurance Surcharge (NIS) for the whole year from 3.5 to 2.5 percent—effectively, a 1 percent reduction in payroll;
2. raising tax thresholds by 2 percent more than the rate of inflation; and
3. increasing some specific duties at a rate less than that of inflation.

The reduction of the NIS was urgently pressed by the Confederation of British Industry (CBI) and was echoed by back-benchers.[30] Politically,

29. So far as I know, the only economist to acknowledge publicly that his prediction was wrong was the economics editor of *The Times*, David Blake. This he did with candor and grace.
30. The bitter complaints by the CBI and others about the crippling effects of the 3.5-percent NIS seemed rather strange in view of the 21.4-percent increase in average earnings in the manufacturing industry from third quarter 1979 to third quarter 1980. Of course, the reduction in NIS affected labor costs of all firms, whether they were making profits or losses; it was a lowest common denominator—probably a normal outcome of CBI discussions.

it was an astute measure. It was partly offset by the increase in the employees' National Insurance Contribution. This could be rationalized on the arguments of the actuarial basis of the scheme. The package had all the appearance of reducing industrial costs and thus improving the financial conditions of industry at the expense of the household sector.

But the household sector did have an offset to the NIC in the form of the overindexation of the tax thresholds. This made a start toward getting real thresholds back to their earlier levels.

It is interesting to note that, in theory, whether one reduces NIS imposed on business or NIC imposed on employees makes no difference to the incidence of the tax in a competitive system. As a tax on employment they have precisely the same effects. Yet in practical budgeting they are regarded by the Treasury, politicians and the media as though the incidence falls on those who pay. Nice balances are drawn up between the corporate sector and the household sector, and the 1982 budget was judged in such terms.[31]

The main innovation of the budget was the introduction of the principle of indexation for capital-gains tax. This measure was deemed practical and affordable because it allowed only inflation offsets after March 1982 and excluded the first year. The actual rules of indexation, as first promulgated, were rather bizarre. The increase of prices from March 1982 were applied to the *base* year of purchase of the asset. This had to be amended by subsequent measures.

To sum up, considerable progress was made in the 1982 budget toward reforms that most people accepted as desirable but had hitherto found untouchable. A little progress was made toward the raising of real-tax thresholds and relieving the low wage-earners of the high marginal tax rates. Yet it was still true that, although the poor and the wealthy had benefited—at least as first round recipients—from the combination of threshold movements and NIC rises, some people in the lower ends of the middle-income ranges were made very slightly worse off.[32]

31. Some such division could be justified if one were clear that the results were only a transient phenomenon with conditions of stickiness of wage adjustment and substantial monopoly power. Yet, what increase in business profits takes place this year is likely to be more than eroded in subsequent years, which one should logically take into account. I remain puzzled by this practice.
32. In the debates on the Finance Bill, there was considerable confusion, including some on the government benches, about the combined effects of all the personal tax measures and the NIC. This illustrated the complex mess into which the tax benefit system had degenerated, rather than the lack of briefing by the Treasury officials.

Certainly it could not be claimed that the budget was the opening shot in the election year of 1983. On the contrary, it was quite centrally pitched in terms of the MTFS. In the months that followed, which brought such events as the Falklands conflict (April–June) and the sharp downturn in Germany and Italy in the second quarter, the budget provided a sheet anchor for the stable financial conditions which Britain enjoyed during this tumultuous time. But the growth rate in the first quarter of 1983, over the first quarter of 1982, exceeded 3 percent. Britain was clearly growing faster than the combined rate of other OECD countries.

## The Budget of 1983

It was widely expected that this would be the final budget before the election. This was the last big chance. In electioneering theory, one would have expected a "give-away" by substantial cuts in taxes where they would gain the largest expected harvest of votes.

At first blush, the budget seemed to do just that. The main measure was to raise income-tax thresholds by 14 percent, compared with the 5.5 percent required by inflation. Thus, real thresholds were increased by 8.5 percent. (Even so, this was still not sufficient to restore the pre-1981 real value of the thresholds—they were still some 4.5 percent short of those values.) At the same time there was an increase in the National Insurance Contribution (calculated from the actuarial "requirements") of between 0.2 and 0.6 percent. A second important element was the 0.5 percent reduction of the National Insurance Surcharge to 1 percent. A miscellaneous collection of other tax reductions—many intended to stimulate business, such as the Business Expansion Scheme—provided additional "expansionary" stimulus.

Yet, in spite of these tax reductions, it seemed that the Chancellor remained firmly wedded to the MTFS. The projected PSBR was only £8 billion—2.75 percent of GDP and still only 1.25 percent more than the 1.50 percent predicted for this financial year when the MTFS was inaugurated in 1980. The Chancellor might with propriety have claimed that this adjustment to the original strategy was consistent with the fact that the economy was still far from its normal level of employment.

The Chancellor managed to pull off this trick of reducing taxes and maintaining MTFS integrity largely by resort to what many commentators regarded as sleight of hand.[33] The PSBR for 1982/83 had included

33. See, for example, John Kay, "Fiscal Policy in 1983: Retrospect and Prospect," in J. Kay (ed.) *The Economy and the 1983 Budget,* Institute for Fiscal Studies, London, 1983.

a contingency reserve of £2.5 billion. At the time of the budget preparations there were good reasons for regarding this as excessive; thus, the Chancellor decided to reduce it to £1.1 billion—giving him the opportunity to make tax reductions of about £1.4 billion.[34] Similarly, there were claims that the departments would underspend their planned totals by about £1.6 billion, or at least it was thought that this would be the most likely outcome. In the event, this hope was frustrated by a late spending spree, and in July 1983 the new Chancellor was quick to announce remedial measures, consisting of additional asset sales and a reduction in cash-controlled expenditures.

## Was Fiscal Policy Too Tight? A European Comparison

In assessing answers to this problem, one has the eternal difficulty of relating actual policy to some feasible *ideal* policy. We have already discussed one aspect of this ideal in terms of the level of the structural deficits—and, particularly, the very high level (7 to 10 percent) during the election year 1979.[35]

But let us ignore the instability and erosion of confidence occasioned by this large deficit overhang, and let us discuss the tightness of fiscal policy in terms of the *changes* in the adjusted deficits, relative to some norm. In other words, let us adopt the implicit assumption of Buiter and Miller (1983) that the structural deficit in 1979 of 7 to 10 percent was ideal.

One sort of norm is to compare the UK cumulative changes in the adjusted deficit during the slump with the same measures for other countries.[36] The Commission of the European Communities has published changes in adjusted budget deficits for all member countries from 1981 through 1984 (forecasts).[37] Thus, we can compare the behavior

34. In his Autumn Statement 1983 the new Chancellor made it clear that he was going to restore the contingency reserve for 1984/85 to £3.0 billion.
35. In 1979, the PSBR was 6.6 percent of GDP at market prices. If we add the adjustment suggested by the IMF for cyclical correction (2.3 percent), we get 8.9 percent. Kay (1983) suggests, however, that the cyclical adjustment should be some 4 percent, which would bring the structural deficit up to 10.6 percent.
36. This is, as we have seen, the chosen method of Buiter and Miller, where they compared the UK with other OECD countries as a group. To judge from OECD reports, IMF publications, and reports of the Commission of the European Communities, this methodology is widely used.
37. In addition to allowing for cyclical elements of the budget, "the effect of changes in activity," the Commission also adjusts for "the effect of changes in net interest payments." Commission of the European Communities, "Annual Economic Review 1983–84," *European Economy* 18, November 1983, Brussels, p. 109.

Table 5.2 Change[a] in adjusted budget deficits, EEC and member states, 1981–84 (% of GDP)

| | Change in adjusted deficit | | | | Total |
|---|---|---|---|---|---|
| | 1981 | 1982 | 1983[b] | 1984[c] | 1981–84 |
| Belgium | −0.6 | 2.2 | 1.5 | 2.5 | 5.6 |
| Denmark | 1.5 | −1.9 | 2.7 | 2.2 | 4.5 |
| Germany | 0.8 | 2.6 | 1.5 | 1.2 | 6.1 |
| Greece | −3.9[d] | 4.7[d] | 0.8[d] | −0.2[d] | 1.4 |
| France | −0.9 | −1.1 | 0.9 | 1.0 | −0.1 |
| Ireland | −2.3 | 1.7 | 4.6 | 2.1 | 6.1 |
| Italy | −1.2 | 2.6 | 1.9 | 2.7 | 6.0 |
| Luxembourg | 0.1 | 1.7 | 0.9 | 1.8 | 4.5 |
| Netherlands | −0.1 | 0.5 | 1.3 | 0.2 | 1.9 |
| UK | 2.8 | 0.8 | −0.7 | −0.2 | 2.7 |
| EEC | 0.1 | 1.0 | 1.0 | 1.1 | 3.2 |

*Source:* Commission of the European Communities (*op. cit.*), p. 109.

a A plus sign indicates a reduction in general government borrowing requirements, a minus sign indicates an increase.
b Estimates.
c Forecasts.
d Including the effect of net interest payments.

of the UK with those similar economies of Europe with whom we compete and cooperate (Table 5.2).

Since it is known that the outcome of deficits in a particular year has on the average a large deviation from intent, it is clearly better to judge fiscal policy by aggregating for the four yearly changes in the expectation that these "errors" will be muted. The cumulative differences will give a fair idea of the thrust of fiscal policy during the recession—covering both the decline and the hesitant recovery. As before, the higher percentage, the tighter the fiscal conditions.

The most striking feature of Table 5.2 is the fact that the *United Kingdom has pursued an easier fiscal policy than the EEC* (either including or excluding the UK). Britain reduced its adjusted borrowing by 2.7 percent of GDP whereas all the EEC countries reduced theirs by 3.2 percent. Furthermore, if we compare Germany with the United Kingdom, on the argument that these two countries are similar in industrial structure, in markets, and in size, then it is clear that German fiscal policy has been much more contractionary than that of the UK. The Federal Republic's deficit has contracted cumulatively by 6.1 percent over the years 1981 to 1984, more than twice that of the United Kingdom.

Indeed, the United Kingdom pursued fiscal policies which in the

Community were exceeded in ease by France (−0.1), Netherlands (+1.9), and Greece (+1.4).[38] On normal fiscalist principles, the French performance is about the minimum of what should be done; it may not be the fiscalist ideal but it more nearly approaches it than any other EEC country. In fact, in the years to mid 1983, French policy was expansive (the 1981/82 changes totaled − 2.0 percent), consistent with fiscalist notions of countercyclicality. By mid 1983, however, France was forced, or at least thought it wise, to change her expansionary policy.

Let us return now to the UK. Since we have shown that, relative to Europe, British policy was over the four years expansionary in the statistical sense accepted by fiscalists, one might still object that the *time profile* of the deficits was inappropriate. The tightening was all done in one year—1981. Indeed, the sharpness of the fiscal contraction in March 1981 provoked the most intense and bitter criticism from the economics profession and from the most prestigious former chief economic advisers to the government.[39] However, granted that reform of the structural deficit was required, it seems that it is best to get it over with as soon as possible. Germany (in 1982), Italy (in 1982 and 1984), Denmark (in 1983), Greece (in 1982), and Ireland (in 1983) have all experienced a similar or even larger fiscal contraction in recessionary conditions not very different from those of the UK in 1981. However, these contractions excited little or no criticism from British academic economists and ex-advisers.

The general conclusion of this comparison is that during the Thatcher government the general stance of fiscal policy was, compared with the rest of the EEC, relatively loose or at least less tight than our community trading partners. This is almost certainly the opposite of the general protestations of so many economists over the years. Of course, it is possible to adopt different statistical adjustments to show that the United Kingdom was among the tightest of the main countries.[40] But

38. As the crudest possible measure of the effects of such fiscalist counter-cyclicalism in these countries we may note that the unemployment rates all *increased* from 1981 to 1984, 7.8 to 9.7 in France, 7.1 to 17.6 in The Netherlands, and 4.1 to 8.7 in Greece, p. 33 *et sequenta* of EEC *Annual Report*, 1983–84.
39. Since their criticism was leveled at a deficit reduction which was planned, rather than the much larger one that was achieved, consistency would require that they be even more upset by the outcome from which the figures in the table are derived.
40. This appears if we use the OECD adjustment procedures, which do not take into account the interest-rate adjustment used by EEC, and adopt a different cyclical adjustment calculation. The OECD results show that over the four

all this illustrates the fragility of figures on fiscalism—that would be an alternative conclusion. It is also, in the context of the debate between fiscal and monetary policy, an interesting one. Critics of monetary policy and monetary targets have frequently argued that there is a very large number of alternative definitions of the money supply, which are unlikely to give the same signals. Many go on to argue that this makes monetary policy a very blunt instrument and that we should use the sharp, more delicate, and more immediate scalpel of fiscal policy instead. From recent years, it is clear that the arbitrariness of fiscal measure exceeds that of monetary aggregates.

## Appendix: Government Spending as a Fraction of GDP Adjustments for Employment

Success in the UK government's announced policy of reducing the fraction of government spending in the economy has been judged with respect to the percentage of GDP which constitutes government spending (including net interest payments). This is shown in Table 5.3.

However, these are misleading indicators of the extent to which the economy has become "de-publicized" or "privatized." In the first place, the fraction is much affected by the cyclical oscillation in income and employment. The recession increases the real value of the numerator because of the increase in benefits paid to the unemployed, whereas the denominator, real GDP, declines as output falls. Secondly, even apart from the cyclical variation, the ratio reflects the *trend* in "natural" rates of unemployment which are brought about by technological change. This is that change in employment which would have occurred whatever the degree of public-sector involvement.

In a similar vein, the rate of inflation much affects the debt-interest part of expenditures. Nominal interest rates tend to rise when inflation rises. The nominal-debt service charge rises—but much is front-end loading and represents repayment of principal rather than interest cost.

Unfortunately, it is not possible to calculate the effects of these factors with any high degree of confidence and conviction. However, a rough measure which eliminates the cyclical effects would be to compare trough with trough and peak with peak. This can be done, for example, by comparing

---

years we were almost exactly as contractionary as Germany. (See OECD *Economic Outlook* No. 34, December 1983, Table 10, p. 14.) Similarly, to drive the UK into the severe contractionist camp, one could pursue a comparison with OECD which includes, *inter alia*, the United States and Japan—two economies that are very different from the United Kingdom and, as Buiter and Miller (1983) did, make 1979 par at zero. To press it further, one can use the inflation adjustment of public debt.

Table 5.3. Public expenditure as a percent of GDP

| | |
|---|---|
| 1974/5 | 46.0 |
| 1975/6 | 46.0 |
| 1978/79 | 40.5 |
| 1979/80 | 40.5 |
| 1980/81 | 42.5 |
| 1981/82 | 44.0 |
| 1982/83 | 43.5 |
| 1983/84 | 42.5 |

*Sources:* HM Treasury, *Autumn Statement,* 1983 and 1984, HMSO, London.

1974/75 with 1981/82—which shows that there has been a small reduction of the size of the public sector from 46 to 44 percent.

But such measures must span periods of around five years—the average length of the cycle. They are of little use for judging the success of particular governments. In the case of 1974/75 to 1981/82, for example, the success of reducing the relative size of the public sector was indeed largely an achievement of the Labour government 1974–79, particularly in 1977.

Another alternative indicator which eliminates the cyclical effect is to calculate a ratio standardized for *trend employment*. The difficulty is, of course, to determine the trend.

It is probably easier to stabilize the ratio with respect to *unemployment* rather than employment. Then not only can the cyclical effect be eliminated, but there can also be an allowance for the increase in the *core* of unemployment due to the technological changes of the 1970s. The natural way of adjusting the ratios is to calculate the ratios—say, from 1970 to 1982—*assuming that unemployment remained at the level of 1979* (roughly 1.3 million).

The recalculation has to take account of the financial cost of the additional unemployed person (roughly £4000 per annum in 1982 values) in the numerator and the GDP loss per person employed in the denominator (about £7000 a year in 1982—assuming it is at the *average* wage).

As a rough calculation consider the adjusted ratio in 1982. Unemployment was about 3 million, thus the excess over 1979 was 1.7 million. We adjust the numerator by deducting 1.7 million × £4000 per annum = £6.8 billion. This amendment to the numerator accounts for about 6 percent of total public spending (£113 billion). Thus, the ratio for 1982/83 would be reduced from 43.5 to about 40.5 percent.

This adjustment is, of course, without allowing for the addition to GDP which, assuming a constant labor force, the additional job would have produced. Adding an additional £ (1.7 million × 7000) to the denominator would bring the adjusted ratio in 1982/83 to about 38 percent. Therefore, compared with 1979, there has been a noticeable decrease (2.5 percentage points) in the relative size of the public sector from 40.5 to 38 percent.

Now an adjustment must be made for the interest rate on public debt. Since the interest rates on conventional debt in 1982/83 were about 1 to 1.5

percentage points below those of 1979, and since net debt interest in 1982/83 constituted about £8 billion in 1982 and would have been above £9 billion in 1979, this would imply a decrease of about £1 billion in public spending. Furthermore, indexed debt of the order of £10 billion was added in 1981–83, saving interest payments of some £0.7 billion. Thus, the reduction is modified slightly to 38.5 percent or perhaps 39 percent in 1982/83. The fall in the adjusted ratios is from 43.5 to 39 percent. Clearly, these adjustments—and particularly the one for employment—are of crucial importance for a sensible appraisal of one of the main aims of the government—the reduction of the size of the public sector. Additional work should be carried out on these indicators.

# II
# MONETARY POLICY

In Chapter 6, we first explore the background of monetary policy in the postwar years. In the 1950s and early 1960s it was widely believed, following the Radcliffe Report, that monetary policy was ineffective. Opinion changed in the late 1960s and 1970s, partly due to the accumulation of evidence in academic and other studies, but above all due to the experience of the inflationary consequences of excess monetary expansion, particularly in the 1971–74 period. Yet the efficacy of monetary policy largely depends on the stability—and most monetarists would assert, *long-run* stability—of the demand for money. This evidence is briefly reviewed in the second section of the chapter. The broad conclusion is that there is a stable demand for money and that monetary expansion has its main effect not on real output but on prices in the long run. In the third section we raise the issue of the definition of the money supply and, in particular, whether one should use a broad or narrow target for monetary control. There is a sharp distinction between money (the stuff with which one pays one's bills) and credit (which enables one, for a time, not to pay the bills). The main conclusion is that narrow or transaction money, which excludes credit instruments, is the best instrument for monetary control. We demonstrate that narrow money was the appropriate criterion by which to judge monetary conditions in 1979–81 and that broad money, dominated by interest-bearing term accounts, was misleading. Thus, monetary policy was tight—not loose—during the early years of the Thatcher government.

101

Finally, we review the monetary aspects of the Medium Term Financial Strategy (this follows as the counterpart to the fiscal aspects of the MTFS which were examined in Chapter 5). The main thrust of the strategy was to bring down the rate of inflation gradually to low and stable levels, and at the same time to avoid any severe liquidity crunch. The main problem was to gain credibility for the policy. Despite difficulties in the first year or so, mainly due to the adoption of a £M₃ target, it appeared that by the end of 1981 the policy had passed the crucial test of credibility. There was to be a sustainable reduction in the rate of inflation.

Chapter 7 reviews a hardy perennial issue—the monetary effects of Britain's proposed membership of the European Monetary System (EMS) and other aspects of exchange-rate targeting. (Strictly speaking, the UK is a member of the EMS but is not a party to the Exchange Rate Mechanism; that is to say it does not intervene to keep rates within specified limits.) The first section discusses a fundamental flaw in the EMS arrangements under conditions of substantial freedom of capital movements and credit markets. Fixed exchange rates require equality of nominal interest rates which will tend to induce those countries that are inflating rapidly to add fuel to the inflation, whereas those countries with very low inflation will be subject to an additional monetary squeeze. The "pure" EMS system promotes not convergence but divergence. The second section examines alternative systems of exchange-rate targets which do not involve reliance on the behavior of the German economy. Although such targeting may be preferable to joining the EMS, there are severe problems in interpreting exchange-rate movements. The main conclusion is that the exchange rate reflects political alarms and events which have little or nothing to do with domestic monetary policy. It does not seem sensible to make monetary policy dance to the wild jig of the exchange rate. But, as we reflect in the fourth section of Chapter 7, there will be little alternative if the market is convinced that the government will react strongly to exchange-rate movements. Then monetary policy will be driven willy-nilly by exchange-rate pressures. The issue again is one of the credibility of policy—and once such credibility is lost, it is very difficult to regain.

In Chapter 8 we review British monetary policy in the years 1979 to 1983. First, we examine the tightening of monetary growth (at least in terms of narrow money) in 1979 to the last half of 1980, and the slightly easier conditions in 1981. The monetary policy of 1979–81 was reflected in the reduction in the rate of inflation from mid 1980 to the

5-percent rate of 1983. Although it is a matter for conjecture, it seems likely that the recovery which began in mid 1981 was assisted by the easing of monetary growth that preceded it. Secondly, we discuss the performance of monetary policy in the environment of the sharp squeeze in the United States from mid 1981 to mid 1982 and the collapse of the European economies in the second quarter of 1982. Yet the authorities held broadly to the policy of the adjusted MTFS—and Britain's recovery continued, albeit at a much-reduced pace but faster than any other country in Europe. Finally, we examine monetary policy on the run up to the election of mid 1983. The evidence suggests that there was little of the monetary laxity that is thought to be a part of the election tactics of incumbent governments. The reward was an election victory and continued low (5-percent) inflation.

# 6

# Monetary Policy:
# Arguments and Designs

## The Background—1950–79

In many ways the discussion of monetary policy (and particularly monetary instruments) has followed a course similar to that of fiscal policy. But over the years there has been a substantial change in the relative importance attributed to monetary and fiscal policy. In the years after World War II, money virtually never entered into the discussion of macroeconomic policy. The attempts to bring back so-called monetary measures (they were actually credit restrictions and controls) as part of a package in 1955–58 were seen to be an unredeemed failure and led to the establishment of the Radcliffe Committee and its Report of 1959.[1]

The Radcliffe Report was thought to show that monetary policy was ineffective. It argued that the financial effects of policy were exerted by a concept which it could never define called "liquidity." The quantity of money was thought to be relevant only insofar as it was a component or affected the "liquidity" of the financial system. The Radcliffe Committee believed that, since credit markets were not perfect, direct controls on bank lending and hire purchase were the most powerful and quick-acting financial instruments to be properly employed in inducing

1. Committee on the Working of the Monetary System, the chairman of which was Lord Radcliffe, a prominent judge; the committee was dominated by Richard Sayers, professor of economics at the London School of Economics and Sir Alec Cairncross (later to be head of the Government Economic Service). In 1968 Lord Radcliffe told me that he was persuaded that there were serious flaws in the approach. He thought that he had made a mistake in allowing the academics so much influence in shaping the Report.

104

the economy back to its low inflation, full-employment state or to reduce an unsupportable pressure on the pseudo-fixed sterling exchange rate.

In the early 1960s the government did not even prepare any statistics on the quantity of money. But there were elaborate data on bank lending, hire-purchase credit, and the like.[2] The first intimations of monetarism came soon after the Labour Party won power in 1964. Because of the initial expansionary policy associated with the National Plan (1964) and with the government's refusal to devalue sterling in 1964–66, the balance of payments absorbed large quantities of foreign exchange reserves, and the government was forced to ask for assistance from the IMF. The IMF had some considerable experience with other monetary systems and had developed its own particular medicine for overheated economies. Ceilings were imposed on *domestic credit expansion* (DCE) in the letter of intent to the IMF in 1968. Even so, the mechanisms of credit rationing went on substantially as before.

Like any other system of controls, the allocation of credit caused considerable distortions and inefficiency. Banks, and particularly the clearing banks, bore the brunt of the regulation—but this merely resulted in the normal banking business leaking out to the unregulated nonbank sector. For example, companies lent directly to one another rather than allow their money to be caught up in the web of controls in the banking system.

Competition and Credit Control (CCC), introduced by the Heath Government in 1971, intended to sweep away the quantitative and qualitative controls on credit markets. The Governor of the Bank said, "Basically, what we have in mind is a system under which the allocation of credit is determined by its cost. . . ."[3] The CCC regime lasted but two years. Yet in that period there was the most rapid monetary expansion in the history of Britain. CCC had clearly *failed,* and the evidence of the extent of the failure accumulated rapidly as inflation accelerated to 14 percent in 1974, successive funding crises developed, and the current account balance of payments degenerated into a record deficit of £3.3 billion. The reasons for the failure are many. Perhaps the main

2. It is of some interest to note that in 1961–62 when Noel Kavanagh and I applied for a Houblon Norman research grant from the Bank of England in order to develop statistics of the quantity of money in the UK, the application was rejected, partly, I was told, on the grounds that the quantity of money was of little interest in formulating financial policy. The Bank accurately reflected the opinion of the profession and Radcliffe.
3. "Key Issues in Monetary and Credit Policy," *Bank of England Quarterly Bulletin,* Vol. 11 (2), June 1971.

reason was the fact that the authorities were unwilling to impose the rates of interest which would contain the monetary aggregates. A secondary reason was that the government, believing that monetary and fiscal policy could be regarded as largely independent, had embarked on a massive program of fiscal stimulus in an attempt to avoid an imminent increase in unemployment to the magic figure of one million.

The CCC period left many long-lasting impressions on monetary management. The first was that rapid increases in monetary aggregates should be avoided; and the system should be changed to prevent such explosions. The second lesson was that monetary policy must be considered in conjunction with fiscal policy; they should not be planned as though they were independent instruments. Although these two lessons were long-lasting and remain as central principles of monetary policy today, the immediate reaction was the reintroduction of controls. True, they were imposed on the liability side of the banks' accounts, rather than on bank credit, but that was only a matter of form. The quantitative constraint took the form of a control over the "interest bearing eligible liabilities" (IBELS) with suitable penalties if these were exceeded. Like most controls, it seemed an initial success; but as time wore on the financial community found many ways of circumventing the mechanism. Like its nickname "the corset," it squeezed the controlled sector of the financial body but redistributed the fat into the uncorsetted areas; it made the financial system seem trimmer and fitter than it really was. But appearances matter—particularly in political discussion—and the corset remained girdling the financial markets until it was abolished in mid 1980.

The introduction of the first explicit monetary targets in Britain was in the April budget of 1976. This followed a period of reckless expansion from the first election of 1974 to the sterling crisis of July 1975, particularly in public spending. Contrary to many accounts, the monetary targets were not imposed by the IMF, although they were much influenced by the troubled state of sterling. Perhaps the main reason for monetary targets was the burgeoning belief that monetary control was necessary to avoid inflation. The lessons of 1971–74 had been heeded.

The choice of $M_3$ as the only target variable seemed eminently sensible, in spite of the fact that more than half of the total consisted of interest bearing deposits. The $M_3$ aggregate had the singular advantage of being closely related to the fiscal variables, and particularly to the

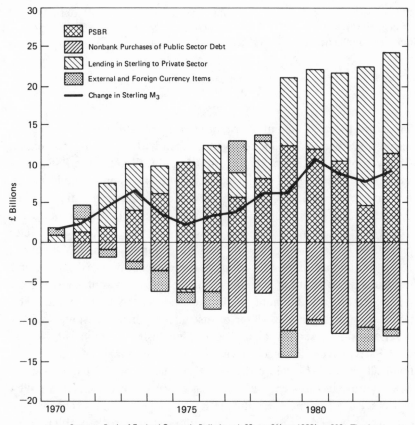

Sources: *Bank of England Quarterly Bulletin*, vol. 23, no. 2(June 1983), p. 203. The data for 1982 and 1983 have been added from *Bank of England Quarterly Bulletin*, vol. 24, no. 2 (June 1984).

Figure 6.1 Counterparts to monetary growth, 1970–83.

PSBR. Treasury and Bank officials could readily translate a constraint on $M_3$ into a maximum PSBR and, thus, into limits on public spending. True, there were many slips between cup and lip, but the general flow of the argument was unmistakable.

Yet, there was another important institutional reason for embracing $M_3$. The rationing of credit had been the form of financial control for many decades, and statistics of lending, particularly by banks, had been the main triggers of the regulatory system. (See Figure 6.1). And the definitions were such that the increase in $M_3$ could be easily translated into its components on the credit side:

| PSBR less sales of debt to the nonbank domestic sector | plus | Sterling lending to the private sector | minus | External financing of public and private deficits |
|---|---|---|---|---|
| | minus | Increase in non-deposit liabilities | | |

These are the credit counterparts of sterling $M_3$.[4] It was natural to interpret the main task of monetary control in its $M_3$ or $£M_3$ context as simply another version of the control of credit. Granted the PSBR was substantially funded, the major item was the extension of credit to the private sector. Cynically speaking, we were still securely entrenched in the business of credit control—it had merely been relabeled "money."

The first experiences with monetary targets were entirely favorable, particularly after the signing of the IMF letter of intent in December 1976. Yet confusion over the ultimate objectives of financial policy, and particularly the desire to keep the exchange rate from appreciating, soon led to sterling $M_3$ booming well in excess of the target limit.[5] The political paralysis of the winter of discontent, when widespread strikes paralyzed public service, as well as the increasing acrimony in the Labour Party, gave little encouragement for the continuation of a resolute financial policy. (Certainly the rapid expansion of the money supply was absurdly inconsistent with the final phase IV of the incomes policy which set a 5 percent norm for the rise in wages. In the event average earnings increased about 13 percent in the last year of the Labour Government—but that left much pent-up wage inflation ready and waiting for the Thatcher Government.)

## The Evidence

The accumulation of evidence on the effects of the monetary mechanism in the UK really dates only from the first half of the 1960s. Many of the early ideas were borrowed directly from the United States and particularly from the Chicago School. The first issue was clear: could one identify a stable and largely predictable function for the demand for money? If the demand for money were random and could not be forecast with

4. Sterling $M_3$ differs from the traditional $M_3$ in excluding sterling balances held by foreigners and the foreign-currency deposits of residents.
5. In the financial year 1977/78 sterling $M_3$ grew by more than 15 percent compared with the target range of 9 to 13.

any consistency or certainly, then we could all stop going on about it and turn our minds to more important matters.

In this monograph, however, I cannot give anything like a *complete* survey and evaluation of the evidence. All I can do is give a broad summary of the state of debate, and indicate where I believe the balance of evidence falls.[6]

Empirical studies of the demand for money in the 1960s suggested that, contrary to what had been asserted by generations of economists and by the Radcliffe Report (1959), there was convincing evidence that the demand for money was a stable relationship. The precise form of the relationship whether short run as well as long run, and the dynamics of causation were still open issues of much dispute. But it seemed clear that, whatever the outcome of such arguments, money, money income and interest rates were not unrelated. In fact, it was convenient frequently to carry out such analyses in terms of such traditional concepts as the velocity of circulation or its reciprocal, the so-called Cambridge "k," which is the quantity of money divided by National Income, or GDP or GNP. The results of the work in the 1960s showed that, for the long-run relationship, the income elasticity of demand for money was nearly unity and the elasticity with respect to the interest rate on consols was about 0.5 to 0.6 percent.[7] With this long-run relationship seemingly secure, analysts turned much of their attention to the more difficult problems of the nature and dynamics of the transmission mechanism.[8]

The mid 1970s experience, however, appeared to provide convincing evidence to contradict the notion that stability was a characteristic of the demand for money in the UK. The period after the introduction of the CCC saw a sustained increase in the ratio of money to GNP (that is, a decline in velocity) and a sharp increase in the yield on consols. This ran counter to the normal movement that had been observed over the previous half a century.

This effect can be seen most readily by plotting the data for the "old $M_2$" divided by GNP against the yield on consols (both averaged over

6. A thoughtful discussion of the present state of knowledge is to be found in David Laidler, *Monetarist Perspectives,* Harvard, Cambridge, 1982, Chapter 2.
7. In Kavanagh, N. J., and Walters, A. A. (1966), "The Demand for Money in the United Kingdom, 1877–1961," *Bulletin of the Oxford University Institute of Economics and Statistics,* Vol. 28, pp. 93–166, for the more reliable data in the period post-World War I, the elasticity with respect to income was +0.96 and with respect to the consol rate −0.55. There was also considerable support from the analysis of short-run (usually quarterly) data. See Laidler (1982).
8. For my own attempt see "Monetary Multipliers of the United Kingdom," *Oxford Economic Papers,* 1966.

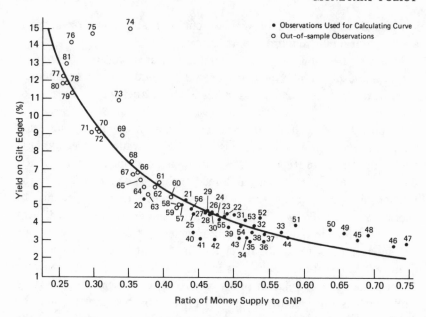

Figure 6.2 Interest rates and the demand for money, 1920–81. From Artis and Lewis (1984).

the year). The data produced in Figure 6.2 have been adapted directly from Artis and Lewis (1984) (AL).[9] The years 1973–75 appear as a marked aberration from the fifty years or so which preceded them. There is simply no other period like it. This deviation from the historical relationship had a considerable effect on monetary analysts and eroded some of the faith in monetary control which had been built on the stable results for the last fifty (or even one hundred) years.[10] It seemed that yet another great stable relationship of macroeconomics had become unhinged.[11]

The AL graph, however, shows that the abandonment of monetarism's

9. Michael Artis and M. K. Lewis, "How Stable is the Demand for Money in the United Kingdom?" *Economica,* November 1984, p. 474. Artis and Lewis use the "old $M_2$" which comprises currency outside of bank holdings and the sterling deposits of London Clearing Banks, and they report that this amounted to about 86 percent of $M_3$ in June 1982. This definition of "old $M_2$" makes it easy to get long series of comparable money-supply figures from 1920 onward. Essentially, the Artis and Lewis analysis is an extension of the work that Kavanagh and I did in 1966.
10. See David Laidler, "Monetarism: An Interpretation and an Assessment," *Economic Journal,* 91, No. 361, 1981.
11. Readers will recall that the stability of the (Keynesian) consumption function also disappeared in the maelstrom of the early 1970s.

claim for demand stability was a little premature. The deviations of the early 1970s proved to be transitory. From 1977 through 1982 the observations were so uncannily close to the predicted values from the AL fit from 1920–57 that, as AL point out, the 1977–82 forecast values have a much smaller deviation from the true values than the average deviation for the sample 1920–57. Hence, to forecast so accurately the outcome of 20 years is a remarkable performance—perhaps even a unique performance—in prediction with economic time series.

The picture of stability that emerges from the AL figure pertains of course to the long run. We are not able to adduce any such stability for short-run, month by month, or quarter by quarter periods. Little or nothing can be learned about the dynamics of adjustment. But, in any progressive program of research, it is important to establish the long-run constraints that obtain. If long-run velocities conform to a stable pattern, then those who make monetary policy will ignore these relationships at their, or rather the country's peril.

The most detailed analysis of the long-run velocities has been carried out by Friedman and Schwartz (FS) for the United Kingdom and the United States.[12] The methodology they use is directed toward averaging out, through taking business-cycle phase averages, the variability in the short and medium run in order to highlight the long-run underlying relationships. Friedman and Schwartz analyzed the data from 1867 to 1975. Thus, their analysis finished with the great aberration of the early and mid 1970s. Nor did they take into account the "return to the monetarist fold" of 1977–82. Nevertheless, FS claim to have found some remarkable stability in the velocity over the previous 100 years or so. The FS claim is supported by scholarship of the highest possible kind in which the data have been checked and exhaustively analyzed for alternative hypotheses. It is a comfort that they tell broadly the same story as the crude data plotted by AL in Figure 6.2. But there are some differences—probably the most important is that FS ascribe less importance to the interest-rate variable than appears in my analysis (Kavanagh and Walters, 1966) or the Artis and Lewis figure.

The FS results, however, have been subject to stringent and sweeping criticisms, primarily because of their statistical or econometric properties by Hendry and Ericsson (HE).[13] HE argued that contrary to what

12. Milton Friedman and Anna Schwartz (*op cit.*) 1982.
13. D. F. Hendry and N. R. Ericsson, "Assertion without Empirical Basis: An Econometric Appraisal of . . . Friedman and Schwartz," *Monetary Trends in the U.K.*, Bank of England, London, October 1983.

FS assert, velocity is better described as a "will-o'-the-wisp" and is not distinguishable from a "random walk." Essentially, HE argue that the observations of velocity contain less information than Friedman and Schwartz believe they encompass. This is because the particular observations of velocity are not like "independent drawings" from a system which produced the velocity curve like that of AL. On the contrary, the velocities are systematically related to history, as HE demonstrate elegantly and exhaustively in their Equations (20) to (29) and Table II, p. 73.

This can be seen by simple inspection of the observations in the AL figure. Generally, the progression through time is from low velocities (high $M/Y$) to high velocities (low $M/Y$), and correspondingly from low to high interest rates—and from low inflation in the interwar years to the increasing inflations of the years after World War II. But around this general time trend there are many "loops" which betray some underlying dynamic process not captured by the long-term relationship. The most striking is the long loop during and after World War II. From 1939 to 1947 the money supply, relative to income, expanded rapidly at yields on consols which were all rather above the value forecast by the fitted equation. After the war, the monetary stock relative to income steadily declined at interest rates which were again all somewhat above the expected values. This is merely one example of the distinct patterns in the residual deviations of the observations from the line.

Nevertheless, notwithstanding the great weight of sophisticated econometric testing that HE has brought to bear, it is difficult to accept that the observations in Figure 6.2 are a will-o'-the-wisp. Is it a mere accident of history that we have wandered on our random walk from the low velocities of pre-World War II to the high ones of the postwar years? We might, according to the random walk explanation, have wandered in the other direction to even lower velocities. Like Dr. Johnson, when told that he could not refute Bishop Berkeley's proposition that reality, in the form of a large boulder, did not exist, promptly hit the boulder with his stick saying "I refute it thus . . . ," one feels inclined to believe the graphical evidence rather than be persuaded that one is being deluded by optical illusions.

But even more clinching is the evidence of 1977 onwards. The Friedman and Schwartz analyses refer to the period up to and including 1977.[14] However, from 1977–82, there is an uncannily close relation-

14. HE, however, extended their analyses to include 1978–82.

ship between forecast and observed velocities. Obviously, the astonishingly tight fit is something of a fluke. But if one relied on the systematic relationship calculated from the 1920–57 data, one would have done much better in predicting the outcome of the late 1970s and early 1980s than if one had projected it as a random walk. The critical test of a proposition lies in the accuracy of its predictions outside the period of fit rather than the extent of correspondence of predicted and true value within the sample period. Visual inspection shows that the model passed with flying colors.[15]

The early 1970s, however, remain to be explained away. The rationalization that comes readily is to suggest that it was due to a dramatic change in monetary policy starting in 1971 and running through to 1976. The unprecedented size of the increase in the rate of growth of the money supply over these years, and particularly from the last months of 1971 through to the end of 1972 associated with unprecedented deficits was a "shock" to which the financial system had to adjust in the ensuing years. Expectations of very rapid inflation, large demand for credit (to finance the deficits of both public and corporate sectors) and far higher interest rates than would historically pertain to monetary conditions of this kind—all suggest that the economy was driven off its long-run demand for money as it adjusted to the inflationary policies of the 1970s.[16]

This is a superficially attractive explanation. But it is also unsatisfactory. If sharp and sustained changes in monetary growth cause such large deviations from the long-term stable relationships, then the forecasts of monetary conditions will be wanting in accuracy just when one most needs them.

Ironically, the monetary model did in fact forecast the inflationary consequences of the early 1970s far better than any other model. Poor

15. A kind but anonymous reader has pointed out that the HE hypothesis is not inconsistent with the policy measures which are discussed in these chapters. In particular, HE cannot reject the hypothesis that velocity can be represented as a random walk with "drift" which is itself a random walk but with a different variance. Then monetary policy should (a) tolerate some monetary overshoot—as in 1979–80–81, but (b) when it became clear that drift had occurred, it should revise the monetary targets upward as in 1981 and 1982. I accept that one can have HE's statistics and this sort of adaptive monetary policy, but at this stage I still find HE's results to be inconsistent with the evidence of *my* eyes.

16. The early 1970s, with the decreasing velocity, were a little like the wartime years when velocity similarly decreased. But in the late 1940s interest rates remained low; this probably represented the widespread belief in the long-run stability of the price level. This was eroded in the 1950s and 1960s and shattered in the 1970s.

though its performance may have been, alternative models performed even worse. Towards the end of 1971 and in early 1972, I forecasted that on the basis of the increase in the rate of growth of the broad money supply (from approximately 9 percent to over 20 percent per annum), the rate of inflation in 1974 would be "over 10 percent and perhaps as high as 15 percent." In fact, it was 14.7 percent.[17] Other forecasters had suggested that the rate of inflation would increase little from the 1971 value (some even thought a fall was likely).[18] Thus, in spite of the deviations recorded in the AL figure, the simplest version of the monetarist model performed relatively well during the great monetary explosion of the early 1970s.

The long-run relationship between velocity and the consol yield, although giving a framework for monetary analysis, did not tell us anything about the relationship between money, real income, and the price level. Nor does it say much, if anything, about the chain of causation.

The classical argument, as old as economics, is that an increase in the supply of money which exceeds the demand for money at current prices and real income levels, will merely increase prices in the long run; there will be no effect on output. This result emerges clearly from the Friedman/Schwartz analysis (op. cit., pp. 7–8) and indeed, more dramatically from the history of the last fifteen years of the great inflation. This is of course a long-run result. In the short run, for cyclical effects, the evidence is less clear cut. Friedman and Schwartz find that the quantity theory approximation is a good one; monetary variation has little or no effect on output, the effect being entirely absorbed in the variation in velocity (and the variation in interest rates). Finally, FS

17. "Inflation, Inflation, Devaluation, and More Inflation," *Sebag Gilt Edged Review,* May–June, 1972. This article followed quite closely a memorandum I had submitted as a part-time employee of the Central Policy Review Staff to Lord Rothschild for the attention of the Prime Minister. The article also forecast that there would be a current balance-of-payments deficit of "as much as one billion pounds" in 1974 (it turned out to be more than 3 billion) and that in a year's time (from May–June) the government, in spite of their protestations to the contrary, would be driven to impose price-incomes controls (this actually occurred in July 1973).

18. For a post mortem, see Michael Intrilligator (ed.), *Frontiers of Quantitative Economics,* Vol. B, North Holland 1977. The main explanation advanced by the principal critic, Mr. David Worswick (then Director of the National Institute of Economic and Social Research), was that I had been lucky since the increased rate of growth of the money stock had just preceded the great increases in the price of imported raw materials and, later, oil. (Ibid., p. 829.) Perhaps so. I hope I continue to retain my lucky star.

find that there is a *negative* relationship between the phase average growth of output and the rate of change of prices in the United Kingdom—a result which appears less surprising today than it would some decades ago. Inflation, whatever its cause, is not "good for growth" over the phases of the cycle.

The "chain of causation" is perhaps the issue that generates most differences of opinion and emphasis. At one extreme is the Kaldorean or Cambridge view that the money supply is virtually entirely an endogenous factor. The money supply simply responds to the needs of trade. If the private sector want more money they can easily "manufacture" it for themselves, by mutually extending credit.[19] The causation is entirely from income and activity to money. This stands in stark contrast to the Friedman and Schwartz paradigm, where their analysis is dominantly in terms of the government (or authorities) determining the quantity of money, with stable velocity and income and prices as the consequence of adjustments by agents in the economy.

Both extreme versions are caricatures of reality. But the FS version approaches more nearly the messy process of monetary control. Through all recent history, the authorities in the United Kingdom have had neither the instruments nor the will to control directly the quantity of money—however that concept is defined. The authorities have normally used as their main instrument the short-term interest rate (variously labeled Bank Rate, Minimum Lending Rate, and currently the dealing rate for bills). The market is supplied with whatever quantity of money it wants at this interest rate.[20] The authorities, over the years, have had different, and often mutually exclusive, objectives in fixing interest rates—and it is only in recent years that the quantity of money has been among the list of desiderata. There will be some considerable impulses which flow from income to money demand and supply at these controlled interest rates, a fact which Friedman has frequently acknowledged.[21] He argues, however, that the main movements of the money supply have been exogenously determined by the authorities through processes such as those employed in the early 1970s of pegging the interest rate too low. Historically, there is no doubt that the great expansion of 1971–73 was not

19. In Lord Kaldor's trenchant illustration: if his waist expands, he lets out the seams in his trousers—he does not go on a diet.
20. This case has been most cogently put by Tim Congdon "Has Friedman Got It Wrong?" *The Banker,* July 1983, pp. 117–25.
21. See, for example, Milton Friedman and Anna Schwartz "Money and Business Cycles," *Review of Economics and Statistics,* 1.2, 1963, pp. 32–78.

due to accidental effects transmitted on the demand for money through transitorily high incomes.[22]

Nor is there any doubt, however, that if the main effects of money are exerted and best measured in terms of the *quantity* of money, then control of that magnitude through the manipulation of short-term interest rates seems hardly an efficient way of managing policy. The relationship between money and interest rates is never very precise, and there is bound to be many a slip between cup and lip. The appropriate interest rates are rarely obvious. Yet, as Congdon points out, the mechanism of supplying the market with liquidity has many advantages—particularly in times of liquidity crises—and it should not lightly be set aside. (We return to this problem in the next section.)

The conclusion is that there is a usefully stable demand function for money balances, which seems to temporarily fail only when there is a drastic change of regime. Secondly, the main effect of monetary growth is on prices and not on output. On the contrary, there is some weak evidence that inflation and output growth are negatively related.

## Money—Wide and Narrow

One of the crucial distinctions made by monetarists and many monetary economists is between credit and money. The essential point about money is that it is used in transactions. You pay your bus fare with money; you do not offer the fare collector a promissory note. A transfer of money discharges obligations; an extension of credit *delays* the discharge of obligations. Money is used to pay bills; credit is used to delay paying them. However, since most money in modern economies is also credit—usually extended by the holder to the government (for example, paper currency)—it is easy to confuse the two.[23]

Money is that limited class of credit instruments which are customarily and widely used in the buying and selling of goods and services. Thus, one would clearly not count £50,000 negotiable CDs as money; so far as I am aware no one would ever accept such an instrument to pay an

22. The Kaldor argument, of course, goes much further than this. Essentially, it says that money is a private credit arrangement over which government can have little, if any, control. Monetary changes are an incidental result rather than a contributing cause. Then, indeed, government policy with respect to monetary control would not matter—and so it is difficult to see why there is such debate over what is regarded as harmless.

23. The exception to this general rule is coins of precious metals where the intrinsic value is near to its exchange value.

outstanding expense. Money is then naturally defined in terms of currency (notes and coin) and checkable accounts held in financial institutions such as banks and building societies.

Obviously, there is no way in which one can define for all time the instruments that are used as money; over time they change. For example, it is only recently that building societies have offered checkable deposits; hitherto deposits in such institutions were not functioning as money. And on the other hand, not all checkable deposits should be counted as money; some are wholesale deposits on which interest is paid and can only be encashed in terms of large denominations. Although the boundary does shift, the criterion for deciding what is and what is not money is fairly straightforward and causes difficulty only when the categories are passing through some metamorphosis. Over the years, the UK approximation to transactions money has been $M_1$, that is currency plus sight deposits of the banks. But recently the changes in the financial system have induced the authorities to develop a "new $M_2$."[24] This counts in the checking accounts of building societies but nets out large interest bearing sight deposits. It approaches much more closely the concept of transactions balances.

It is money in this transactions sense that plays the central role in the theoretical structure and the propositions of monetarism. Credit has but a minor role. Yet for much of the empirical analysis, many of the studies have used indicators for "money" which have included substantial credit instruments which are never or very rarely used for transactions purposes.[25] Indeed, the definition that was adopted in the MTFS was for sterling $M_3$—about 60 percent of which is interest-bearing credit instruments which are not used for transactions purposes. True, much of this credit was highly liquid and could be rapidly and almost costlessly transformed into checking-account balances or cash. But some other person or agency had to supply the cash or checking-account balance. It was, in the IMF phrase, quasi-money and not transactions money.

There were many reasons for embracing a wider definition of money. First, and of dominant importance for the comparable studies of FS, it was easier to get long runs of comparable data on somewhat wider definitions of money. Secondly, and particularly important in the case of the United Kingdom, it was possible to relate the wide £$M_3$ to the mar-

24. In the Bank and Treasury documents this is referred to merely as $M_2$—but we need to distinguish it from the old $M_2$ that appeared in the AL figure and which consisted of currency plus the deposits of London Clearing Banks.
25. In FS, for example, money includes the time deposits of commercial banks.

kets for credit, and the impact of the demand for credit by the public sector. This provided a degree of continuity with the regime of credit monitoring and rationing . . . *plus ça change.* Thirdly, and most important for monetary analysts, up to the early 1970s all the monetary measures moved in close harmony. When Kavanagh and I investigated the data from the 1870s to 1961, we found that the definition of money, whether broad or narrow, had largely only scaling effects in the equations.[26] Consequently, it did not much matter which definition of money was used, the statistical results when suitably rescaled were more or less the same. The choice of £M$_3$, therefore, encountered little or no resistance from monetary analysts.

The wide £M$_3$ measure received an additional fillip with the analysis of the genesis of the great inflation of the mid 1970s. The £M$_3$ measure had been a somewhat better predictor of the inflation than any of the narrow measures, particularly M$_1$.[27] Thus, the arguments in favor of adopting one broad £M$_3$ target appeared quite cogent if not overwhelming.

In retrospect this appears as remarkable capitulation of monetarist principle to institutional continuity. True, the harmony of the statistics provided a good excuse and, so far as I know, no monetarist put up a fight for a money, as opposed to a credit, measure. Thus, the MTFS and political reputations were based on the volatile credit base of £M$_3$.

A parable will illustrate the problem. Consider an economy which consists of two sectors—Household (H) and Corporate (C)—each of which is substantially self-financing, so that there is no flow of credit between them. Now consider some event occurring that makes the H sector rich and the C sector equivalently poor for a specific period (say one year), after which the situations are reversed for the same period and we get back to the status quo in the third year. Clearly, there will be an increase in savings of H and the accumulation of financial assets—

26. This was not discredited by the more detailed work of David Sheppard, *The Growth and Role of U.K. Financial Institutions, 1880–1962,* Methuen, and the exploration of adjustment hypotheses in Laidler, D. and Parkin, J. M., *The Demand for Money in the United Kingdom, 1956–67, Preliminary Estimates,* Manchester School, 38, September 1970.

27. I had accurately predicted the 15-percent inflation of 1974 by using M$_3$ statistics in 1971–72. Mr. Barber and Mr. Heath at that time argued that, from the data on M$_1$, there was little, if any, monetary laxity. However, any rational review of the record will show that, although M$_3$ performed somewhat better during this period, both M$_1$ and the monetary base M$_1$ also predicted with fair accuracy the arrival of the increase in inflation of about 7 percentage points.

and a decrease in savings and an increase in the liabilities of C. The banks, acting as intermediaries, will take interest-bearing deposits from H and lend them out to C. Bank deposits and credit will expand. But there is no reason why this expansion of credit and interest-bearing deposits should be associated with an increase in nominal income and an increase in the price level. Transactions and narrow (transactions) money balances remain what they were before—only the quantity of credit has changed.[28] Thus, the quantity of credit can change without having any effect on aggregate demand.[29]

This description serves as a useful caricature from 1979–81 in the United Kingdom. Because of the mixture of high real-wage increases, the appreciation of sterling and the beginning of the international recession, the corporate sector was in dire financial straits.[30] Correspondingly, the household sector was enjoying higher real incomes. Personal savings increased from 10.8 percent of disposable income in 1977 to 15.6 percent in 1980. The natural corollary was an expansion of bank credit and interest bearing deposits, which largely found their way into the $M_3$ aggregate.[31]

The attempt by the authorities to contain the burgeoning £$M_3$ statistics took the form of raising short-term interest rates through the Minimum Lending Rate (MLR) mechanism in an effort to sell more government debt to offset the additional bank lending. But as an inadvertent outcome, the MLR increase induced a severe squeeze on *transactions* money $M_1$ and the monetary base.[32] No doubt the increases in interest rates contained and curtailed to some extent the growth of bank credit,

28. In principle, there is no reason why the rate of interest should change since the additional demand and supply of credit are equal. A necessary condition of the expansion of credit and deposits is that the banks can acquire reserves at nonpenal rates which makes intermediation profitable.
29. In principle, the additional intermediation would involve some additional demand for cash. Thus, with a predetermined supply of cash, this increased demand would result in an additional squeeze of the already stringent monetary conditions.
30. The normal financial surplus of industrial and commercial companies—about £1.0 billion in 1978—became a £1.6-billion deficit in 1979 and a mere £558-million surplus in 1980.
31. There were at times many other factors also working to increase the degree of bank intermediation; the elimination of the "corset" with effect from July 1980, the virtual extinction of the corporate debt market by inflation, and the reluctance to engage in rights issues with the equity market so "low," *inter alia*.
32. From a growth rate of almost 17 percent from the end of III/77 to the end of III/78, $M_1$ growth fell to virtually zero from IV/79 to III/80.

but this effect appeared to be small compared with the severity of the effects on transactions balances.

One of the main lessons to be absorbed from this experience is the primacy of the transactions definition of money for monitoring and control purposes. Money matters much more than credit. However, this does not mean that there is no knowledge of monetary conditions to be gained by monitoring such credit magnitudes as $M_3$, etc. Nor can anyone doubt that if bank credit to the industrial and commercial companies had been curtailed by effective rationing devices or yet higher interest rates, there would have been considerable repercussions on real output and the level of prices. A credit crunch can be effective but at fearful cost. Clearly, there is much to be gained from keeping a weather eye on bank credit. Similarly, one can use other indicators of monetary and credit conditions, such as the exchange rates, interest rates, inflationary expectations, etc., to check consistency. Although, as we shall see, they are often very difficult to interpret—and this has to be borne in mind when using such data.

## Monetary Policy and the MTFS

The role of monetary policy varies according to the time period considered. However, it is clear from all the empirical evidence accumulated over these many years, that our knowledge of long-run effects is far more secure than for short-run consequences.

In the *long run* a persistent increase in the rate of growth of the money supply is transmitted into an increase in the rate of inflation. But how long is the run? Alas, there is no precise answer. It seems, however, that an increase in the monetary growth which occurs for some six months and is then reversed in the following six months will have little or no effect on the rate of inflation. On the other hand, we are virtually certain that if the higher monetary growth is maintained for three years, then higher inflation will result. Therefore, for control of inflation, we need to plan low increases in the monetary aggregates over a period of at least three years, and we had best try to ensure that growth of money does not get substantially off course in any rolling period of more than one year. For practical planning purposes we might regard the long run as four to five years—the so-called medium term.

In the period covered by the *business cycle,* the main role for monetary policy is to avoid exacerbating the cyclical swings. The combination of the unpredictable timing of the cycle and the fact that monetary effects are slow and uncertain in the lags means that monetary variations are unsuitable for countercyclical policy. All that can be done is to ensure that monetary policy does not become procyclical and make the swings wider than they otherwise would have been.

In the *short run,* that is to say in the day-to-day operation of monetary policy, the main objective is to ensure the liquidity of the financial system. The authorities will be called upon daily to relieve shortages or to syphon off surpluses on the money markets. But more important if there is a liquidity crisis and a run on the banking system (or on a large bank), then the authorities should be ready to supply liquidity—or if there is a run on deposits, to supply currency—to restore the public's belief in the integrity of deposit liabilities.[33]

The MTFS was primarily concerned with the problem of moderating inflation (and budgetary imbalance) and restoring a low and stable rate of inflation. It was a medium term program in the monetary sense that it anticipated a permanent reduction in the rate of inflation. As for the cyclical effects, it was never part of the policy to vary the money supply targets to counter expected cyclical oscillations.[34] It rejected "fine tuning," "touches on the tiller," etc., as likely to be procyclical and ultimately inflationary. However, the MTFS recognized the essential day-to-day requirements of maintaining the liquidity of the financial system. But if there was a need to expand the money supply to ensure the liquidity or even to counter a run on the banking system, then any increase could be readily offset before it had a chance of promoting inflation.

Since the monetary targets of the MTFS were set in terms of $£M_3$ (for broadly the reasons discussed above), there was a crying need to show that they were compatible with the planned budgetary policy. In addition to the extension of bank lending to the private sector, one of the main demands for credit comes from the government's PSBR, which in turn arises mainly from expected public spending and tax revenue. Thus, the $£M_3$ target had to be consistent with the targets for public spending and revenue.[35]

33. This is a sort of lender-of-last-resort function of monetary policy, and in its banking crisis manifestation it is often called "Bagehot's Rule." There are many problems of moral hazard with these arrangements.
34. This is distinct from the PSBRs in the MTFS where it was thought that some modest overshooting should be allowed if the economy were in a recession. In combination with the monetary targets this implied additional sales of gilts in a recession to cover the increased deficit.
35. There are other volatile elements in the equation. The overseas contribution—for example, by residents switching from sterling to foreign currency de-

Such consistency is, however, in its turn entirely consistent with considerable year-to-year variations in the PSBR and in the growth of $M_3$. One would not expect them to march in step, although with controlled and "sticky" interest rates one might contrive some annual correlation. But in the long run, or even medium run, there must be some consistency since, if the government runs higher and higher PSBRs, then it must continue reducing the price of its gilts in order to fund the deficit and maintain its $M_3$ targets. But there is a limit to the extent to which the private sector will absorb gilts. And as has been repeatedly demonstrated, the attempt to force large sales of gilts down the throats of unwilling portfolio managers gives rise to very damaging oscillations in interest rates and the price of government debt. Funding strikes and financial crises are the consequence of high PSBRs and low $M_3$ targets.[36] The MTFS sought to, and from 1981 onward through to 1984 did, avoid any sustained funding strike and financial crisis.

This consistency provided a necessary but not sufficient condition for the *credibility* of the policy. Another precondition for credibility was that the authorities had or were willing and able to acquire and wield the instruments to bring this policy into being. Apart from the fiscal instruments, the main control on the monetary side was the manipulation of the short-run interest rate. Although monetarists had long argued that interest rate controls were a most inefficient and difficult way of controlling monetary aggregates, this had been the main form of control in Britain for, literally, centuries. During most of that period there had been no persistent inflation, and over long periods there had been pervasive but gentle deflation. However, in view of the recent experience following CCC in 1971–73—when the government deliberately pegged interest rates, from political motives, and allowed the inflation to explode—there was initially considerable doubt about the performance likely from the Thatcher government. The cynics sighed—*plus ça change.*

In some extreme versions of the theory of expectations (so-called rational expectations), the announcement of a policy by government

---

posits—may have a considerable effect on £$M_3$ in a period. But over the longer run these elements will tend to cancel out. Similarly, the net addition of non-deposit liabilities may exhibit volatility in the short run, but little in the longer time span. Perhaps the most volatile element—and the one most difficult to forecast—is bank lending in sterling to the private sector, as discussed above.

36. See House of Commons, Treasury and Civil Service Committee, *Memorandum on Monetary Policy* (July 1980), in which both Lord Kaldor and Milton Friedman gave evidence from somewhat different points of view.

would have wonderful effects. People would quickly adjust their behavior to the new parameters of policy, including the low inflation rates to be achieved by the MTFS. But such theories should be regarded as parables or ideals; they should not be taken as recipes for reality. If one judges only by the historical record, it is indeed more rational *not* to believe a government will implement its protestations on policy.[37] Politics seems inevitably to be one long painful path of U-turns.

And there were good technical as well as political reasons for doubt if not cynicism. In addition to the optimistic targets for public spending, discussed above, many monetary economists were doubtful about the ability of the authorities to control the growth rate of sterling $M_3$.

The opposition to the MTFS by those economists and commentators who still believed in substantial discretionary policy and targets in terms of real variables, such as growth of GDP, level of unemployment or employment, etc., was entirely understandable; their opinions had a Bourbon predictability. However, what was more surprising was the opposition, albeit on technical grounds, from many monetarists.[38] While these critics usually embraced the targeting of sterling $M_3$—largely on the empirical grounds that it was marginally better than other aggregates in the recent past—they believed that the use of interest rates as an instrument was clumsy, inefficient, and perhaps ultimately ineffective. They argued that the best method was Monetary Base Control (MBC).[39]

There was, however, some ambivalence, perhaps inconsistency, in the position taken by the monetarist critics. A monetary base control *method* combined with a sterling $M_3$ *target* would be efficient only if there was a close and predictable relationship between the monetary base and sterling $M_3$. While the relationship was valid for long runs—say, more than three years or so—the monthly and yearly variation in the ratio of the monetary base to sterling $M_3$ was considerable.[40] There is little or no point in trying to use the MBC system to control $\pounds M_3$. How-

37. Readers will recall that a certain indicator of the imminence of devaluation was the frequency and vehemence with which the Chancellor denied that he had any such thoughts in mind.
38. Economists such as Brian Griffiths and Roy Batchelor at the City University Centre for Banking and International Finance were the most prominent critics, and they were joined by many of the most disinguished monetarists in the United States, such as Allan Meltzer.
39. See, for example, Allan Meltzer, "Central Bank Policy: Some First Principles," *Annual Monetary Review, No. 2* (1980), City University, London.
40. In fact, the monetary base was very well contained during all the years of the Thatcher government. But the ratio of sterling $M_3$ to the monetary base expanded probably faster than any period in recent history.

ever, there is a logically consistent argument for MBC if the monetary base is used as the *target* as well as the control. Then the argument is that, provided the monetary base is held at a suitably low rate of growth (say 0 to 2 percent), it is very unlikely that there will be any substantial persistent inflationary pressure.[41] This was, however, a far cry from the MTFS, but the issue of $M_0$ will be taken up later in this narrative.

41. This was a fair representation of the positions taken by many distinguished monetarists such as Karl Brunner and Allan Meltzer, as well as the late William Fellner.

# 7

# Monetary Policy
# and the Exchange Rate

## Interest Rates and Divergence
## in the European Monetary System

There have long been aspirations to form some monetary union of the European Community, which would correspond to the trade and fiscal harmonization implicit in the Treaty of Rome. The breakdown of the Bretton Woods system of more or less fixed exchange rates, and the erosion of confidence in the stability of the dollar, added to the European view that there should be some substitute for the role of reserve currency. The initial "snake," introduced in early 1972, was modeled on the late lamented Bretton Woods, with exchange rates "fixed but adjustable."[1] The European Monetary System (EMS) was introduced in early 1979 and included all the major currencies of Europe except sterling.

The essence of the EMS consists of agreeing central rates, with respect to the European Currency Unit, which obtain until the next "realignment." The member countries then use policies of intervention and monetary control in order to keep their rates within a band ± 2–2.5 percent, except Italy where the band is ± 6 percent. In practice, however, the rates are usually maintained fairly close to the central value. Although the system has many of the features of a mini-Bretton Woods, there is no systematic relationship of any currency, including the D mark,

1. The snake had a checkered history, with the early defection of three of the four major currencies, leaving only the German mark and its satellite currencies. However, by the time of the introduction of the EMS, the snake had become bloated and very permissive indeed and had few pretensions to be a fixed-rate system; adjustments were large and frequent.

to the U.S. dollar. The most important exchange rate in the trading world, the D mark/dollar rate, was excluded from the EMS.

In assessing the effect on monetary policy of EMS membership one must initially draw a sharp but essential distinction between the ideal system and the real system. First, we shall examine the ideal: If the objectives meant anything, then they would have required the exchange rates to be virtually fixed with respect to one another for a specific period (say, one year) before the next realignment. If this is the case, and assuming there are no oscillations around the central values, the markets can expect periods of up to one year when the exchange rate between the Italian lira and the D mark are fixed.

However, if the exchange rate is fixed for an average of six months, then this will imply that the rates of interest on financial assets with those maturities will be roughly the same. If, after six months, I can exchange my lira for Deutsche marks at the same rate at which I bought them, I will find it profitable to switch into lira deposits if the interest rate in Italy is a tithe above that in Frankfurt. Thus, nominal interest rates for those maturities must be approximately equal; portfolio arbitrage will ensure the outcome.[2] It follows that by joining the EMS, as in any fixed exchange rate system, Britain would have to forego a substantial degree of sovereignty over her monetary policy.[3]

This interest rate equality illustrates one of the main difficulties—an inherent contradiction, no less—with the EMS. One of the objectives of the EMS was to produce "convergence" of the rates of inflation of member countries—and in these terms it meant converging on the inflation rate of Germany. Thus, it was hoped that Italy, with an inflation rate of about 15 percent, would eventually converge to the German inflation rate of about 3 percent. But the requirement that, under a fixed-exchange rate, Germany and Italy have the same nominal interest rate—say, 9 percent—means that the real interest rate in Germany is high and positive (6 percent), whereas the real rate in Italy is negative at minus 6 percent. If the monetary authorities operate an interest-rate regime in controlling their domestic money supply, there will be a great pressure to expand

2. There will be some transmission of this effect to other maturities so the level of the yield curve will be largely determined by this arbitrage, but we leave that aside for this argument.
3. The government would have a number of other monetary instruments—such as reserve ratios and varying the maturity structure of public debt—which could be used, but there is no doubt that interest-rate policy is the primary weapon.

money and credit in Italy, whereas in Germany there will be a substantial financial squeeze.

This is precisely the opposite monetary policy to that which would move toward "convergence." Monetary policy has not been merely neutralized by the fixed exchange rate system, it has been made perverse. If countries still seek convergence, then this must be achieved mainly through fiscal policy, and indeed fiscal policy will have to offset the malignant effects of the EMS monetary policy. It is often claimed that the EMS has had a substantial effect in inducing member countries to take stringent fiscal action which they would not have entertained had they not been members of the EMS. This is true. But it is odd to credit the EMS with discipline that arises from its distortions.[4]

In reality, however, the EMS diverges substantially from the fixed exchange rates with free capital markets that we have outlined above. First, there are substantial restraints on the free flow of capital—particularly, by France and Italy—so that arbitrage is nowhere near perfect. Indeed, in the case of France and to a lesser extent in the case of Italy the capital constraints became considerably more stringent since France has been a member of the EMS. One must be wary of *post hoc ergo propter hoc,* but this evidence is not inconsistent with the fact that France would not have needed such controls if she had not been constrained by the pseudo-fixity of exchange rates. Willy-nilly, regulation of capital flows has enabled considerable deviations in interest rates between member countries, so the countries have been able to pursue more appropriate monetary policies than those which were implied by a strict EMS.

Secondly, even over quite short-term horizons, the exchange rates have not been fixed. This is partly because of the width of the band within which currencies can move—up to 5 percent for all except Italy which can move as much as 12 percent.[5] But the main reason is that changes in the exchange rate have been frequent and sometimes quite sudden. The average percentage change (ignoring sign) from month to month (end) in the exchange rate of the French franc and the Italian

4. Am I alone in finding it odd that exchange-rate fixity and the concomitant equality of interest rates is described as "closer monetary cooperation . . . in Europe"? Commission of the European Communities, "Five Years of Monetary Cooperation in Europe," Brussels, March 1984. Fixing exchange rates and interest rates will produce divergent monetary policies.

5. It must be noted that the *practice* of countries was to attempt to keep their exchange rate, on the average, close to the central value and not to bump against ceilings and floors.

lira from 1979 to 1983 was 0.8 percent.[6] If the movement is all one way, as it was (substantially) in the case of Italy, this represents about a 10 percent depreciation of the lira during a year. Although currencies outside the EMS exhibited greater month to month variability, on this measure, there were many more negatives canceling out positives, rather than the more-or-less steady downward drift of Italy and France.

The forward markets reflect all these uncertainties about future rates of exchange. And it is noticeable that the forward discounts for France and Italy in the EMS group, with respect to the D mark, were and are usually larger than the ones pertaining to the United Kingdom.[7] Being inside the EMS did not seem to reduce the insurance premium one had to pay to avoid the exchange-rate risk. On the contrary, insuring against exchange risk would cost more if you were in Italy, France or Eire than if you were outside—in the United Kingdom or the United States. Although the EMS has removed some of the short-term, month-by-month unsystematic "random" variations in exchange rates, it has not reduced significantly the systematic variation which can be forecast by the market.[8] This variation in EMS exchange rates together with capital controls has enabled the countries to pursue monetary policies, as manifest in their interest rates, which were not entirely counterproductive in inducing "convergence." The basic inconsistency between fixed exchange rates and convergence remains.

In the rather messy EMS system, there has been no evidence of convergence. As the CEC paper admits, the mean absolute deviation between annual price inflation *increased* slightly from 4.2 percent in 1979 to 4.4 percent in 1983, although as always great things are expected for the years to come. So far, the record on convergence is rather dismal,

6. See "Five Years of Monetary Cooperation in Europe," Table 1.
7. Thus, on March 27, 1984, three-month forward dollars commanded a 5-percent premium in D marks, and a 6-percent discount in the lira. This corresponds to the annual 10-percent drift of the lira against the D mark in 1983. Sterling, however, was at a premium of only 1.74 percent. And, of course, three-month interbank rates reflected these at 5.85 in Germany, 17.4 in Italy, and 9 in London.
8. The CEC study, "Five Years of Monetary Cooperation in Europe," measures exchange-rate instability by the size of the average monthly absolute change in percentage terms. It is worth noting, therefore, that the same measure of variability (i.e., 1 percent per month) would apply to the following two series. In Series I there is one big 12-percent fall (not atypical of the EMS realignments), whereas in the other Series II there is a plus-one minus-one pattern for each month (see Figure 7.1). Additional uncertainty in Series I arises from the fact that no one knows *when* the big fall will take place. Thus, the same measured result masks a very distinct and different reality.

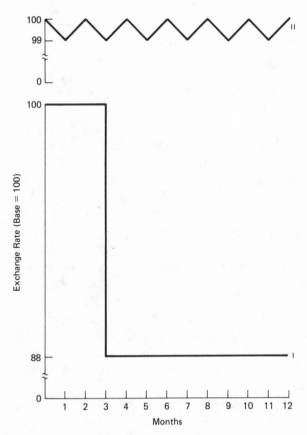

Figure 7.1 Exchange-rate "variability."

but more important is the fact that the EMS has buttressed the latent argument for greater capital controls and reductions in the degree of convertibility. It has also provided a rationalization for trade restrictions.

The EMS was also presented as a step in the grand process of monetary integration of Europe—perhaps ultimately toward one central bank, one currency, and one economic policy. If one entertains such ultimate goals, then the EMS seems to me to be a step backward. Fixing prices (like exchange rates or, indeed, agricultural prices) creates centrifugal forces and divergence, not centripetal forces and convergence. The road to convergence is to harmonize the great *quantity* determinants of monetary conditions—namely, the rate of growth of money, and the budget deficit. If the members each pursued policies of similar low monetary growth then there would be the basis for eventual convergence. A medium-term financial strategy is the right approach.

It has been claimed that the EMS is one way in which member states will accept the fiscal and monetary discipline required for convergence. The policies of France in the period of the socialist government 1981–84 are presented as an example of such discipline. And it is true that the expansionary program of the Mitterrand government from the assumption of power in 1981 ran only until March 1983. Then after successive devaluations in October 1981, June 1982, and March 1983, the government instituted an austerity program, aimed at reducing the budget deficit to 3 percent of GNP and monetary growth to 9 percent. Of course, one cannot be sure what policy the French government would have pursued if they had not been members of the EMS. But we do know that the behavior of the British Labour government in the period 1974–76 was quite similar. Unbridled expansionism in 1974–75 was followed by a substantial squeeze in 1976. Ironically, in spite of the fact that Britain was not in the "snake," the exchange rate against the dollar was pegged over this period! Thus, protestations that the French government were largely or even significantly induced to the austerity of 1983 by membership of the EMS must be viewed with skepticism. It is entirely understandable that the supporters of the EMS should claim such credit as falls their way.

The conclusion is that it is difficult to see what the United Kingdom would gain from joining the EMS. Certainly under the Thatcher government, and conceivably under alternative governments, there has been no need to bolster the anti-inflationary policies with pseudo-fixed parities of the kind practiced in the EMS. At most the EMS might reduce the very short-term (weekly or monthly) variations in the exchange rate against the EMS currencies. But research suggests that because of thick and almost perfect forward markets such short-term movements have little if any effect in inhibiting trade.[9] On the other hand, those who seek eventual monetary union of Europe had best pursue it through quantitative convergence rather than exchange rate fixity. Britain will best

9. A survey of firms by the British North American Association showed little concern with the short-term variability of exchange rates, and firms were apparently well-versed in buying forward cover. Under floating conditions the firms could either buy certainty in the forward market or take their chances on the spot market. With a real fixed-rate system that choice is denied them. For a contrary view, however, see M. A. Akhtar and R. Spence Hilton, "Effects of Exchange Rate Uncertainty on German-U.S. Trade," Federal Reserve Bank of New York, *Quarterly Review* 9, 1 Spring 1984, pp. 7–16.

serve monetary union in Europe by urging the right policies rather than embracing the wrong ones.

Finally, the EMS failed, indeed it was bound to fail, in insulating policies from politics. One of the great attractions of fixed parities of the past, such as the gold standard, is that the rules determined policy. If, for example, there was a run on the gold stock, then no one doubted that a monetary squeeze was on the cards, as manifest in the Horsley-Palmer rule. The room for political discretion and dissembling was small.

It would be nice if the great nations of Europe periodically discussed the existence and rationale for the fundamental disequilibria in exchange markets, and then proceeded to a rational conclusion. Such ideals are far from reality. In the EMS the periodic realignments are grand political events which present many opportunities for horse-trading, threats, counterthreats, bluff, etc. *Quid pro quos* are extracted for any "concession" on exchange-rate parities. And exchange rates became another pawn in the grand game of Europe. Indeed, it would be naive to expect anything else. (The same characteristics emerged in the Bretton Woods system, and eventually led to its demise.) At the very least one may claim that it is not clear that the pseudo-fixed rates and other policies that emerge from this political bargaining process are "superior" to the free-market solutions.

## An Exchange-Rate Target

Of course, it would have been possible for the government to pursue an exchange-rate target without joining the EMS.[10] The set of possible exchange-rate targets is virtually infinite. However, if one is seeking stability, not merely in terms of foreign currency but also in terms of domestic monetary-fiscal policy, one should choose that currency, or a combination of currencies, together with appropriate rules of reaction, which are thought likely to give rise to such stability. If we restrict our search, for the time being, to particular currencies—suppose it is the US dollar—then the targeting is an act of faith in the greater likelihood of the United States pursuing suitable stable policies.[11]

10. Logically, it could have pegged at a central rate with respect to the EMS currencies and behaved *as if* it were in the EMS, without the political hassle of the realignments, etc.
11. The experience of pegging to the United States in effect through gold in 1925–31 and in the Bretton Woods system after World War II to 1971 is not reassuring. In the period from 1947 to the 1960s it was complained that the United States was exporting deflation, whereas from the mid 1960s onward,

The choice of the EMS is essentially a decision that the German economy is, in the future, likely to be managed in monetary terms so that it is a suitable model for the United Kingdom. Perhaps it will. The postwar years have certainly seen Germany pursue the most stable of monetary and fiscal policies. But things may change, especially with the transformation of the SPD and the emergence of persistent unemployment.

If there was a desire, however irrational and misplaced, for more stable exchange rates in the United Kingdom, then it would have been more sensible and consistent with the objectives if the exchange rate target had been expressed in terms of the effective rate rather than the EMS/ECU package. This takes the exchange rates and weighs them according to the composition of trade of the United Kingdom. Thus, targeting an effective rate, compared with the EMS regime, would enable us to avoid following the D mark slavishly as it depreciates (or appreciates) with respect to the dollar, and so, by stabilizing with respect to the D mark, introducing greater instability with respect to the dollar.

In the long run an effective exchange-rate target would ensure that the United Kingdom inflated, with respect to the prices of traded goods, at roughly the same rate as her trading partners; whereas an EMS target that did not suffer periodically large one-way "realignments" in respect to the D mark would ensure that we inflated at the same rate as Germany.

## Interpreting Exchange-Rate Movements

One of the main criticisms of adopting either a fixed exchange rate, or an exchange-rate target, is that the value of a currency reacts—sometimes dramatically—to many factors besides monetary behavior. The exchange rate is the relative price of liquid financial assets. Although the stocks and changes in the stocks of such assets are important determinants of the relative price, they are only part of the story. The exchange rate is much affected by anticipations, expectations, and uncertainties, which are in turn affected by political events, rumor, and report. In effect the exchange rate has many of the characteristics of the price of an ordinary share of a corporation. One must expect a fair degree of volatility in free markets for foreign currencies.

Consider, for example, the effects of targeting an exchange rate during the periods of particularly large political uncertainty such as the run

---

they were said to be exporting inflation. In the 1970s under the dirty floats they were said to be exporting both. And in 1984 few would claim that the United States is a paragon of financial prudence and stability.

up to the general election. A conservative government committed to a policy of sound finance will find the exchange rate coming under increasing downward pressure. The markets will take a view of the likelihood of Labour government and the consequential fall in sterling (or combination of exchange controls and regulations). Provided there is a high enough probability of a Labour government being reelected, the markets will anticipate the event.[12] The higher the likelihood of a Labour government being elected, and the greater the differences between the expected monetary and fiscal policies of the two parties, the greater the depressing effect on the exchange rates in the year or months before the date of the election.

Suppose the authorities were pursuing an exchange-rate target for monetary policy. Then in the year before the election the authorities would increase rates and induce a monetary squeeze in order to maintain the parity. This is likely to result in a decline in real growth, and perhaps a decline in real output, together with other effects such as an increase in unemployment—hardly the sort of policy which any government would wish to impose during the election year. Furthermore, the greater the difference between the parties—the Conservative "sound policy" and the Labour "profligate policy"—the tighter the squeeze. Worst of all, the greater the likelihood of a Labour government, the higher interest rates must go to deliver the exchange-rate target, and so the policy will increase still further the probability of a Labour government being elected. Thus, a good chance of a Labour government may be turned into a sure thing.[13]

Clearly the exchange-rate target for monetary policy is bad political economy.[14] But even if it were not, there are strong objections to a mone-

12. In the 1983 general election the chances of a Labour government, as reflected in the polls, was virtually zero.
13. The bias induced by this policy to elect profligate governments is still present in the case where the existing government pursues an inflationist policy. If the alternative Conservative government were believed to be in favor of sound finance, and if they had a good chance of being elected, then this would have a favorable effect on the exchange rate of the Labour government and so enable them more easily to pursue an appropriate expansionist policy in the run-up to the election.
14. It is, of course, conceivable that an exchange-rate target may be proposed precisely to offset the normal temptations of governments to expand and inflate during the run-up to the general election. But, according to the argument in the previous footnote, it would have the *opposite* effect on an incumbent profligate government, making it yet more inflationary on the approach to the election. It will restrain only the government that pursues, relatively speaking, a sound monetary policy.

tary policy that routinely reflects all the alarms and excursions that affect exchange rates. If, for example, the United States, in order to contain the inflationary impact of the large Federal deficit, induces a very tight monetary squeeze so that the dollar-sterling rate comes under great pressure, why should the United Kingdom respond in a like manner, in order to defend the parity? It may well be that the domestic monetary conditions in the United Kingdom are entirely satisfactory and do not call for any such squeeze. The exchange-rate target will induce artificial oscillations and additional instability in monetary conditions in order to preserve stability of exchange rates.

Granted that it is undesirable to make monetary policy a consequence of the vagaries of exchange-rate movements, it is worthwhile considering whether the movements in exchange rates can be used to interpret and get useful assessment of prevailing monetary conditions. If, for example, a high exchange rate meant that monetary conditions were "tight" and a low exchange rate implied that monetary conditions were "loose," then the exchange rate could rank along with interest rates, both nominal and real, as a measure worthy of close attention but not targeting. The exchange rate could provide corroborating evidence for our main targets, the monetary aggregates.

The difficulty with this subsidiary role for exchange rates is one of interpretation. One would need to identify the causes of movements in the exchange rate before it could be used safely for monetary analysis. One would need to filter out those movements which are due to political factors, changes in the policies or prospects of our trading partners, accidents and the vagaries of nature, market "confidence," etc., which account for a substantial fraction of the variation of the exchange values. This is difficult. There is no repetitive historical record so that one can isolate such effects.

Exchange-rate movements must, therefore, generally be considered as rather dubious indicators of monetary conditions. There are exceptional circumstances where very large exchange-rate movements, combined with other evidence, may be used as a clinching argument. (I shall argue that this was the case in the winter of 1980–81.) But one should not look to exchange rates for any subtle interpretation of monetary conditions.

## Exchange Rates and Credibility

Although the authorities may decide to eschew exchange-rate targets and concentrate on delivering a target for monetary growth, it will be difficult to ignore the exchange-rate effect if the market still believes that the authorities will react to exchange-rate changes. The authorities will be driven by the market. Again one finds that the critical element in the policy is its "credibility."

Consider for example conditions which, as we shall see, broadly apply to the United Kingdom. The authorities announce that the level of short-term interest rates will depend primarily on the assessment of the movements in the monetary aggregates. The exchange rate is to be the object of benign neglect. However, the markets are not convinced that the politicians and central bankers can so readily jettison their concern for the level of the exchange rate. (There are many in the Bank of England who have made no secret of the fact that they believe it would be appropriate to pay much more, not less, attention to the exchange rate.) The question will be put: "Can ministers stand idly by as the exchange rate sinks (or rises) with all that that will entail?"

Whatever the reasons for the market's distrust, portfolio managers will act on the basis of these beliefs. Thus, suppose that there is a rise in the United States dollar brought about by some draconian tightening of monetary conditions in the United States. The authorities, surveying domestic monetary conditions, observe no surge of monetary growth and broadly believe that monetary conditions are "right." The market, however, sees sterling sinking against the dollar and anticipates that there is a good chance that the authorities will be driven to raise interest rates to stop the precipitous fall. The expectation of the authorities increasing interest rates substantially will be enough to generate falls in the price of financial assets. Portfolio managers will be induced to sell gilts in the expectation that they will be able to buy in later at a lower price. Similarly, the discount market will reduce the price that it offers for new bills. Thus, there will be all the appearances of a "gilt strike!"

Broadly speaking, the authorities have two choices. First, they could stick to their announced policy and not ratify the market moves, or secondly they could follow the lead of the market and behave as if they were defending the parity of sterling. The first path is a difficult one. Changing ingrained expectations is a harrowing business. The authorities would have to sit out the funding strike and use other sources of funds—such as running down foreign assets or borrowing from foreigners.[15]

It would be wise to avoid monetizing any of the borrowing require-

15. The implications for the exchange rate are clear and need not be elaborated here.

ment and so inflating the monetary aggregates, but as a temporary measure this might be a last resort. The dangers of such a policy choice—the possibility of inciting inflationary expectations, and indeed the fact that the authorities may lose the confrontation—are clear and present.

The second choice seems to avoid all such risks. If the authorities raise interest rates so that there is no risk of them going up further, then the funding strike is over and the flood begins; and sterling will return to the range at which there are no market fears of authority reaction. The temptation to follow this seemingly obvious path is clear.

But this will simply *validate the market's expectations that there is an exchange-rate target*. The next time the rate comes under pressure, the authorities will be locked ever more closely into the exchange-rate target by the more certain expectations of the market. Believing it is so makes it so. All that is needed for an exchange-rate target is the belief, however acquired, in the market that the authorities just could not tolerate substantial depreciation of sterling. Then the authorities can argue that they cannot fight market pressure—or at least it would be foolhardy to do so. Thus does rumor beget policy.

In one sense, the second alternative of capitulation to the market has many attractions for government and monetary managers. The markets and foreigners can be blamed for the painful oscillations in interest rates as well as the instability of exchange rates. It avoids eyeball to eyeball confrontation of the authorities and the market, and the government is unlikely to get a bad press if it does what is expected. The older heads in the corridors of Whitehall and the City will recall that in battles between the authorities and the City (not to mention the gnomes, etc.) it is the latter that always wins.

But the markets may take the view that some pressures on the exchange rate cannot be effectively countered by feasible movements in interest rates. Portfolio managers may be convinced that, on fundamental grounds of purchasing power parity, the exchange rate must move. Their guess about the intentions of the authorities is reciprocated by the authorities trying to adduce what the market foresees or wants, and so on . . . As in all game-theoretic strategies, such behavior defies any neat analysis. The extent to which the authorities were driven unwillingly by market expectations cannot be easily assessed from overt behavior. The attempts to attribute causation in the following pages are tentative. The subject deserves more analysis and reflection.

# 8

# Monetary Policy in 1979-83

## The Squeeze (1979–80) and the Easing (1980–81)

On coming into office the Thatcher government inherited very high rates of growth of narrow money (called hereafter $n$-money). All the $n$-money aggregates were telling broadly the same story. In 1978 both $M_1$ and noninterest-bearing $M_1$ (NIBM$_1$) were growing at about 20 percent per annum, and the monetary base was expanding at the rate of 15 percent (on a year-on-year basis). Had these rates of growth persisted, they would have been consistent with inflation rates of over 15 percent.

For reasons discussed in Chapter 6, however, the attention of the authorities was concentrated on the broader aggregates and, particularly, sterling $M_3$.[1] These were somewhat less alarming. The rate of growth of sterling $M_3$ in 1978 was about 14 to 15 percent, but, nevertheless, this was thought to be consistent with inflation rates exceeding 10 percent.

In the budgets of June 1979 and 1980 there were two important provisions that explained much of the behavior of the monetary aggregates and the banks that produced them. First, there was the speedy abolition of all exchange controls in 1979. This created complete freedom for residents in switching between sterling and foreign exchange. The banks were no longer constrained in the dealings in sterling and foreign-currency accounts. Secondly, the removal of the regulation of and discrimination against bank interest-bearing eligible liabilities

---

1. In 1978–79 there were no published compilations of the monetary base o of $M_2$.

Table 8.1. Monetary targets (% growth)

|                        | 1979/80   | 1980/81 | 1981/82 | 1982/83 | 1983/84 |
|------------------------|-----------|---------|---------|---------|---------|
| 1979 budget (i)        | 7–11      |         |         |         |         |
| 1980 strategy (i)      |           | 7–11    | 6–10    | 5–9     | 4–8     |
| 1981 strategy (i)      |           |         | 6–10    | 5–9     | 4–8     |
| 1982 strategy (ii)     |           |         |         | 8–12    | 7–11    |
| 1983 strategy (ii)     |           |         |         |         | 7–11    |
| Actual rise in sterling $M_3$ | 12 (iii) | 19 | 12 (iv) | 11 (iv) | 8(iv)  |

*Source:* Official statistics and Treasury Committee report on the 1983 Budget.

*Notes:* (i) These ranges apply to sterling M3 only; (ii) these ranges applied to M1 (the narrowly defined money supply, cash and bank accounts) and the broader aggregate PSL2 (private-sector liquidity, including building society deposits) as well as to sterling M3; (iii) eight months to mid-February 1980 at an annual rate; (iv) 12-month changes to banking April excluding public-sector deposits.

(IBELs)—inelegantly called "the corset"—in mid 1980 enabled the banks to compete, without handicap, for the interest-bearing deposits from which they had hitherto been largely excluded. For example, in order to avoid the corset, large corporations had developed a considerable market in deposits between corporations. This avoided the intermediation, and regulation, of the banking system. The abolition of the corset did much to bring this market back to its natural habitat in the banking system.

The precise effects of these two acts of deregulation can never be known with any certainty. The presumption, however, is that the deregulations would lead to, on the average, a larger value of deposits (and loans) of the banking system.

The monetary target for sterling $M_3$ in the 1979 budget was set at 7–11 percent. (See Table 8.1.) Subsequently, in the introduction of the Medium Term Financial Strategy (MTFS) in the March 1980 budget, targets for sterling $M_3$ for the subsequent four financial years were announced. These showed a gentle decline of 1 percent per year in the growth rate of sterling $M_3$. Thus, it was very much intended to be a gradualist program with the implicit objective of achieving by 1983–84 a rate of inflation less than 10 percent, yet still very likely to be exceeding 5 percent.[2] However smooth and gentle the path in the period 1982

2. This is allowing for lags in a trend in sterling $M_3$ velocity of 1.5 percentage points per annum, roughly the experience of the period 1964 to 1979. One of the problems arises from the fact that the definition of £$M_3$ has been refined over time—particularly with respect to the eventual exclusion of public-sector deposits.

onwards, the policy implied a considerable squeeze in the initial period 1980–81. Financial conditions of the private sector were already quite tight by the end of the financial year 1979/80. The erosion of the private sector's financial assets by increases in interest rates and inflation was accompanied by a substantial increase in personal savings. At the same time the big demand for credit by the corporate sector (and the overseas sector) saw the banks intermediating to meet the increased demands for liquidity.

As in the caricature discussed in Chapter 6, the banks took interest-bearing deposits from the flush personal sector and supplied loans to hard-pressed industry. This increase in interest-bearing deposits was one of the main causes of the burgeoning of sterling $M_3$. Up to July 1980, although sterling $M_3$ was running rather high, it did not appear to be beyond the pale. However, the removal of the penalty on banks issuing interest-bearing liabilities (i.e., the removal of the corset) was followed by a very rapid increase in such deposits.[3] For example, the intercorporate market for deposits, which had developed to avoid the restrictions of the corset, largely came back to the banks. From the summer of 1980 through June of 1981, sterling $M_3$ growth was up to the Heath-Barber figure of 20 percent (see Figure 8.1).[4]

Attempts to moderate the rate of growth of sterling $M_3$ through reducing public expenditure were largely frustrated. (See Chapter 5.) The authorities' main alternative weapon was interest rates. The object was to reduce the demand for bank credit by the private sector.[5] The effect of the large increases in interest rates in 1979 and the first half of 1980 did not appear to have a substantial, or at least speedy, effect on the demand for credit.[6] It was widely thought that "distress borrowing" by corporations was insensitive, at least in the short run, to servicing charges.

On the other hand, the *supply* of interest-bearing deposits did appear

3. Estimates of the effect of the removal of the corset vary. I suspect that some 3 percent addition to $£M_3$ is about correct.
4. Over the target period, running from mid February to mid April, the annual percentage rate of growth of sterling $M_3$ (seasonally adjusted and excluding public-sector deposits) was as follows: 1980–81, 19.9 percent; 1981–82, 12.9 percent; 1982–83, 11.0 percent; 1983–84, 9.7 percent.
5. Base or Minimum Lending Rates were as follows: *1979:* April 16, 12 percent; June 15, 14 percent; November 16, 17 percent. *1980:* July 4, 16 percent; November 24, 14 percent.
6. However, corporate borrowers at base rate plus one were still enjoying *negative* real-borrowing rates after tax. See *Bank of England Quarterly Bulletin,* Vol. 23, No. 4, December 1983, p. 472.

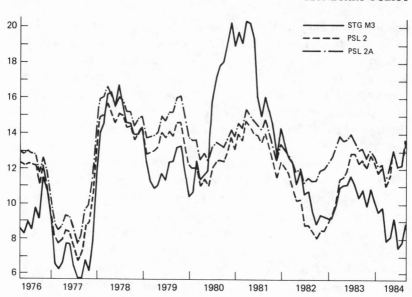

Figure 8.1 Growth in broad money (annual percentage changes, seasonally adjusted).
*Source:* Bank of England.

to expand in response to the higher yield. The private sector sought ways to economize on checking (current) accounts and cash, and earn interest on time deposits.[7] The high interest rates appeared to have a more serious and immediate negative effect on narrow money. From the late summer of 1979, the rates of growth of all indicators of narrow money fell precipitously. For example, the rate of growth of $M_1$ fell from about 13 to 14 percent in the best quarter of 1978 to 3 or 4 percent (on a year-on-year basis) in the spring of 1980. Such a sharp reduction of the rate of growth of $M_1$ had no precedent in recent monetary history. Furthermore, since the rate of inflation peaked during the early summer of 1980 (on a year-on-year basis it was 22 percent in May 1980), the fall in the level of real $M_1$ was quite unprecedented.

The nominal monetary base showed a somewhat less precipitate but still marked decline. The effect of the squeeze on the real monetary base can be seen in Figure 8.2 which shows the base in real terms. The fall in the real base was even sharper both in absolute and (even more) in relative terms than that of 1973–76.

To any scholar who had studied monetary behavior in countries other

7. The increase in nominal interest rates probably had some effect in raising the personal savings ratio to 14.8 in 1980. But there are many competing explanations for this phenomenon.

than the United Kingdom, this combination of statistics would have been construed as evidence that there had been a substantial and sharp monetary contraction. However, there was also much secondary and subsidiary corroborating evidence: the decline in the level of activity, the rapid rise in unemployment (or, more convincing, the fall in the level of employment), the increase in the number of bankruptcies, and widespread reports of the distress of British manufacturing industry. The exporting industries suffered in particular from the rapid appreciation of sterling.

This appreciation to a high of more than $2.40 masked an even higher real appreciation, which on various calculations amounted to 20 to 40 percent from its low in 1975.[8] This appreciation occurred primarily dur-

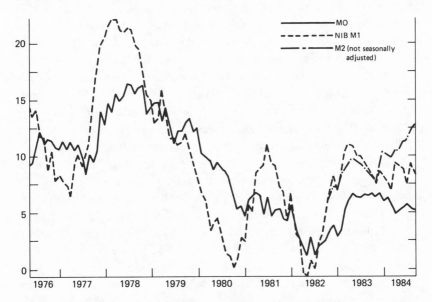

Figure 8.2 Growth in narrow money (annual percentage changes, seasonally adjusted).

*Source:* Bank of England.

8. See Buiter and Miller (1983) and Jürg Niehans, "The Appreciation of Sterling—Causes, Effects and Policies," SSRC Money Study Group Discussion Paper, Social Science Research Council, London, 1981. In my view the calculations of real exchange rates from official price indices overestimated the appreciation. This was primarily because there was a considerable improvement in the quality of British exports over the period which was not adequately reflected in the statistics. This, of course, is only a conjecture, but it is consistent with, first, the high level of U.K. exports that persisted in the aftermath of the appreciation (considerably in excess of the predictions of all models), and, second, the relatively high prices of exports (in terms of purchaser's currency).

ing a period of the most rapid inflation in 1980 and appeared puzzling to the Bank and the Treasury as well as the media. If sterling $M_3$ were a measure of the degree of monetary constraint, it was quite impossible to argue that the pound had appreciated because of a sharp fall in the quantity of (real) sterling $M_3$. But the soaring value of sterling was entirely consistent with the evidence of the precipitous fall of the real narrow aggregates. The rise in sterling was part and parcel of the squeeze.

Indeed, it is likely that, as Niehans argued, sterling in 1980–81 went through a phase of "overshooting" in response to the steep increases in nominal interest rates. The nominal yield on sterling financial assets (such as bills and CDs) was much above that to be obtained on similar US dollar assets. This gave rise to a demand for spot sterling, increasing its spot-exchange value relative to the US dollar. However, the market anticipated an increase in the supply of sterling (and demand for dollars) in the future as asset-holders got back into dollars. This gave a corresponding discount in the forward market for sterling, so that the rate of return, when one allowed for the cost of forward cover, was roughly the same in the United Kingdom as the United States. A transitory overshoot—lasting for some months—was a corollary of the high interest rates in the sharp monetary squeeze.

Thus, all the evidence seemed to be consistent with the "tight money" hypothesis—except for the rogue aggregate sterling $M_3$. The authorities, however, had such a commitment to sterling $M_3$ that they naturally sought nonmonetary explanations for the high exchange rate. And there were good reasons for believing that part of the appreciation was due to the increase in the price of oil in 1979. The real question was how much could be attributed to oil prices? So fas as I know, there was no rigorous effort to examine critically the proposition that the oil-price increase accounted for virtually all the appreciation.[9] Niehans conjectured that only some 20 percent of the appreciation could be attributed to the rise in the price of oil—and I still find no good reason to disagree with that figure. It was clear that the monetary squeeze was the dominant cause of the appreciation.

The authorities soon acknowledged, albeit implicitly, that the sterling $M_3$ statistics were misleading. In the wake of the great sterling $M_3$ ex-

9. If it were true, then one would similarly observe an appreciation of the currencies of other oil-rich countries. From my casual survey of the evidence, no such result emerged. But it is fair to add that no one forecast the behavior of exchange rates with any degree of accuracy and, to this day, it is very difficult to explain all.

pansion in July 1980, after the removal of the corset, the authorities did not attempt to increase interest rates. MLR stayed at 16 percent, until November when they were reduced again to 14 percent, in spite of the fact that sterling $M_3$ continued to increase at a rate of nearly 20 percent per annum.

In the fall of 1980, the Treasury and the Bank instituted a wide-ranging inquiry into the monetary aggregates, their meaning and means of controlling them.[10] The general conclusion from the inquiry was that sterling $M_3$ had indeed been misleading, and that in the interpretation of monetary conditions it would be best to take into account other evidence, including the narrow aggregates (at the time mainly $M_1$). But at the same time it was thought that monetary conditions had erred on the side of laxity.[11] There was no recognition of the fact that there had been a very considerable monetary squeeze. Many remembered the genesis of the Heath-Barber inflation of 1971–73 and recalled that $M_1$ had not given an adequate signal of the monetary expansion and the incubating inflation. (As discussed in Chapter 6 above, I believe this view was mistaken.)

The alternative of switching to a narrow aggregate was difficult for all sorts of reasons. Politically, it would have created a furor. But there was also good reason for believing that as interest rates fell the $M_1$ aggregate would rapidly expand. True, it would be in the nature of a once-and-for-all adjustment of transactions balances to the lower yields on time deposits, but it would have seemed like a "frying-pan-into-fire" switch to a narrow aggregate.

Another alternative was to impose an exchange rate target of a sufficiently narrow band to imply binding constraints on interest-rate policy. (This approach need not necessarily have been associated with a decision to join the EMS.) With a falling sterling the authorities would intervene, without sterilization, by buying sterling and running down official stocks of foreign exchange. This would reduce domestic monetary aggregates, other things being equal, and so put some upward pressure on the exchange rate. If such operations run the reserves down to dangerously low levels, then the authorities will have to increase do-

10. See Keegan (1984) for an account of this inquiry, although since his sources seem to be mainly from the Bank there is some selectivity in his evidence. A Green Paper on Monetary Control was published in 1980.
11. The view that monetary conditions were lax was strongly argued by Professor Brian Griffiths, Geoffrey Wood, and Roy Batchelor at City University.

mestic interest rates to ensure that a sufficient inflow of foreign exchange reserves is secured. This increase will of itself depress the monetary aggregates, and so assist in the adjustment process.

It was always reported that the Bank was keen on an exchange-rate target. The autumn and winter of 1980–81 had seen the unexpected combination of appreciating exchange rate *and* £M₃ overrun, and the Bank feared similar conditions could persist into 1981 leading to the decimation of the trading sector of the economy. The Bank's emphasis was on stemming the decline of output rather than on controlling inflation. It was perfectly clear that it would be absurd to peg the rate at its $2.40 or DM4.7 level. Some large devaluation (say to a $2.00 or DM3.8 parity) was the sine qua non, with even larger expansions of "money" (as in 1977) to maintain the parity.

On November 24th, interest rates were reduced 2 percentage points to 14 percent, but the Chancellor did not change his targets or indeed the numerical value of the existing sterling M₃ target. That was deferred to the 1981 budget-day financial statement. But the autumn statement did herald considerable changes in monetary arrangements. Although the statement did not embrace any ultimate objective of Monetary Base Control (MBC), it did set out a number of changes, desirable in their own right, and which would facilitate a move toward MBC if that seemed to be the appropriate policy.

The Bank was to reduce its discount window lending. Cash was to be injected or withdrawn entirely through open-market operations in the bill market—normally through buying and selling, but occasionally through repurchasing agreements. The objective was to control the interest rate on seven-day money within an unpublished 2-percent band. The market was to have more of a role in determining interest rates of longer maturities, so that the pressure of demand and supply would be exerted through the yield curve and the associated expectations.

As the new arrangements bedded down in the first half of 1981, the operational pattern was somewhat different from that predicted. First, authorities controlled the seven-day rate much more tightly than anticipated, and the unpublished band was really otiose. The market operators, long used to a rate-of-interest control system, and knowing that there was no alternative quantitative control on bank reserves, would deal at the rate fixed by the Bank.[12] Secondly, although the market pressures were supposed to work through the yield curve and to induce the

12. Minimum Lending Rate was suspended in August 1981.

Bank to adjust its dealing rate (in band I, as the short rates were called), the Bank found it impossible to restrict its large operations to the seven-day rates. In order to maintain the liquidity of the financial system in the seasonal and extraordinary shortages and gluts, at the controlled dealing rates, the Bank built up a very large portfolio of bills (as much as £9 billion by 1984), which waxed and waned with the seasonal patterns of liquidity conditions. Contrary to the original intention, the Bank was operating in the longer market (up to three months). It could not allow the market to determine the yield curve since it was such a large participant. In practice the Bank maintained a flat yield curve for bills during most of the period under review. This caused considerable difficulty in dealing with the anticipations of the market, and occasionally gave opportunities for arbitrage in the interbank market.

These changes in technical arrangements, however, did not much affect the actual thrust of monetary policy, except insofar as they reduced the degree of politicization of decisions about interest rates, and led to a somewhat speedier recognition of the need to move.

The last phase in the easing of monetary policy in 1980–81 came with the budget of March 1981. This tightened fiscal conditions considerably and allowed the Chancellor to reduce MLR by 2 percentage points to 12 percent. In the preparation for the budget it had been accepted that not only had monetary conditions been much tighter than had been indicated by sterling $M_3$, but they had been tighter than one would have proposed in any "gradualist" policy.[13]

13. In his account of this period, Keegan has sketched in a role which I played in the arguments about the exchange rate and monetary conditions. Before I came to No. 10, I had already given a seminar and briefing in the United States in October and November when I argued that monetary policy was, if anything, too tight in 1979–80 and not too loose as indicated by sterling $M_3$. The appreciation of sterling and all events other than the broad aggregates seemed to me to corroborate this view. I was pleased to find that when I tested my judgments with the late Dr. William Fellner—then of the American Enterprise Institute, and an economist for whose insights I had the highest regard—he fully agreed with me. Subsequently, this view emerged from the study by Jürg Niehans which was commissioned by the Centre for Policy Studies. Niehans, however, did contemplate the possibility of massive intervention (the "imperial guard") to knock sterling off its $2.40 perch in January 1981, using the arguments deployed by Fritz Leutwiler, President of the Swiss Central Bank, when he cut down the overshooting of the Swiss franc in 1978. I was opposed to this measure. It involved many more dangers in the situation of the inflating United Kingdom than in stable Switzerland. It seemed to me likely that the exchange rate would fall as a consequence of the monetary easing which had started in November of 1980, and was required to be extended in the budget. So it did.

Meanwhile, there was a need for a "stock adjustment" in narrow money and transactions balances to restore them to their normal-trend level in real terms. The surge in the growth rates of $M_1$ to 10–12 percent, and the halt in the fall of the growth rate of $M_0$ were welcome consequences of the easing of the tight monetary squeeze.

## Steering "Blind" and the Short Squeeze of 1981–82

Even while Britain was easing her monetary constraints in the period from November 1980 through March 1981, the United States embarked on a monetary contraction.[14] This monetary contraction coincided with the trough of the business cycle; yet interest rates remained very high in nominal terms (US Treasury bills were around 15 to 16 percent). The fall in the rate of US inflation meant that real interest rates actually increased substantially.

The dollar-sterling exchange rate had already begun its fall at the end of the first quarter of 1981 and this continued through the second quarter.[15] Much of this fall could probably be associated with the end of the "overshoot," but some was due to the more relaxed monetary conditions from the end of November 1980. The value of sterling was certainly nearer to its purchasing power parity with respect to the dollar. The profitability of export industries rose quite sharply from the abysmal levels which had accompanied "overshoot." The tightening of monetary policy in the United States from July onward put additional pressure on sterling. The average three-month Eurodollar rate was 18.4 percent in the third quarter of 1981.

The authorities reacted in September to the expected shortage of funds by allowing the market to push up interest rates and MLR by 2 percentage points to 14 percent. Shortly after, on October 1st, the authorities clearly *led* an increase in interest rates of two more percentage points so that MLR was back to 16 percent. The occasion for this further increase was an association of a sagging currency and hesitations among buyers of gilts who were expecting some such reaction. It

14. Phillip Cagan says "The decline in monetary growth after the mid-year was sharp and thus explains the fall in real GNP in the fourth quarter." See his essay "Monetary Policy and Subduing Inflation" in *Essays in Contemporary Economic Problems: Disinflation*, 1983–84 edition, edited by William Fellner, American Enterprise Institute, Washington, D.C. p. 34.

15. The average dollar exchange rates for the quarters for 1981 were: *I*, 2.31; *II*, 2.09; *III*, 1.84; and *IV*, 1.88.

seemed like a "Duke of York"—a steep and sudden increase in interest rates so as to provide for a period of gradually rising gilt prices.[16]

It was widely thought that the authorities had adopted surreptitiously an exchange-rate "target." Although this was not true, there was some substance to the view. Because of industrial action by civil servants, the preparation of statistics on the money supply (and on many other magnitudes) was much delayed and distorted. The only monetary aggregate that was readily available without distortion was the monetary base. Since $M_0$ was in the process of being defined and explored, and since little work had been carried out on the relationships between various definitions of the base and other aggregates and money income, the authorities were reluctant to lean very heavily on the base as an indicator of monetary conditions.[17]

One indicator of monetary conditions was available from hour to hour—the exchange rate. Yet it was widely admitted that the adjustment from the peak of $2.40 to the four-year low of $1.756 on August 10th was entirely justified in purchasing power parity terms. What alarmed the Bank and concerned the Treasury was the speed at which sterling fell.[18] Old campaigners recalled catastrophic declines when it was felt that it would never stop falling, such as in 1975–76. Expectation of further falls inhibited gilt buyers, and the familiar combination of falling sterling and funding strike loomed ominously.

Did the fall in the exchange rate indicate that monetary conditions had become too lax? As we have frequently seen, the exchange rate reflects many things besides monetary conditions. And to use it as an

16. Base rates were:

| Oct. 1, 1981 | Oct. 14 | Nov. 9 | Dec. 3 | Jan. 22, 1982 | Feb. 25 | Mar. 12 |
|---|---|---|---|---|---|---|
| 16 | 15.5 | 15 | 14.5 | 14 | 13.5 | 13 |

and so on to the low of 9 on November 4th.

17. Although I did not share in the great reluctance to use the base as a very important indicator, the absence of any substantial research to back up one's views meant that they could hardly be adopted by the skeptics.

| | Exchange Rate | | | | |
|---|---|---|---|---|---|
| | 1979 May | 1981 March 10 | 1981 Aug. 28 | 1981 Sept. 29 | 1981 Dec. 11 |
| Dollar | 2.06 | 2.21 | 1.85 | 1.79 | 1.88 |
| D-mark | 3.93 | 4.66 | 4.53 | 4.15 | 4.25 |
| Effective index | 86.3 | 98.6 | 91.3 | 87.0 | 89.8 |

18. This was assisted later in the month by the widespread cutting of oil prices and the breakdown of the OPEC price-fixing arrangements.

indicator of monetary conditions often requires subtleties of interpretation beyond the wit of economists and central bankers. The exchange rate was undoubtedly reflecting the severe monetary squeeze in the United States, rumors about the price of oil, and political uncertainties in the future of the government. In retrospect, however, it might well be argued that the easing of monetary conditions from November 1980 onward had gone too far. $M_1$ growing at 10 to 15 percent was not consistent with the policy of reducing inflation into the 5- to 10-percent range by 1983. Although a surge of narrow money growth had been expected, it could not be allowed to continue.[19]

Although the evidence (ex post) of monetary laxity is not overwhelming, it is sufficient to justify some of the increase in interest rates and, indeed, some case for arguing that the rapidity of the fall in the exchange rate was correctly interpreted. It is, however, much more debatable whether the situation needed the rather drastic medicine of a 4-percentage-point increase in interest rates to 16 percent. The precipitous decline in noninterest-bearing $M_1$ and $M_1$ in the third quarter of 1981 is corroborative evidence that the squeeze may have been overdone.[20] $M_1$'s rate of growth declined about 6 or 7 percent, and $NIBM_1$ fell even more steeply.

Within two weeks of the date of the final 2-percent increase in interest rates, the authorities started easing them down by half a percentage point per month to the low of 9 percent on November 4, 1982. Possibly, the situation called for a fall in interest rates, similar to that of March 1981, so as to avoid a secondary contraction.[21] In the event, however, the authorities were not persuaded of the need for speed. The gradual Duke-of-York process of adjustment created the longest bull market in gilts that anyone in the City could remember. The policy undoubtedly built up considerable confidence in the financial markets, which was maintained and even improved during the exigencies of the Falklands war.

The year 1982 saw the first convincing fruits of the counterinflation

19. It is worth noting, however, that the monetary base grew at 6 percent or so during the period from the third quarter of 1980 through to the end of the calendar year 1981. The decline in the rate of growth of the base was arrested in October 1980 but there was no evident surge as in the $M_1$ data.

20. Tim Congdon, a distinguished City economist, at the time argued that the first 2-percent increase in interest rates could be justified. But he was certain that the additional 2 percent was overdoing it, and would inhibit the fragile recovery. The figures (particularly, the broad measures) were distorted by the civil-service strike.

21. After growing quite vigorously in the second half of 1981, industrial production stagnated and manufactures actually declined.

policy. Retail prices were increasing at 12 percent when the year began, and only 5 percent when the year ended. This disinflationary process was entirely consistent with the monetary squeeze, interpreted in terms of the narrow aggregates, which began in the last quarter of 1979.[22] The decline in interest rates broadly followed the decline in the rate of inflation so that short-term real interest rates remained roughly constant. The fall in the inflation rate also helped restore the depleted level of real balances.

Over the 1981–82 period it was widely conjectured that the authorities had departed from their monetary targets. Most commentators suggested that there was really an exchange-rate target. Certainly, the overt evidence could not be used to discredit that proposition. One of the remarkable features of the period was the great stability of the effective exchange rate. From September 1981 to October 1982 it remained in the 90 to 92 range (1975 = 100).

An alternative hypothesis, suggested by Mr. Gordon Pepper and others, was that there was really a monetary base target—perhaps in preparation for the introduction of Monetary Base Control. Again there was good evidence to support his conjecture, since the growth of currency and, to a lesser extent, the monetary base exhibited considerable stability over those months. Yet others suggested that the authorities had a real short-term interest-rate target—again, they had some considerable stability to point to. Finally, there were suspicions that the government was really targeting the growth of nominal GNP, which again appeared to be declining in a steady course.[23]

All such suggestions were mistaken. The authorities were behaving according to their announced policy, of paying particular attention to the monetary targets, but also taking into account other indicators of monetary conditions. The idea that the authorities were targeting the exchange rate was presumably scotched by the decline in the effective

22. During 1981 I had become convinced that inflation would be down to 5 percent by 1983. My colleagues, and the media (following the inevitable leak), were rather incredulous, but I was applying the old lessons to the new situation. After 1982 it was then widely predicted that the reduction in inflation was only a transitory phenomenon and that it would soon assert itself—and many said to figures above 10 percent. I thought although it would wobble about a bit, it was unlikely to go up or down for a year or two. This also turned out to be roughly correct.

23. During 1982 there was considerable momentum behind the idea of a nominal GNP (or GDP) target. Professor James Meade put his intellectual weight behind the idea, and Sam Brittan publicized the advantages in the *Financial Times*.

rate from 92 (1975 = 100) in October 1982 to less than 80 in February 1983. (This fall was even sharper than that of 1981.)

The conjecture of Mr. Pepper, however, was more prescient, if a little premature. $M_0$ was included among the targets from March 1984 onward. Similarly, one can point to substantial increases in short-term real interest rates in January 1983.

Alas, boring though it may be to media men, the authorities (broadly speaking) carried out the policy consistent with the principles that had been announced; it is odd that few believed them.

## The Approach to the Election 1982–83

In his 1982 budget speech the Chancellor announced that instead of a target only for sterling $M_3$, the objective would be broadened to include the narrow aggregate $M_1$ and the alternative broad aggregate PSL2—but both would have the same target band (8–12 percent) as sterling $M_3$. One of the remarkable coups of Sir Geoffrey Howe's tenure of the Chancellorship was to deliver all aggregates within the target range in 1982–83. The real sector of the economy responded quite encouragingly—the recovery proceeded at a steady, if unspectacular, pace. And, contrary to the Jeremiahs, inflation remained at a low level. At last it appeared that the authorities had produced that stable financial framework that had been promised and pursued with such determination. The achievements of this period are the more remarkable when judged not only against the rapid contraction in Europe (particularly Germany) and the United States in 1982, but also against the backdrop of an impending election to be held before June 1984 and a possible change of regime.

It was clear that if there was to be a change of party, then there would immediately be a rapid depreciation of sterling, an inflationary expansion of public spending, and more drastic regulations and controls. Although the Conservatives had a clear lead in the opinion polls, it was just possible that the polls may either be wrong or they may turn. And in any case the government was not invulnerable to banana skins.

One main effect of a rise in the probability of a Labour government would be a flight of capital, in anticipation of the imposition of stringent exchange controls. Portfolio switching to insure against such risks would have the effect of putting considerable pressure on the exchange rate and on government funding. The availability of indexed gilts, although clearly a help, was not on such a scale that it could provide an important haven for funds.

Speculation about the election uncertainties was one of the factors that lay behind the 15-percent devaluation in the effective rate (both nominal and real) from November 1982 to March 1983. There were, as always, other contributing factors. Possible cuts in oil prices produced the usual bouts of nerves. More important, however, was the generally ambient view that interest-rate reductions by November to 9 percent had gone perhaps a "bit too far" and that there was some looseness in the monetary stance. There was some evidence of this in all the aggregates—particularly in the third and into the fourth quarter of 1982.

The authorities were faced with the subtle task of making a small tack in monetary policy, but at the same time resisting the pressures to fight the fall of sterling. The policy, as so often announced, was to ensure that the monetary conditions were consistent with the gentle but insistent disinflationary pressure. As far as the rumors of elections or oil price changes were concerned, the exchange rate would be allowed to take the strain. Fortunately, both economic and political arguments were in agreement. It would have been a great mistake to allow the electoral (and oil) rumors to lead the government into a substantial monetary squeeze in order to defend an exchange-rate target.

Nevertheless, by January the markets, by nudging the modestly reluctant authorities, had moved interest rates up by 2 percentage points to 11 percent. This 2-percent increase contrasts with the 4-percent increase in late 1981; correspondingly, the devaluation was even sharper and greater in the 1982–83 period than in 1981. Furthermore, in 1983 the exchange rate was nearer to its purchasing-power parity, so such an adjustment was less needed. In retrospect, however, it is fairly clear that the 1982–83 policy was somewhere near the appropriate one. The monetary aggregates behaved themselves quite well (Table 8.2) and provided a suitable sense of stability in the conduct of monetary policy.

This in turn served to increase the probability of a Conservative victory in the election. It became clear that the likelihood of a Labour victory was very small, at least as judged by the lengthening odds at Ladbrookes. This paved the way for a series of one-half percentage point reductions in base rates to 9.5 percent on June 14th, just after the election.

It is interesting to contrast the pre-election period of 1982–83 with that of 1978–79. The monetary aggregates clearly show that the Labour

Table 8.2.  Growth of monetary aggregates
(Percentage increases (annual rates); seasonally adjusted)[a]

| Banking months | Sept. 82–Nov. 82 | Dec. 82–Feb. 83 | Mar. 83–May 83 | June 83–Aug. 83 |
|---|---|---|---|---|
| Wide monetary base | 6.2 | 5.4 | 4.7 | 3.6 |
| Noninterest-bearing $M_1$ | 15.6 | 4.9 | 10.6 | 10.5 |
| $M_1$ | 15.9 | 11.3 | 16.5 | 12.1 |
| $M_2$ | — | — | — | 8.8[b] |
| Sterling $M_3$ | 12.4 | 8.6 | 13.8 | 11.1 |
| PSL1 | 9.3 | 8.0 | 17.2 | 8.6 |
| PSL2 | 10.0 | 11.9 | 18.4 | 11.7 |
| $M_3$ | 13.3 | 13.4 | 11.4 | 11.4 |

*Source:* Bank of England *Quarterly Bulletin,* September 1983, p. 337.

a These figures are calculated by adding the increases in the money stock for the three-month period and dividing by the stock at the beginning of the three-month period.
b Change over twelve months to mid-August 1983 (not seasonally adjusted).

government embarked on a rapid expansionary program—presumably, in the belief that this would enable them to win the election.[24] The government of Mrs. Thatcher, however, clearly eschewed such expansionism. The monetary aggregates were kept under control both up to and beyond the polling date.

24. There was good reason to believe that monetary expansion helps turn a few votes to the incumbent government; the familiar story of (then) Harold MacMillan turning the 1959 incipient defeat into a massive victory on the basis of his expansionary policy is one of the oft-repeated tales of politics. Similarly, the Labour party will never cease to blame Roy Jenkins for the contraction of 1968–69, which, they believe, cost them the election of 1970.

# III
# SOME CONSEQUENCES

Part III is devoted to an examination of some of the consequences of the policies outlined in Parts I and II. These chapters are highly selective—even a little quirky—in the choice of subject matters and analysis. Certainly, they do not pretend to be at all comprehensive let alone a definitive study of the efficacy and effects of the British government's financial policy during these years. I have examined only a subset of those questions which many influential commentators thought to be critical or at least important in any assessment of policy.

Chapter 9 examines first the widely held Keynesian view that the 1979–81 fierce fiscal contraction was the main cause of the sharp fall in GNP. The evidence suggests that the traditional Keynesian explanation is not consistent with the evidence; indeed, the economy seemed to behave in the *opposite* way to that which many a Keynesian confidently predicted. The abiding impression, consistent with account in Part I, is one of the high power and positive effects of monetary policy compared with the seemingly perverse effects of fiscal policy. Chapter 9 then pursues the proposition that the main effect of the government's financial squeeze was on the exchange rate through making (net) exports unprofitable and through a deteriorating current balance. The evidence shows, per contra, that there was an astonishing buoyancy of exports (indeed, of manufactured exports) in the wake of the very steep rise in the real value of sterling's exchange rate. Furthermore, the current account surplus increased to record levels. It is tentatively suggested that

153

this creditable behavior of exports and the current balance might have been due to the "cold shower" effect and the clear evidence that sterling's height was only a transitory phenomenon.

Chapter 10 then examines the suggestion that the reforms of 1979–81 have generated substantial beneficial changes in British industry—in particular, it discusses the rapid advance in productivity in 1980–83 and whether this is merely a "flash in the pan" or some evidence of permanent change. Finally, but alas most inconclusively, we review the causes and cures for the high unemployment that emerged in 1979–81 and persisted throughout the recovery.

# 9

# *Financial Policy, Sterling and the Current Balance*

The previous chapters have been concerned with the principles and practices of fiscal and monetary policy during the period 1979 to 1983. Although on occasion the account of the theory and the decisions on policy necessary implied some judgment about the efficacy of the policy or the desirability of the outcome, I have not attempted to answer the great questions which have so occupied the media discussion and the many economists who spend their time on current policy issues. For example, one of the questions that has dominated discussion can be put simply: "Was Mrs. Thatcher's policy responsible for the recession from 1979?" Or was it largely due to oil prices, trades unions, foreigners, technical change, the European Community, and so on?

In one sense these are the most interesting questions of policy—but they are also the most difficult. Economic policy does not depend entirely or even primarily on economic principles and evidence. Political, social and psychological factors must play a considerable part in any successful policy. Yet all an economist can do is to examine critically the economic ideas which lie behind a particular policy; he will have only a sketchy idea of the other determinants of policy. Similarly, the assessment of a policy—such as that so loosely but evocatively described as Thatcherite—must be in terms of an *alternative feasible* policy. Alternatives derived from some economic text or econometric model may be useful for the classroom, but to serve as an alternative standard they

155

must satisfy political, social, and indeed psychological conditions of credibility and acceptance.[1]

However, it is worthwhile reviewing some of these questions. We shall be able to settle little, although it may clear the ground for some later reflections.

The underlying thrust of policy was the great disinflation from 1980 to 1983—from 20 percent to 5 percent. Any disinflationary policy was bound to be associated with *some* dislocation of activity, although it is both arbitrary and irrelevant to attribute such dislocation to the process of disinflation rather than the inflation which preceded it. Similarly, to suppose that one could have avoided the adjustment costs by continuing the inflation, at perhaps an accelerating rate, is clearly inconsistent with the evidence of history (as, one may add, is the presumption that incomes policy would have achieved costless disinflation). The ambience of the discourse in this chapter is this disinflationary process. All the judgments of fiscal vs. monetary policy, of the effects of sterling's appreciation, of productivity growth, and of unemployment must be seen in the context of the pressures of changing entrenched expectations of inflation.

## Fiscal Policy: The Cause for the Recession?

Fiscal policy is probably the most accepted reason for the recession itself and, certainly, for its depth.[2] Some quotations from Buiter and Miller (1983, p. 327) illustrate the argument:

> The cyclically adjusted budget change is thus a 7 percent shift to surplus over the four calendar years 1980 to 1983. . . .
>
> By Keynesian principles of the determination of aggregate demand and

1. In M. J. Artis, R. Bladen-Hovell, E. Karakitsos, and B. Dwolatzky, NIESR *Review* 2/84 No. 108, May 1984, pp. 54–67, "The Effects of Economic Policy 1979–82," the most sophisticated test of the effects of fiscal policy in the period 1979-I to 1982-IV compared the actual policy with what would have happened if the government had expanded public spending at a rate of 1.8 percent per annum and had not raised tax rates. This would have increased the budget deficit substantially and, on the basis of the arguments discussed in earlier chapters, would have eroded confidence both in the economic management and in the political credibility of the existing government and its policies. Of course, no such effects can be included in any econometric model—as the authors implicitly acknowledge. One should treat such calculations as exercises in modeling rather than as any evaluation of policy.
2. The 365 signatories to the *Times* letter of 1981 clearly subscribed to that broad view. See also Buiter and Miller (1981, 1983).

output, the depth of the depression in the United Kingdom can be partly explained by the tight fiscal stance, induced by the MTFS. . . .

The . . . demand effect of the government's spending and tax program has fallen almost 4 percent behind the potential growth of the economy. . . .

The first problem with this interpretation of events is that of *timing*. There is little doubt about the timing of the upper turning point of GDP: on all measures this occurred in the second quarter of 1979. Similarly, the lower turning point occurred exactly two years later in the second quarter of 1981. If the fiscal hypothesis is correct, then we should have observed a contractionary fiscal policy in 1978 and 1979 and a switch to an expansionary policy in 1980 through to 1981.[3]

We observe, however, precisely the opposite. The years 1978 and early 1979 saw a markedly expansionary fiscal policy that preceded the slump, whereas the beginning of the recovery in the second quarter of 1981 was preceded by a severe contractionary fiscal policy from the summer of 1980 throughout 1981. In particular the budget of March 11, 1981 clearly announced the sharpest fiscal contraction in recent history. Yet the economy not merely ceased its precipitate fall, but actually reversed and grew.

This result is so striking that it is necessary to ask whether the many alternative definitions of fiscal policy would give rise to different interpretations. Unfortunately, as we have seen, the enormous variety of adjustments that have been suggested make it impossible to survey the whole field. Restricting the enquiry to the EEC and OECD cyclical adjustments discussed in Chapter 5, however, suggests that the conclusion would not be changed, and indeed, would be fortified—especially with respect to the lower turning point in 1981.

It is obviously tempting to stand the fiscalist proposition on its head and ask whether the fiscal expansion in 1978–79 *caused* the downturn and the contraction of 1980–81 *caused* the upturn of 1981. Considered as isolated policy changes, without reference to other (particularly, monetary) conditions, no such claim can be entertained. Simple one-to-one causation is unlikely to give one insights into the cause and cure for the slump. However, if the argument that the ambient level of confidence was as important as I (quoting Keynes) have argued, then the timing

3. This timing is consistent with the widely held view among fiscalists that the effect of an increase in the deficit is felt within a quarter, and the effect persists for two years or so. See quotations from Modigliani and Ando, p. 48 in this book.

of Healey's expansionary fiscal policy in 1978–79 and the sharp Thatcher contraction in 1980–81 surely were important contributions. Confidence lost and then regained.[4]

The fiscalist arguments that the tightness of fiscal policy (the MTFS) caused (or lengthened or deepened) the recession have understandably not dwelt on the timing of the swings of fiscal policy. They have concentrated on the *cumulative* tightness over a number of years. There are sound reasons for accumulating the observed financial deficits or borrowing requirements over the years. In any particular year, let alone quarter, there is usually a substantial deviation between aim and achievement. Errors are endemic. Analyzing the results over, say, four or five years will filter out some of the noise. So one has a better idea of the average fiscal conditions by cumulating changes over the five-year period.

Unfortunately, this cumulative approach negates one of the central principles of fiscalism. As Ando and Modigliani (1976) explain, the fiscalists offer to boost demand and output only in the two-year period—after that the effects are a "curiosum" and may even be negative. Timing is everything in countercyclical fiscalism.

Even so, as we argued in Chapter 5, the record of the United Kingdom over the years 1979–84 cannot be identified readily as one of unremitting fiscal squeeze. Using the "adjustments" of the EEC, the data indicate that the United Kingdom pursued a policy which was fiscally *looser* than that of other member countries. And if the OECD adjustments are taken as the standard, then the fiscal stance of the UK was only just about as tight as that of Germany over these years. Thus, the evidence of a differential Thatcher fiscal squeeze over the four- or five-year period is not sustained.[5]

4. This 1981 type of experience in the UK was manifest in Germany in 1983. Again, a sharp fiscal squeeze in 1983 was associated with a turnaround of the economy and a renewal of growth.

5. Those who argued the fiscalist case have usually pressed the "relative squeeze" point in the years up to 1981. This was the year before Germany and the rest of Europe, the United States, and Japan suffered a sharp decline in activity and employment in spite of the preceding expansionary budget policies. Similarly, the inclusion of high-saving, large-deficit Japan in the OECD is helpful to the fiscalist case. Nevertheless, it is perfectly true that the UK entered the recession before the OECD countries and, after the budget squeeze of end 1980 to early 1981, recovered earlier.

## Monetary Policy

An alternative explanation for the recession is thought to be the tight monetary squeeze from 1979 to 1980. The recovery from 1981 onward was then largely due to the easing of monetary policy in November 1980 through the fall of 1981. In terms of the *timing* of events, monetary policy clearly has a rather better claim than fiscal policy to be considered a prime mover. As we have seen, however, the interpretation of monetary policy was, at the time, dominated by the concentration of attention on the wider aggregate, sterling $M_3$. And if one accepted that wide money was the only—or even the best—indicator of monetary conditions, then the timing was seemingly all wrong.

In this final summing up, however, I shall assume that the wide vs. narrow argument is settled in favor of the narrow. Then it is certainly true that there was a very sharp monetary squeeze from the first quarter of 1979 onward, which was maintained throughout 1980. The rate of growth of $M_1$ fell from about 15 percent at the end of 1978 to about 4 percent at the end of 1979—and stayed below that level, on average, throughout 1980.

The turning point in GDP occurred in the early summer of 1979. This is consistent with the proposition that a sharp monetary contraction has its effect on real output within a fairly short period of 3–9 months. Of course we do not *know* that the monetary squeeze *caused* the turning point in output—that downturn might have occurred in any case. But it is worth considering the hypothesis that monetary policy was a prime mover in the onset of the recession. Or to put the point another way, if monetary policy had persisted on its 1978 course, might the recession have been substantially different? Might its onset have been delayed for some months, and might its pattern have been different—perhaps shallower but longer? With the persistence of the 1978 policy, there is little doubt that inflation would have continued to run in the early 1980s, at about 15 to 20 percent. As it turned out the monetary squeeze may have heralded, more or less according to the expected schedule, the low inflation rates of 1982.[6]

The timing of monetary policy in 1980 and 1981 is also consistent with the proposition that the upturn in GDP in mid 1981 was caused or at least assisted by the modest easing of monetary stringency in Novem-

6. In 1980 there were very few who dared to suggest such a low inflation rate from the end of 1982 onward—Professor Patrick Minford was the notable, and much derided, exception.

ber 1980 and March 1981. The peculiar interest in this period arises from the combination of massive fiscal squeeze and modest monetary ease. It is also worth reflecting on the extent to which the reductions in interest rates reflected the confidence of the gilt-owners that the markets were not going to be flooded with government debt; thus was the monetary ease engineered by the fiscal squeeze. But perhaps monetary policy dominated the real outcome.

It would be possible to trace the effects of the modest monetary tightening in the latter months of 1981 in the slowing of the recovery in 1982. This was followed by the easing again in the second and third quarters of 1982 through to the middle of 1983. These were, however, either relatively small changes in direction or, if sharp (as at end 1981), they were short-lived.

But leaving that record for more detailed dissection on another occasion, we might turn to the great question that has puzzled and vexed some scholars. What is the transmission mechanism for monetary policy? Can we trace the effects through the intermediary variables to see how monetary policy affects real output and prices?

## The Appreciation of Sterling, Oil and the Current Balance

In an open economy like the UK, most economic theorists would argue that a main transmission mechanism for changes in domestic circumstances or policy is through the foreign exchange. With a more or less free exchange rate, any substantial monetary squeeze will be reflected in an appreciation of sterling. The relative reduction in the supply of sterling, compared with other alternative currencies, will cause its value to rise. Furthermore, it has been argued that under conditions of a relative monetary contraction, the currency will go through a transitory period of "overshooting" before it settles down to the new level consistent with the new monetary conditions.[7]

Certainly, sterling did appreciate sharply in nominal terms during the period from early 1979 through to the first quarter of 1981 as can

7. The increase of interest rates in the UK, relative to foreign rates, means that to preserve equality of rates of return sterling must be expected to fall at some time in the future. But if it is thought that sterling will settle at a future value consistent with the new monetary stringency, then currently sterling must rise above the future value in order to be able to decline and offset the higher yield on sterling financial assets. This will preserve the equality of covered interest rates in money markets.

Table 9.1. Sterling exchange rates

Quarterly average (US dollars)

| | | |
|---|---|---|
| 1978 | I | 1.9273 |
| | II | 1.8347 |
| | III | 1.9317 |
| | IV | 1.9843 |
| 1979 | I | 2.0157 |
| | II | 2.0801 |
| | III | 2.2318 |
| | IV | 2.1587 |
| 1980 | I | 2.2536 |
| | II | 2.2849 |
| | III | 2.3811 |
| | IV | 2.3856 |
| 1981 | I | 2.3101 |
| | II | 2.0813 |
| | III | 1.8365 |
| | IV | 1.8837 |
| 1982 | I | 1.8471 |
| | II | 1.7799 |
| | III | 1.7253 |
| | IV | 1.6497 |

Source: IMF *International Financial Statistics*.

be seen in Table 9.1. However, since the United Kingdom suffered a rate of inflation substantially larger than that of the United States and those of the majority of its trading partners, the appreciation in the *real* effective exchange rate was even more dramatic. This can be seen, in its most relevant manifestation, in the calculations of the movement of the producer prices and labor costs of Britain relative to those of our competitors (primarily in the OECD countries). Even if one ignores the sharp peak of January 1981, the real appreciation of sterling clearly exceeded 30 percent—and perhaps the best figure to bear in mind for this period is a real appreciation of some 35 to 40 percent.[8]

The classical process of a currency appreciation is to decrease the sterling prices of goods that are traded or tradeable relative to those that are not traded. Domestically, people will substitute tradeable goods for

8. In his excellent analysis of this period Jurg Niehans pointed out that the real appreciation of sterling was even greater than that experienced by the Swiss economy in 1978. Then, however, the fault lay not so much in tight Swiss monetary policies as in the inflationary monetary policies being pursued in the United States. See Jürg Niehans, *op. cit.*

nontradeables—or, in other words, imported goods and services for the output of domestic industry. The relative fall in the sterling price of exports will make exports less profitable and induce producers of exports to switch resources from low-profit exports in order to supply the domestic market; thus, more goods will flood onto the domestic market and depress (relatively) the prices of nontradeables.

The net effect is to increase imports and reduce exports, thus, causing the current balance to deteriorate.[9] This will reduce aggregate demand and augment aggregate supply. Similarly, the relative fall in the sterling price of traded goods will be partially transmitted through factor costs to the prices of nontraded goods. So inflation will be reduced.

Before we review this process at work in the UK, it is convenient to consider an important variation on this theme. This is the so-called Dutch disease explanation of Britain's allegedly severe recession. This denies that the appreciation of sterling is largely due to the monetary squeeze. It is thought to be due almost entirely to the combination of Britain emerging as a substantial oil producer in the late 1970s and a net oil exporter in 1980, and the rise in the price of oil in 1979.[10] From the mid 1970s oil was expected to "replace" a quantity of manufactured exports in the current account. The mechanism of this substitution of oil for manufactured exports is the appreciation of sterling.

The plausibility of the oil explanation as a major cause of the appreciation of sterling has been criticized, and I think effectively, by Niehans (1981) and Buiter and Miller (1981). Additional evidence, however, has been adduced recently to support the oil explanation of the appreciation.[11] It has been claimed that the appreciation began well before the Thatcher monetary squeeze of 1979.[12] Indeed, if oil were a main explanation of exchange-rate movements of the 1970s, then the exchange rate would have clearly appreciated from the middle of the 1970s or perhaps earlier when it became clear that the North Sea was going to be a major contributor to the oil balance of the UK. Professor Chrystal

9. Assuming that the elasticities of demand for imports and supply of exports are sufficiently large. (These are the Marshall-Lerner conditions.)
10. P. J. Forsythe and J. A. Kay, "The Economic Implications of North Sea Oil Revenues," *Fiscal Studies,* Vol. I, July 1980, pp. 1–28. See also K. Alec Chrystal, "Dutch Disease or Monetarist Medicine? The British Economy under Mrs. Thatcher," Federal Reserve Bank of St. Louis *Review,* Vol. 66, No. 5, May 1984, pp. 27–38.
11. I am not discussing here whether the appreciation had the effects claimed: that issue is taken up later in this chapter.
12. Chrystal, *op. cit.*

sees such an effect with respect to the sterling/dollar exchange rate from 1977 onward, well before the monetary squeeze. He is misled, however, by taking the sterling/dollar exchange rate. In *effective* terms sterling *depreciated* from 1976 to 1978.[13]

To avoid misunderstanding, I would not argue that the presence and price of oil has *no* effect on the exchange rate. The point is that it is likely to be relatively small and highly transitory. There seems to be no reason to dispute Niehans's conjecture that not more than 20 percent of the appreciation of sterling can be explained by the oil factor.

Let us now leave this oil-diversion and return to the main argument that the transmission mechanism of the appreciation of sterling, caused by monetary policy, was the main cause of the depths of the recession. The effects appear primarily in the decline in exports and the flooding in of imports—that is a decline in the current balance of payments. Yet there was no decline from the deficit inherited by the government in 1979. In striking contrast, the current balance became highly positive.[14] This requires some explaining away.

13. The annual average exchange rates of sterling were:

|  | 1975 | 1976 | 1977 | 1978 | 1979 |
|---|---|---|---|---|---|
| $ | 2.22 | 1.81 | 1.75 | 1.92 | 2.12 |
| EER (1975=100) | 1.00 | 85.7 | 81.2 | 81.5 | 87.3 |
| IMF wage costs | 70.0 | 65.0 | 63.5 | 68.3 | 80.1 |
| Real exchange rate of US$ | 100.00 | 111.7 | 105.8 | 95.6 | 84.8 |

In 1977–78 the dollar fell sharply against virtually all OECD currencies. The IMF series for wage costs suggest that there was a small appreciation in the real sterling exchange rate from 1976 to 1978—but, compared with 1975, it had declined. *Sources:* CSO *Economic Trends* No. 367, May 1984, p. 50; John Williamson, "The Outlook for the Future of Sterling Real Exchange Rate, Proof of Evidence to Sizewell B. Power Station Enquiry," May 1984.

14. The current balance was in current £ bn:

| 1974 | 1975 | 1976 | 1977 | 1978 | 1979 | 1980 | 1981 | 1982 | 1983 | 1984 (fore-cast) | 1985 (fore-cast) |
|---|---|---|---|---|---|---|---|---|---|---|---|
| −3.3 | −1.5 | −0.8 | 0.1 | 1.2 | −0.6 | 3.7 | 7.3 | 5.5 | 3.0 | 1.9 | 3.0 |

Thus, for the three years after the 1974 lower turning point of GDP, Britain suffered a cumulative deficit of £ −5.6 bn. If this were transformed in constant (1982) price terms, the deficit in 1974–76 would be about doubled to £ −12 bn; whereas the three years after 1981 has a total surplus of £ 15.8 bn. This comparison, of the three years after the lower turning points of GDP in 1974 and in 1981, eliminates much of the cyclical effects and many random elements in the yearly figures. It suggests that the total turnaround was from an annual £ −5 bn (in 1982 prices) to £ 5 bn in an average change of £ 10 bn. We may anticipate the future argument by noting that

Traditionally it is argued that, for a short period, the price effect of the appreciation of sterling will be most important, because although import and export prices will move quickly (downward), it will take some time for the quantities to adjust.[15] One would expect, therefore, an immediate improvement in the current balance followed in a few months by a deterioration that will carry the balance well below the underlying status quo ante.[16] No such pattern emerged. In spite of persistent "overvaluation" of sterling, on a purchasing power parity basis, the current account remains (and was still in 1984) stubbornly in surplus, thus contradicting forecasts to the contrary by the most prestigious institutions.

A ready explanation may be that the increase in the current balance was largely due to oil, and that the slump was brought about by the exchange rate operating on nonoil exports. It seems to be wrong to ignore the resource implications of the North Sea.[17] But willy-nilly, let us provisionally accept the picture of an oilless Britain in examining the effects of the appreciation of sterling. The argument has been further refined, not merely to nonoil trade but down to *manufactures*.[18] It is on

---

this considerably exceeds the increase in government revenues from oil (in 1982) prices which averaged above £ 7 bn over 1981–83. It was roughly equal to the net balance of payment effect of oil. See F. J. Atkinson, S. J. Brook, and S. G. F. Hall, "Economic Effects of North Sea Oil," *National Institute Economic Review*, 2/83, No. 104, May 1983, pp. 38–44. To this current surplus we ought to add an estimate of the general underrecording of surpluses. In 1983, according to IMF statistics the world had an aggregate deficit of $74 billion. Taking Britain's share at about 7 percent means that the surplus was underreported by about $5 billion or £ 4 billion. (This adjustment was suggested by John Williamson as being the most appropriate).

15. One may note something of a paradox here. The same economists who make the argument about the relative high speed of price compared with quantity adjustment also tend to argue that in domestic terms prices and particularly money (or sometimes real) wages are "sticky" and adjust more slowly than quantities.

16. The (inverted) J pattern is the economist's word for it. It takes about 18 months or two years for half of the effect of a price change to appear in quantity adjustment. Hence, we have tended to use the years 1981–83 as a measure of the effect of the exchange-rate appreciation from 1977–80. In mid 1981 and the end of 1982 there were sharp depreciations which probably affected the 1983 trade figures. Occasionally, therefore, we have restricted the examination to 1981 and 1982.

17. This would be equivalent to ignoring the opening of the prairie in nineteenth-century America or Argentina, or the coal industry in nineteenth-century Britain, or oil in twentieth-century Abu Dhabi.

18. Nonoil nonmanufactures, particularly service exports, seemed to bear up quite well during the appreciation of sterling.

Table 9.2. Export of manufactures

|  | UK Av. vol. index (1980 = 100) | Av. shares (%) of total world exports of manufactures | | |
|---|---|---|---|---|
|  |  | UK (%) | France (%) | Germany (%) |
| 1974–76 | 89 | 9.0 | 9.7 | 20.8 |
| 1981–83 | 94 | 8.4 | 8.9 | 19.0 |
| Change 1974–76 to 1981–83 | +5 | −0.6 | −0.8 | −1.8 |

*Source: National Institute Economic Review 108, May 1984, pp. 78, 81.*

the exports of manufactures that the Thatcher appreciation of sterling is alleged to have wreaked its havoc in deepening the recession into a slump.

Again, however, the evidence does not bear out such an interpretation. First, the performance of manufactured exports compared with the pre-Thatcher period is illustrated in Table 9.2. In order to reduce cyclical and random components, we calculate the average exports for the three years dating from the recovery years 1974 and 1981. The volume index shows that there was no fall in manufactured exports—on the contrary, there was a slight *increase* in spite of the massive appreciation of sterling (column 1). Perhaps the buoyancy of exports is explained by the fact that exporters continued to hang on to markets in the expectation that sterling would fall and exporting would become again profitable. However, this cannot explain the *persistence* of both high exports and the overvaluation of sterling. But I suspect it does account for the lack of any sharp movement in exports.

It might be objected, however, that the effect of the sterling appreciation on manufactured exports would appear in the sharp deterioration of the *share* of world (or more accurately of OECD) manufactured exports.[19] Clearly, total world trade expanded over this period and the main effects would be illustrated in the loss of its share of the total market. In fact the United Kingdom did suffer a decline in its share of exports from 9.0 percent to 8.4 percent (see Table 9.2). But, as can be seen in columns (3) and (4), France and Germany suffered a *greater* loss of share—not only in terms of the percentage of the share, but also in terms of the percentage of their exports.

These results are very difficult to rationalize in terms of the patterns of exchange rates. Obviously, a comparison with the EEC partners Ger-

19. This interpretation was suggested by Professor John Williamson.

many and France is more appropriate than with countries such as Japan, the United States, or Australia. The composition of manufactured exports is broadly similar and they compete in the same markets. Furthermore, sterling appreciated even more sharply in 1979–80, in real terms, against the deutsche mark (perhaps more than 40 percent) than against the dollar and the average basket of currencies. One would have expected a very sharp deterioration of Britain's share relative to that of Germany and France, rather than the relative improvement observed in the table. Furthermore, the long term trend of the UK share has been down, whereas the long trend of Germany and France has been up. So the movement is countertrend. One main counterargument is that this period was coincidental with the main effects of Britain joining the Common Market. One would have expected a structural change in trading patterns involving an increase in manufactured exports which would be independent of exchange-rate movements. But this hypothesis must be left for further study.

One other remarkable feature of the export performance of manufactures is that, comparing 1981–83 with 1974–75, while the production of manufactures fell approximately 15 percent, exports of manufactures actually *increased* slightly, by about 1 percent. Clearly, the manufacturing sector was not decimated by the decline in exports due to the appreciation of sterling.

The main erosion of the manufactures balance of trade took place through increased imports. Britain has long experienced import penetration in manufactures.[20] With the accelerating growth of trade specialization and spreading industrialization, one would expect an increase in the rate of import penetration—especially with the great liberalization of trade that took place in the 1970s.[21] Over the period of 1974–76 to 1981–83, Britain increased her volume of imports of manufactures by 52 percent, whereas recorded world exports of manufactures rose by

20. See James J. Hughes and A. P. Thirlwell, "Trends and Cycles in Import Penetration in the UK," *Oxford Bulletin of Economics and Statistics,* Vol. 39 (4), Nov. 1977, 301–18, where the import to export ratio for manufactures increased at an annual rate of 3 to 6 percent for 1963–74. For the years 1974–82, my rough calculations suggest that the annual rate of import penetration has doubled.

21. This small sensitivity of UK trade to exchange-rate changes, compared with the much larger sensitivity of Germany and the United States, has been noted in work done in the Bank of England. See "The Variability of Exchange Rates: Measurement and Effects," *Bank of England Quarterly Bulletin,* Vol. 24 (3), Sept. 1984, pp. 346–49.

only 30 percent.[22] Britain imported an increasing share. However, partly as a consequence of the appreciation of sterling, her terms of trade in manufactures improved about 16 percent.[23] Thus, if the relative change in export and import prices represents a substantive improvement, Britain could acquire her larger volume of manufactured imports with a smaller resource commitment to manufactured exports.[24]

It is as well to examine the experience of those European countries whose currencies depreciated against sterling, namely, France and Germany. Here we find that over the same period both increased their imports of manufactured goods by about 40 percent over 1974–76 to 1981–83 compared with 52 percent by the UK (i.e., 23 percent less of an increase).[25] Thus, the contention that the main effect of this measured real appreciation was on increased imports has some plausibility. But one must also admit that it had quantitatively little effect—and much less than feared. The effect on the net exports, valued in current US dollars, is shown in Table 9.3.

To summarize, the unprecedented real appreciation of sterling apparently had some effects similar to those which theory would predict—such as the penetration of manufactured imports. In spite of the change in oil prices, the large change on current balance from deficit to surplus and

22. Provided that the percentage bias in the underrecording of exports was the same in the two periods, this figure will also serve as the percentage increase in world imports. The import statistics are rather more difficult to interpret since there are few usable volume indices. We have need to resort to the basic data which are reviewed in the Appendix.

23. Terms of trade for *manufactures* averaged 86.3 in 1974–76 and 100.7 in 1981–83 (1980 = 100). See *National Institute Economic Review*, No. 108, May 1984, p. 77.

24. One interesting aspect is that the prices (or strictly unit values) of UK exports in terms of US $ increased much more than those of any large industrialized country from 1974–80 and remained relatively high compared with European countries. This background to the rather impressive export performance in 1981–83 suggests that there may have been considerable improvements in the *quality* of British exports. It is difficult otherwise to explain why foreigners bought British manufactures rather than German or French when their "prices" had relatively increased. (Improvements in British quality may also partly explain the divergence between the output and expenditure measures of GDP.) Unfortunately, there are no useful independent measures of quality, although there is much anecdotal evidence to keep the idea alive if not quite kicking.

25. See Appendix. Note, also, that we cannot convincingly argue that the differential growth rates of Germany and France compared with the UK explain their greater imports. The growth of both Germany and France from 1973 onward was only a percentage point or two above that of the UK.

Table 9.3.  Trade balances for manufactures, 1974–76 to 1981–82
(annual averages $ US billions)[a]

|         |         | Exports | Imports | Surplus |
|---------|---------|---------|---------|---------|
| France  | 1974–76 | 37.7    | 31.0    | 6.7     |
|         | 1981–82 | 70.9    | 64.0    | 6.9     |
| Germany | 1974–76 | 81.3    | 39.4    | 41.8    |
|         | 1981–82 | 148.3   | 83.1    | 65.2    |
| U.K.    | 1974–76 | 34.2    | 26.7    | 7.6     |
|         | 1981–82 | 65.4    | 61.9    | 3.6     |

*Source: UN Yearbook.*

a Statistical discrepancies are due to rounding.

the buoyant manufactures export performance are difficult to rationalize away. Clearly, there is some missing factor which must be adduced to explain such phenomena. One such factor would be the differential high improvement in productivity in the export subsector of the manufacturing industries. Manufacturers have suggested that the export industries were *forced* to improve productivity more than anyone thought possible. This "cold shower" argument is difficult to develop in terms of standard economic theory. Its leitmotif is in terms of incentives and motivation when the solvency of the firm, or at least the livelihood of the management, is under threat from competitors. It is difficult to find concrete evidence on these issues, but the process clearly deserves some investigation.[26]

The conclusion is that the transmission mechanism of monetary policy through the exchange rate is a weak reed on which to rely for a convincing account of the depths of the UK recession. It is likely that other factors—particularly, the surge in real wage costs—played a much more important role in sharply reducing profitability in 1979–81.

## Appendix: Imports of France, Germany, and the UK 1974–76 and 1981–83

The basic data for manufactured imports into the three countries in current values measured in United States dollars is shown in Table 9.4.[27]

26. The reader may wonder why the import-competing manufacturing firms allowed this market to be penetrated by imports. Did they not have the same incentives as the export sector to increase productivity, lower prices, and stop the rot? It is undoubtedly true that the appreciation of sterling raised real (product) wages and so contributed to the decline of profits and the reduction in employment.
27. We have excluded the heading 68 from the normal SITC 5 to 8 grouping,

Table 9.4. Average value of manufactured-goods imports[a]

| Million US $ | France | Germany | UK |
|---|---|---|---|
| 1974 | 28,036 | 33,608 | 25,577 |
| 1975 | 29,159 | 38,793 | 25,956 |
| 1976 | 35,682 | 45,944 | 28,506 |
| 1981 | 63,792 | 85,014 | 61,366 |
| 1982 | 64,201 | 81,204 | 62,339 |
| 1983 | 59,903 | 83,693 | 65,191 |
| Average | | | |
| 1974–76 | 30,959 | 39,448 | 26,680 |
| 1981–83 | 62,632 | 83,304 | 62,965 |
| Increase in value (%) | | | |
| 1974–76 to 1981–83 | 102 | 111 | 136 |
| Increase in quantity (%) | | | |
| 1974–76 to 1981–83 | 39 | 42 | 52 |

Sources: UN Yearbook of International Trade Statistics, Vol. 1, 1976 and 1982; UN Commodity Trade Statistics Staff, preliminary estimates; National Institute Economic Review 108, May 1984, Table 15, p. 78.

a SITC $5 + 6 + 7 + 8 - 68$.

The value of UK imports increased by 136 percent compared with 102 and 111 percent for France and Germany over the period 1974–76 to 1981–83. To get the quantity of imports on a comparable basis we need statistics of the average value of imports or indicators price of imports for these categories. Unfortunately, there are no such statistics which are comparable across countries. As a rough comparison we have supposed that the dollar price of imports was the same in France and Germany as in the UK. We know that the increase in the quantity of manufactured imports in the UK over these two periods was 52 percent (NIESR). Correspondingly, the French and German increases were then 39 and 42 percent, respectively.

These data are consistent with the modest manufactured-goods import boom of the UK compared with Germany and France. But they are based on the assumption of the "one-price" proposition being valid. Although this is perhaps a reasonable assumption to make in tariff-free Europe, it is best to check the statistics with indices of volume.

Using the IMF volume indicators (with 1970 weights) and projecting the figures from 1980, using the World Trade model, gives one a quite different picture. (See Table 9.5.) The increase in imports of manufactures in the UK is remarkably smaller than that in either France or Germany. According to these data, there was no import boom in the UK—on the contrary, France led the increase of imports of manufactures. This reverses the above result.[28]

---

since this heading applies to nonferrous metals and is not normally a manufactured good in the conventional sense.

28. Similar results appear when one uses the export unit-value (in US $) index to deflate the values for trade and OECD tabulations.

Table 9.5. Volume of imports of manufactures (1970 trade weights)[a]

|                  | France | Germany | UK  |
|------------------|--------|---------|-----|
| Average 1974–76  | 165    | 150     | 154 |
| Average 1981–83  | 260    | 234     | 219 |
| Change (%)       | 57     | 56      | 42  |

*Source:* IMF Staff estimates. Value data from United Nations Statistical Office. Unit value index from national sources.

a (1970 = 100).

The exploration of these idiosyncracies of trade statistics is not the purpose of this monograph. However, it seems to me that the basic trade statistics, as tabulated by the United Nations, and the assumption of "one price" is the best basis for judging the relative import experience. The volume series have many difficulties of weighing coverage and interpretation which make them difficult to use. Hence, in Chapter 9 above, I have concentrated on the results derived from the dollar-value tabulations of the UN.

# 10
# Policy, Productivity and Employment

In his book on the 1979–83 Conservative government,[1] Peter Riddell has suggested that one litmus test of the success of the Thatcher policies is the progress of productivity.[2] The record is shown in Table 10.1.

We shall concentrate on productivity in the *manufacturing* industries largely because the measurement problems there are less daunting than in other industries. Much that is said about manufacturing, however, carries over *mutatis mutandis* to the other sectors.

The most striking result is clearly the high level of productivity increases which have occurred since the lower turning point at the end of 1980. Over the three years 1980/81 to 1983/84, the annual increase in output per person has been near 7 percent. (See Table 10.1.) As far as one can determine this increasing productivity trend has continued into 1984.[3]

This is quite an impressive change. Productivity growth per person in the 1970s averaged about 1.64 percent.[4] In the first three or four

1. Peter Riddell, *op. cit.*, pp. 76–79.
2. Severe critics of the policies hardly mention productivity at all. For example in William Keegan (*op. cit.*, 1984), it is dismissed as "not proven" and "not permanent" in 12 lines (p. 203).
3. See *Hansard*, July 12th, 1984, the reply of the Chief Secretary to the Treasury that manufacturing output per head was, in the first quarter of 1984, six percent greater than in the first quarter of 1983.
4. With 1980 = 100, in 1970 output per person was 85.0 and output per hour 80.4. *Source:* CSO *Economic Trends Annual Supplement* 10, 1985, p. 98.

Table 10.1. Productivity in the UK (annual percent change)[a]

|                              | 1980 : 4 to 1981 : 4 | 1981 : 4 to 1982 : 4 | 1982 : 4 to 1983 : 4 |
|------------------------------|----------------------|----------------------|----------------------|
| Mfg. industries              |                      |                      |                      |
| Output/worker                | 10.1                 | 3.6                  | 9.1                  |
| Output/hour                  | 8.1                  | 3.3                  | 7.8                  |
| Total production industries  |                      |                      |                      |
| Output/worker                | 10.6                 | 5.7                  | 8.7                  |

*Source:* CSO *Economic Trends,* June 1985, p. 34.

a Changes to 1984 and 1985 are omitted because productivity was much affected by the strike of the National Union of Mineworkers.

years of the 1980s Britain experienced a more than fourfold increase in the annual productivity gain. The figures suggest that at last, Britain may be starting to catch up with her great European rivals and partners. They may be the first signs of a cure for the British disease and may even herald a minor "economic miracle." This view has been reinforced by many anecdotes from British boardrooms and managers and even from the shop floor.[5]

## Accounting for Productivity Growth

Understandably, this record has attracted close and searching critical scrutiny. The criticisms have generally taken three lines: first, it is said that the productivity growth has been very little out of the ordinary and that similar periods of growth can be found in the last two decades; second, it is argued that the growth will soon (in 1983 or, presumably, 1984) come to a stop; thirdly, it is argued that such productivity growth is bad—or at least no good thing—because it has been achieved almost entirely by reducing output. Let us review each of these points in turn.

First, the "nothing unprecedented" argument. This is given considerable emphasis by Buiter and Miller (1983) and somewhat more muted approval by the National Institute. Buiter and Miller properly pointed out that, in two other periods of 9 quarters, increases in output per worker (or per hour) had been equally impressive. (See Table 10.2.) True. But the story does not end after these periods of nine quarters. In

5. Stories of massive productivity gains abound. The general view is that at last British management and labor have accomplished improvements which should have been done years ago. The overmanning notorious in British manufacturing was substantially reduced. Now all they need is a "bit more demand" to realize even greater feats of productivity.

Table 10.2. "Precedents" for productivity growth

| Period | | Length in quarters | 9 quarters % increase | Annual percent increase next three quarters |
|---|---|---|---|---|
| 1966.4 | 1969.1 | 9 | 15.1 (per worker) | 1.5 |
| 1971.1 | 1973.2 | 9 | 16.8 (per worker) | −5.3 |
| | | | 16.6 (per hour) | 0.6 |
| 1980.4 | 1983.1 | 9 | 16.7 (per worker) | 6.3 |
| | | | 13.9 (per hour) | 5.2 |

*Source:* CSO *Economic Trends Annual Supplement* 10, 1985, pp. 97–98.

the Thatcher years productivity (measured per worker or per hour) continued to grow at the 6 percent rate over the next three quarters of 1983, whereas in the earlier periods productivity growth slumped. Not merely the level but the *persistence* of productivity gains in the 1980s is unprecedented. (*Note:* In his Mansion House speech of October 17, 1985, the Chancellor revealed that productivity in manufacturing has grown 30 percent over the past five years.)

In another respect they are clearly unprecedented because they have been achieved in conditions of a dramatic *reduction* in the rate of inflation. Conditions in the late 1960s and early 1970s saw, however, increasing inflation and the collapse of 1974–75. In 1984–85 no such combination of a fall in GDP and outbreak of 20-percent inflation seems at all likely . . . although nothing can be taken for certain.

The productivity growth was also certainly quite unprecedented if it be compared with Britain's normal performance relative to other OECD countries and particularly to the great European competitors, Germany and France.[6] It is well known that since the revival of the European economies in the early 1950s, productivity growth in Germany and France has been on the average about double that of the United King-

6. The zest that many critics, such as Buiter and Miller, have displayed for OECD or European yardsticks in measuring the performance of the UK economy in matters such as unemployment, budget deficits, taxation, etc., inexplicably disappeared when they discussed productivity. Yet international comparisons of the growth of productivity have normally been at the center of all discussions of Britain's laggardly performance. The yardstick by which to judge the 1980s, according to Buiter and Miller, is Britain in the pre-OPEC period 1966–73 when output per person in manufacturing rose 4.4 percent a year. By any historical standards the 1966–73 period for all OECD countries, but particularly for Europe, was quite unique in its high productivity growth. And apart from postwar recovery periods I cannot easily find similar periods of such high achievements in recorded history. If we are to be judged by such exceptional norms, then we are all damned to mediocrity.

dom.[7] In the 1980s the positions were nicely reversed. Productivity growth in the UK has been about twice that of France and almost 50 percent greater than that of Germany. In terms of output per person or per hour Britain has gone from the laggard to the leader.

Similarly, the productivity increase has defied the normal cyclical pattern. Many distinguished economists argued that it was a "flash in the pan" and that there had been no productivity breakthrough.[8] This takes us squarely on to the second point of the critics—which has been advanced in its most convincing form by Mendis and Muellbauer, namely, that the productivity gains of 1980–81 were merely the compression of the normal productivity gains in a short period of the cycle. In particular, Mendis and Muellbauer argue that reported hours of employment record hours for which wages were paid but little or no work was done. Correcting for this overrecording of labor input in the downswing gives a great (9.0 percent per annum) "corrected" productivity increase from 1980:1 to 1981:1. Thereafter to the end of 1982 "corrected" productivity increased by less than 2 percent. Mendis and Muellbauer predicted that, as paid labor inputs were adjusted to the work to be done, this decline in 1982 would continue in 1983 and would be reflected in the noncorrected index. As the evidence shows, however, their hypothesis was discredited by the sharp 1983 increase in the growth of output per man hour. The bias in measuring labor inputs cannot be the main explanation for the unprecedented persistence of the growth of productivity. There must be some other explanation.

It has also been argued that the reason for the productivity increase has been because of the discontinued production at less efficient plants. More sensationally, Britain has been closing her industrial museums. This raises the average level of productivity gain during the period when such closures occur; but thereafter the old trend rate will reappear. Mendis and Muellbauer estimate that roughly 6 percentage points of the increase in productivity was due to closures in the period of rapid

7. Herbert Giersch, and Frank Wolter, *The Economic Journal,* Vol. 93, No. 369, March 1983, p. 36. National Institute *Economic Review,* No. 108, May 1984, Table 18. Angus Maddison, "Comparative Analysis of the Productivity Situation in the Advanced Countries," in *International Comparisons of Productivity and Causes of the Slowdown,* John W. Kendrick (ed.), American Enterprise Institute, Washington, DC, 1984, pp. 59–92. See also OECD *Economic Outlook 35,* July 1984, p. 45.

8. See Lionel Mendis and John Muellbauer, "Has There Been a Productivity Breakthrough? Evidence from an Aggregate Production Function for Manufacturing," London School of Economics, Working Paper, Centre for Labour Economics, July 1983.

decline of output in 1980 through to the spring of 1981. This was associated with the even larger reduction in manufacturing employment; this was judged to be one of the main proximate causes of the increase in unemployment of labor from the second half of 1979 onward.

There is no doubt that the closure of such inefficient capacity—and the unemployment of much of the labor and capital so freed—has been a marked feature of 1980 and, to a lesser degree, of 1981–83. As Buiter and Miller amusingly not only describe but also judge it:

> . . . the current productivity record . . . is like the cricket team that improves its batting average by only playing its better batsmen. As long as the "tail-enders" score some runs, however, it would surely be better to let them play even if it does lower the sides' batting average.[9]

Of course, the first thing that strikes one is that not *everyone* must play cricket. There *are* other games. The poor "tail-enders" may best give up cricket and play bridge instead. But while they are well paid to wave their bats aimlessly at the ball they will continue to offer their services as batsmen—and sit in the fairly comfortable pavilion drinking tea or something more fortifying, perhaps playing bridge, and waiting for another game. Furthermore, will there not be *some* effect on the performance of the retained batsmen? Or, according to Buiter and Miller, is their performance immutable and quite immune from the rules and rewards of the game?[10]

To the relief of those who feel that cricket is too frivolous or too serious to be so discussed, let us now dispense with bat and ball and get back to mundane manufacturing. The close-the-museums argument may explain the rise in productivity in 1980.1 to 1981.2 as Mendis and Muellbauer suggest. But manufacturing output ceased the rapid decline that began in 1979 and started to rise from 1981.2. Employment, which fell sharply in 1980, settled on a more gentle downward path to the end of 1983. In 1984.2, manufacturing employment rose by 3000. Thus,

9. Buiter and Miller, 1983, p. 358.
10. It must be noted that Buiter and Miller discredit their implicit assumption that high order batsmen will perform only as well as before, when it is admitted (pp. 358–359) that some improvements have occurred in British Leyland, British Steel Corporation, etc. With the same capital equipment and a smaller labor force, output has been expanded dramatically in firms in the automobiles, chemicals, and many other industries. However, BM see little scope for improvement in "management and in cooperation between management and workers" because "they have not been the focus of concerted government policies and actions." Having spent a year or two in the government's concert, I draw precisely the opposite inference.

the museum hypothesis cannot explain the continuing high rates of productivity gain in 1983 and 1984.[11]

One important source of Britain's productivity growth, which has not
been the focus of criticism, may be the increased capital intensity of
industry brought about by increased wage costs relative to the costs of
capital.[12] Although this will be reviewed in more detail later when we
consider unemployment, it is worth noting that such increased relative
wage costs are characteristic of virtually all European economies. Certainly in Europe of the 1970s, increased real wage costs were not
matched by increased productivity. In the 1980s all have experienced
reduced employment but only Britain has enjoyed a sustained differential growth in productivity.

We are left, therefore, with no simple explanations of Britain's productivity. There must be some missing factor—a Thatcher factor?—which
explains this dramatic reversal in Britain's performance. The changes in
attitude of management and labor which many observers have noted
does seem to be a reality which may explain the remarkable record of
the 1980s. The extent to which government policy has contributed to
this outcome is an unknown and perhaps largely an unknowable.

Now to summarize the productivity conclusions:
1. There has been a sharp change in British productivity not merely
   relative to history (that is to say, it is "unprecedented") but also
   relative to the main European economies.
2. Sharply increasing productivity in an environment of disinflation is
   rather a new experience for the United Kingdom, at least in the four
   decades since World War II.
3. Attempts to explain the increase away as a "flash in the pan" which
   soon would be snuffed out have themselves suffered the extinction of
   time's revelations.
4. There remains the Thatcher factor—the compendium of ambient
   macroeconomic stability and microeconomic reform. On general
   grounds it seems likely, to put it no higher, that productivity must

11. The coal strike of 1984 has made the statistics very difficult to interpret.
12. I suspect that the absence of criticism is due to the fact that most economists
    take the view that there has been *too little* investment in recent years. They
    view capital and labor as largely complementary factors, not as substitutes.
    The interpretation of productivity increases as due primarily to increased
    capitalization of production due to high wage costs relative to those of capi-
    tal, would suggest that there has been no fundamental change in British in-
    dustry and labor.

respond favorably under conditions of increased stability and freedom. On such matters, however, one can say a lot but settle little.
Nevertheless, I suspect that if the productivity gains persist, and we
do come near to the productivity in Germany and France, it will be
difficult to attribute causation to any other source.

## Employment and Unemployment

Perhaps no aspect of the performance of the British economy has attracted more attention and alarm than the increase of unemployment
and the persistence of high rates (above 12 percent) even well into the
recovery. Perhaps everyone has been surprised at the calmness, even
equanimity, of British society under these conditions.[13] Yet unemployment remains the most pressing economic problem of the economy.[14]

I shall have little or nothing to say that is new, so I will state the case
briefly, even starkly, and without elaboration or exculpation. First, the
great majority of those who are unemployed, and actively seeking work,
are jobless because wage costs were too high. There is no *demand* for
their services because it is unprofitable for firms to employ them at the
wage costs which they must incur. Secondly, a much smaller increase
in unemployment has occurred because of the lack of profit in *supplying*
work. With the level of benefits and other opportunities available it is
not profitable for the worker to get a job; he will consider himself better
off drawing benefits and supplementing with income from the black
economy.[15]

The belief that the wage-cost/demand effect is much more important
than the benefit/supply effect is based largely on judgment of the underlying relative trends. Between 1973 and 1983 unit labor costs have increased in the UK by 30 percent, compared with the United States.[16]

13. It will be recalled that the Heath government feared widespread social un-
    rest, indeed a breakdown of law and order, if unemployment rose signifi-
    cantly above 1 million (about 4.5%).
14. For an excellent account of the problem and its solution see Patrick Minford,
    *Unemployment—Cause and Cure,* Robertson, London, 1983.
15. This out-of-work income level provides an effective floor to the wages which
    firms will offer since they are unlikely to get many takers if jobs are offered
    at wages below this floor. Hence, there is a lack of low-paying jobs adver-
    tised and on offer.
16. For the rest of Europe the figures are 40 percent for France, 15 percent for
    Germany and 12 percent for Italy. See B. Balassa, "The Economic Conse-
    quence of Social Policies in the Industrial Countries," Lecture at the Institute
    of Weltwirtschaft an der Universitat Kiel, June 1984.

Much of this increase occurred in the great leap forward of earnings (20 to 25 percent) in 1979–80. On the supply side we do find some mixture of marginal benefit and tax increases—but nothing quite as dramatic as the increase in wage costs affecting demand.

At first sight it may seem that the unprofitability of employing labor is a problem which can be solved by boosting aggregate demand. This will increase profits and so increase the amount of labor that can be employed profitably. Much doubt, however, must be cast on such a so-called Keynesian solution.[17] First, since 1981 there has been a very large rise, almost 80 percent from 1981.1 to 1983.4, in gross trading profits for non-North-Sea corporations—a real increase of around 50 percent. And in March 1984 corporate profits had increased 25 percent over March 1983.[18] The CBI 1984 forecast was for a net pretax rate of return of non-North-Sea industrial and commercial corporations of 8.5 percent compared with less than 4 percent in 1981. These data are evidence of a strong increase in aggregate demand from 1981 to 1983. It was increasingly profitable to produce more goods and services—but, alas, not to employ more labor. The number of jobs fell from 1981 to 1984, and the rate of unemployment increased and remained high and is widely expected to stay at around 3 million for some time.[19]

17. Keynes himself would very likely have no truck with the solutions proposed by the latter-day post-Keynesians. For example, in 1937, only one year after the *General Theory* appeared, Keynes had become very worried about inflation and argued that increasing aggregate demand would do little or nothing to help employment but would most likely ignite inflation. Unemployment then was about 11 percent and inflation about 5 to 6 percent. See T. W. Hutchinson, "Keynes vs. the Keynesians," *Institute of Economic Affairs*, London, 1977.
18. See *Hansard*, 12th July 1984, Chancellor's Question Time.
19. This is a stark contrast to the United States where, from the end of 1982 onward, there has been a sharp recovery of profits similar to that in the UK, but also a very large reduction in the rate of unemployment. Many observers of a Keynesian pursuasion have attributed this recovery to the striking increases in the federal deficit. But these increases in the deficit began in mid 1979 to mid 1980—over which the deficit increased about $70 bn—and again another increase of almost $60 bn at the end of 1980 through to 1982.2. The increase in the deficit from 1979 to mid 1981 was about $100 bn. Yet there was a sharp contraction in 1981–82—gross investment fell precipitously from mid 1981 to the end of 1982 and unemployment rose to nearly 11 percent. The addition to the deficit of another $70 to $80 bn in the last half of 1982 was thought by Keynesians to be the cause of the great recovery from December 1982 or January 1983 onward. If the 1982 increase in the deficit were the stimulant of the economy in 1983, why did the $100 bn not work its wonders in 1981–82 rather than lead to the downturn to one of the deepest slumps of the postwar years? On the other hand, monetarists such

Table 10.3. Unemployment and deficits

| | Unemployment (% of labor force) | | Net borrowing of general government (% of GNP) | |
|---|---|---|---|---|
| | 1980 | 1983 | 1980 | 1983 |
| Belgium | 9.4 | 14.5 | 9.4 | 12.2 |
| Denmark | 6.1 | 10.7 | 5.9 | 8.8 |
| Germany | 3.3 | 8.6 | 3.5 | 3.3 |
| France | 6.4 | 9.1 | 0.0 | 3.1 |
| Ireland | 8.3 | 15.3 | 12.8 | 13.4 |
| Italy | 8.0 | 10.8 | 8.4 | 11.9 |
| Netherlands | 4.7 | 15.6 | 3.4 | 6.7 |
| UK | 6.3 | 11.7 | 3.5 | 2.2 |
| Average excluding UK | 6.6 | 12.1 | 6.7 | 8.8 |

*Source:* Commission of European Communities, *European Economy* No. 18, Nov. 83, pp. 204, 226.

Additional plausibility for this wage-cost explanation of high unemployment—or more strictly, evidence on the implausibility of an inadequate-aggregate-demand explanation—can be adduced from the behavior of other countries. At one time, particularly in 1980 and 1981, it was fashionable to contrast the relatively low unemployment of the European and other OECD economies with the higher and more rapidly increasing levels in the UK. This was thought to be explained primarily by the relatively tight fiscal and monetary squeeze of Mrs. Thatcher.[20] However, those countries which had pursued more or less the opposite of Thatcherite policies, with expansions of public spending financed by increased deficits, suffered increases in unemployment in 1981–83 which were just as, or even more, severe than those of the UK. As can be seen in Table 10.3, the differential unemployment effect of 1981 was much muted by 1983.[21]

Whatever their budgetary-monetary policies, all European countries were in much the same boat as far as unemployment was concerned. It

---

as Professor Karl Brunner correctly predicted the recovery on the basis of the sharp expansion in $M_1$ and $M_0$ which began in mid 1982 and persisted through the middle of 1983.

20. See, for example, Buiter and Miller (1981) and William Keegan (*op. cit.*) 1984.

21. Germany had suffered a vast increase in unemployment which was partly disguised by the departing guest-workers. France also ensured that there was a considerable downward bias in her measured unemployment.

appeared that differences in macro policy were reflected mainly in different rates of inflation and not in variations in unemployment.[22]

In any event, it has been largely accepted that the really important measure in the labor market is employment, not unemployment.[23] The concept of unemployment is slippery and the measures wayward. The numbers registered as unemployed depend on the vague categories and shifting interpretations of the administration of the system of benefits.[24] Measures of employment, although they too have shadowy elements, are better indicators of changes in labor absorption.

Although total employment fell and unemployment increased at a faster rate in the UK in 1981 than in any other European country, this pattern was much changed by 1983. Then, although unemployment remained approximately constant or even on a slight upward trend, employment in Great Britain increased by approximately 260,000 in the year to March 1984 (or 1 percent of the employed labor force).[25] This was in contrast with the rest of Europe where the number of jobs continued to decline.[26]

22. I would suggest that, if anything, there is a slight but positive association between the expansionism of macropolicy and the level of unemployment—as manifest in Eire, the Netherlands, Belgium and Italy. But it would be absurd to regard this as any more than the faintest of suggestions. The statistics of unemployment are far too weak to support any such conjecture.
23. Today it is necessary to recall that Keynes' *General Theory* was a theory of employment, not unemployment.
24. See Minford (1983).
25. The pattern of employment and unemployment appears in the following table:

Labor Market (*Seasonally Adjusted*)

|  | UK employed labor force (incl. N. Ireland) (000) | Manufacturing employment[a] (Great Brit.) (000) | Services employment[a] (Great Brit.) (000) | UK adult unemployment (000) |
|---|---|---|---|---|
| 1980 | 25,306 | 6745 | 13,289 | 1561 |
| 1981 | 24,323 | 6122 | 13,097 | 2420 |
| 1982 | 23,987 | 5796 | 13,077 | 2793 |
| 1983 | 23,792 | 5519 | 13,222 | 2970 |
| 1984.1 | 23,981 | 5490 | 13,427 | 2998 |

*Source:* CSO *Economic Trends Annual Supplement 1985 Edition* No. 10, pp. 99, 105.

[a] Note the dramatic fall in manufacturing employment in 1980–81 (almost 10 percent) and the growth in employment in services to the all time high of 1984.1.

26. See Commission of the European Communities, "Annual Economic Report, 1983–84," *European Economy*, No. 18, p. 203.

Among occidental OECD countries the only one that has markedly expanded employment and reduced unemployment is the United States. Whatever interpretation one places on the macroeconomic policies of the United States, there is no doubt at all about the remarkable restraint of real wage costs over the last decade. It is estimated that the EEC real labor costs rose at an average of 3.5 percent during the 1970s, while for the United States the figure was only 1.5 percent.[27]

The proposition that high real wages and real wage costs are the main cause of unemployment may sound perverse to Keynesian ears. For many years it has been customary to argue that increases in real wages *increase* aggregate demand and employment and so *reduce* the level of unemployment.[28] The additional consumer spending that the real-wage increase generates was thought to more than counter the reduction in spending of property owners who have correspondingly lower profits.[29] Consequential substitution of capital for labor was felt to be virtually zero in the short run and of little interest in the longer run.[30] Yet the long run has arrived and in spite of union obstructions there has been enormous capital-for-labor substitution in many industries. I would conjecture that technological advances over the past decade have been primarily concerned with increasing elasticity of substitution between labor and capital—perhaps encouraged by the high and rising real cost

27. Balassa (1984), p. 8. Similarly, he shows that as a consequence of the increased price of labor relative to that of capital, there has been substitution of capital for labor in Europe. Thus, while the productivity of capital has declined by one percent a year, in the United States it has increased by one percent a year throughout the 1970s.

28. A recent example is to be found in M. J. C. Surrey, "Was the recession forecast," in the *National Institute Economic Review*, No. 100, May 1982, pp. 24–28, where Professor Surrey calculates the changes in real wages on aggregate demand and so on GDP (Surrey does not go on to examine the effect on employment, but he clearly believes that real wage, aggregate demand and employment are positively correlated). "The single identifiable factor which prevented the emergence of the recession until 1980 was the rapid growth in real wages," p. 26, and ". . . a factor tending to alleviate the recession, but not fully forecast, was the buoyancy of real wages," p. 28.

29. In Keynesian models the marginal propensity to consume out of wages was thought to be much greater than that out of profits. With the advent of pension funds automatically rising with wages and the majority of industry being owned by such funds, this is unlikely to be clear cut.

30. For a revised Keynesian view see Edmond Malinvaud, "Wages and Unemployment," *Economic Journal*, Vol. 92:365, March 1981, pp. 1–12. It is argued that if the income share of wages is less than the elasticity of substitution between capital and labor, then increases in real wages will depress employment.

of labor.[31] Substitution cannot be swept under the concealing rug of long-run considerations. Common observation suggests that, as a consequence of high real wages, it is a dominant force in the reduction of jobs in the United Kingdom and her European partners.

The final question is why have real wages not fallen—indeed, why have they *increased*—during this period of great unemployment? Why has the classical market mechanism apparently not worked?

Many suggestions have been made. Undoubtedly, the trades unions have played an important role in maintaining and increasing these real rates of pay. The State has contributed through its minimum-wage legislation (the Wages Councils) and through the package of benefits to those in and out of work. The legislation designed to protect jobs—such as inhibitions against unfair dismissal—has undoubtedly destroyed some jobs. The housing legislation has inhibited the movement of workers from depressed to booming areas.

Although some potency must be assigned to all these causes, it is doubtful that they can fully explain the upward trend of real wages. I once conjectured that an important cause of the overshoot of real wages is that both employees and employers were never really *convinced* that the rate of inflation would be as low as that actually achieved. And there is, quite properly, genuine doubt about whether it will hold fast at 4 to 5 percent, let alone meet the Chancellor's intention of stable prices in the long run. Mrs. Thatcher may lose her way or may lose her power. Clearly, a Labour government would embark on a program of inflationary expansion. On the normal cycle of elections a Labour victory cannot yet be dismissed. Yet such an explanation of "unexpected success" in reducing inflation cannot also readily account for the similar experience of real wages in Germany and France. Their record of inflation is different in magnitude and timing from that of the United Kingdom. It is quite implausible to argue that the degree of "surprise" was roughly the same throughout Europe. Nor can the overshoot of expectations account for the continuing rise of real wages in 1984 when inflationary expectations must have subsided.

31. Robots, automation, word processors and the general panopoly of information technology—all suggest that reducing labor inputs is one of the main objectives of technical advance. The reduction in the demand for *unskilled* labor—such as production-line operations—has been one characteristic of this process. As my colleague Lord Bauer has observed, one sees the most enormous investment in labor-saving technology (such as self-service stores and gas stations) at the same time as there is "surplus" of labor as manifest in the unemployment statistics.

In sum, I do not think that we yet have a convincing explanation of the path of real wages; it remains unfinished business. The policy implications are, however, quite clear. The first priority is to remove the impediments to the movements of wages. Easily said, but alas one of the most difficult tasks.

Although this is not the place to review the measures taken by the Thatcher government to help solve the employment problem, it is useful to summarize their main thrust. One main purpose was to put some downward pressure on real wages. Whatever the measure was, it was thought to be important to ensure that it worked *with* the market forces rather than against them. Perhaps the most obvious example of measures which scored highly on such market criteria was the Young Workers Scheme (YWS). Introduced in 1981, this paid a subsidy of 15 pounds a week to an employer who took on a young school-leaver during the first year, provided that the wage rate was less than 40 pounds a week.[32] The purpose was clearly first and foremost to put pressure on nominal wages offered to young workers, and, directly, to induce the potential recipients of the subsidy to expand employment—or perhaps to substitute some of this cheap labor for existing, more expensive employees.[33] Since the catchment area was primarily the nonunionized sector, it was unlikely to promote trades-union power. Similarly, it was expected that it would inhibit the Wages Councils in their activity of pricing youths out of a job—and may even help speed the end of such an anachronism.[34] Later in 1982 and 1983 the Youth Training Scheme (YTS) got under way. This had an overt training element, unlike the YWS, and was much more comprehensive. But it had the same underlying quality that it was designed to work *with* rather than against market forces. Eventually, the comprehensive YTS absorbed the YWS.

These are both measures that address the particular problem of youth unemployment and its attendant problems of wages and training. However, the government did not discover any method of bringing pressure to bear generally on real wage levels and increases. Although ministers clearly identified high wage settlements as the main cause of "pricing

---

32. There was also a provision for a second year at a reduced rate. And for reasons which will remain obscure, domestic servants were precluded.
33. See D. Forrest, and S. R. Dennison, *Low Pay or No Pay?* IEA, London, 1984.
34. Lastly, it was difficult to oppose such a measure since it could obviously be represented as "subsidizing a poor lad, or lass, in his (her) first job when he (she) has so much to learn . . ." This worked *with* the forces in the political market.

themselves out of a job," there was recourse only to remonstration not to regulation. In particular, there was no thought of any attempt to introduce the wage controls which many academics, such as James Meade and Richard Layard, thought an essential ingredient of their desired reflationary package of fiscal and monetary stimulus.[35]

It is difficult to see what else could be done by the government to encourage a rapid adjustment of real wages. No doubt they could have proceeded faster with the legislation on trades unions, abolished Wages Councils, and perhaps restructured the benefits and tax system. But speed would have not been costless, and it is doubtful if there would have been any really large and rapid changes in real wages as a consequence of such measures. Probably, the main direct contribution of the government is to ensure that, unlike 1979/80, the public sector is not the leader in the wage scramble. But the underlying indirect contribution of government was to ensure essential stability in financial conditions. Eventually, everyone may come to recognize that neither government nor the electorate will countenance an inflationary policy again.

## Some Lessons

To conclude this review with a judgment of the success of the Thatcher reform would be premature, not to say presumptuous, considering my involvement in the process itself. It may be thought that I come "not to judge but to praise" Mrs. Thatcher. But the Thatcher government still lives, and balanced judgment must wait for a more detached view of these events. But it is worthwhile provisionally to summarize some of the lessons of the last years, 1979–83, and see what can be learned.

The first main change in the economic environment of 1979–83 was the commitment to contain inflation by the MTFS. The main lesson—still rather tentative—is the power of monetary policy compared with the relative impotence or, in Keynesian terms, even perversity of the effects of fiscal policy. It might be argued that the monetary squeeze of 1979–81 may have exacerbated the downturn in activity just as it laid

35. The evidence remains overwhelmingly against the efficacy of wages controls. The new tax-based incomes policy suggested by Layard and Meade was thought to be an order of magnitude improvement on past error. Perhaps so. But few were persuaded. For my part, I find it difficult to believe that such wage-increase taxes would not be soon incorporated fully into the pricing policies of firms. The supposed antiinflationary effect would sink without trace, but the inequities and inefficiencies of such a pernicious tax would be obvious.

the foundations for the reduction in inflation. Comparative European evidence suggests, however, that the squeeze may merely have moved the recession forward somewhat in time and had little effect on its depth and longevity.

The massive 30 to 40 percent real appreciation of sterling in 1977–80 was perhaps largely a consequence of the monetary squeeze—although some unknown part of the appreciation must have been associated with the oil factor. But the claim that the appreciation of sterling *greatly* exacerbated the recession does not seem consistent with the evidence on the current balance or even the balance of production and trade in manufactures. For reasons which are at present obscure, the massive changes in the value of sterling did not appear to have the devastating effects that many thought to be inevitable. Somehow, the economy of the United Kingdom adjusted to these effects far better than anyone had reason to hope or expect.[36]

One of the elements, in addition to North Sea oil, contributing to the efficacy with which the economy weathered the shock of a high sterling, was the remarkable performance of productivity in the manufacturing industry. It appeared that there was much more room for increases in efficiency than anyone had thought possible. An important element may appear to have been the pressure on profit margins which "forced" change which had hitherto been funked—the "cold shower" effect. But the productivity gains persisted even as corporate profits in real terms rose to a seven-year high. The residual view is that the productivity gains were the result of the many changes in micro policy (elimination of income controls and exchange controls, reductions in the high marginal tax rates) combined with a certain macroeconomic stability. This provided the impetus for such a favorable trend. If this is the true explanation, then it is good reason for believing that the trend can continue for some years. On the one hand, confidence in macro stability is cumulative. On the other hand, there is still much to be achieved in the liberation of the firm and the family from the shackles of state, monopoly, or union restrictions.

Perhaps such microeconomic reforms will go a long way to reducing the persistently high rate of unemployment. The most likely way in which this can be achieved is by reducing the rate of growth of real

36. I am reminded that the German and Swiss economies also seemed to get through periods of overvaluation of the currencies with considerably less difficulty than the basic elasticities would lead one to predict.

hourly wages.[37] Undoubtedly, the increase of real wages in 1979–80 contributed to the sharp decline in profits, the falls in output and employment, and the depths of the recession. The subsequent persistence of high increases in real wages in the face of rising, record levels of unemployment may be adduced as evidence of the extent to which the market mechanism has been eroded by state regulation and monopoly unions. I suspect, however, that part of the explanation for the persistence of high real wages is the realized undershooting of expectations of inflation. But evidence on this is only circumstantial and not convincing. In sum, I can find no plausible explanation for the increases in real wages. There is no point in substituting Aunt Sallies for explanations. At the same time one must be skeptical of forecasts of 3 million or more of unemployment stretching into an indefinite future. If the underlying cause is uncertain, the future is also in doubt.[38]

37. A better alternative would be an even more striking growth in productivity—and, particularly, the productivity of unskilled workers. A more painful alternative would be to reform the benefits system.
38. In the early 1930s no one foresaw the sharp—indeed record—declines in unemployment which actually took place in 1932–37. All forecasts were for persistent, high unemployment. Yet the economy suddenly moved toward rapid growth and striking reductions in unemployment.

# *Index*

187